Agricultural Policy Reform in the United States

T0273287

AEI STUDIES IN AGRICULTURAL POLICY

Agricultural Policy Reform in the United States

Edited by Daniel A. Sumner

The AEI Press

Publisher for the American Enterprise Institute

WASHINGTON, D.C.

1995

Distributed to the Trade by National Book Network, 15200 NBN Way, Blue Ridge Summit, PA 17214. To order call toll free 1-800-462-6420 or 1-717-794-3800. For all other inquiries please contact the AEI Press, 1150 Seventeenth Street, N.W., Washington, D.C. 20036 or call 1-800-862-5801.

Library of Congress Cataloging-in-Publication Data
Agricultural policy reform in the United States / edited by
    Daniel A. Sumner.
        p.   cm. — (AEI studies in agricultural policy)
    Includes index.
    ISBN 0-8447-3913-8 (paper : alk. paper). — ISBN 0-8447-3912-X
(cloth : alk. paper)
    1. Agriculture and state—United States.   2. Agricultural laws
and legislation—United States.   I. Sumner, Daniel A.
(Daniel Alan), 1950–   .   II. Series.
HD1761.A6219   1995
338.1′873—dc20   95-18102
                                                                CIP

1 3   5   7   9   10   8   6   4   2

© 1995 by the American Enterprise Institute for Public Policy Research, Washington, D.C. All rights reserved. No part of this publication may be used or reproduced in any manner whatsoever without permission in writing from the American Enterprise Institute except in the case of brief quotations embodied in news articles, critical articles, or reviews. The views expressed in the publications of the American Enterprise Institute are those of the authors and do not necessarily reflect the views of the staff, advisory panels, officers, or trustees of AEI.

THE AEI PRESS
Publisher for the American Enterprise Institute
1150 17th Street, N.W., Washington, D.C. 20036

Contents

FIGURES

Foreword

In 1995, the U.S. Congress will write farm legislation in the eye of a political hurricane. That is not unprecedented, of course, for we have periodically had economic crises in agriculture that have called for a helping hand from government. But this time the momentum is moving in the opposite direction, toward less government involvement in our lives and toward greater accountability in government policies. No longer will it be assumed that government knows best or even that government is the answer.

Will this movement lead to a totally new farm policy structure in the United States? Not necessarily. But the present structure will be vigorously scrutinized, not only in committee but also on the floor of both houses of Congress. The American public is fed up with all government spending, so subsidies are under attack everywhere. Whether they be direct or indirect, transparent or hidden, this year's legislative process will ferret them out and analyze them. If subsidies cannot withstand scrutiny, they will be phased out or drastically modified. That is precisely what should occur in a democratic society where government has been spending far beyond its means.

This year's debate must also recognize the realities of a global marketplace. Global markets are not coming, they are already here. And they are here to stay. If there is a "domestic" market, it is rapidly becoming all of North America, not just the United States. The distinction between domestic and foreign is becoming ever more blurred and may ultimately disappear. As a result, now we must all compete. We can no longer isolate our farm economy from what others do. We cannot control our own destiny. In fact, we would not wish to do so, for most of our customers are outside our borders.

This reality suggests that 1995 farm legislation should, first, do no harm to our competitiveness and, second, foster it if at all possible. Our foremost objective should be growth in U.S. farm income—from the marketplace, not from the federal Treasury. That will occur only if we continue to reduce unit production costs, add value to raw product here in the United States (for example, through expanded industrial uses), and boost export sales by putting quality food products on the world market at attractive prices. It will take both a vibrant U.S. private sector and an astute, efficient government to bring that about.

We must be more visionary in our policy making. After all, our competitors are not sitting on their hands. If we are not alert and dynamic, they will leapfrog us in competitiveness. We should therefore consider new ideas such as revenue assurance that could provide more flexibility, greater simplicity, and more bang for the buck in our agricultural safety net. As with welfare reform, we need to experiment, even if only on a pilot basis, to see what might work best now or in the future. Let us not be hidebound by farm policy tradition; it is a new world out there.

Through the years we have gradually achieved at least a semblance of harmonization and compatibility among our various farm programs. That trend should continue in 1995. Farm programs need not be identical, but it helps if the fundamental concepts are similar. And let us do something about the sometimes embarrassing anachronisms (peanut and sugar protection, for example).

Finally, this year's legislation should lay the groundwork for another tranche of multilateral trade negotiations, now scheduled for 1999. We were able in the Uruguay Round to expose the most glaring trade distortions of other nations and to persuade those nations to begin to reform. The 1990 farm bill helped generate momentum in those negotiations, and U.S. agriculture will be a major beneficiary of that effort. We now need a similar effort in the 1995 farm bill to set an example for the future and to stimulate others to carry out their own reforms with enthusiasm and commitment. That, coupled with another successful negotiation in 1999, would provide a rewarding future for American farmers as they enter the next century.

CLAYTON YEUTTER
Former Secretary of Agriculture
and U.S. Trade Representative;
Counsel to Hogan & Hartson

Contributors

DANIEL A. SUMNER is the Frank H. Buck, Jr., Professor in the Department of Agricultural Economics at the University of California, Davis. He was the assistant secretary for economics at the U.S. Department of Agriculture, where he served as the chief economist in policy formulation and analysis on issues facing agriculture and rural America from food and farm programs to trade, resources, and rural development. Mr. Sumner was a member of the Board of Directors of the U.S. Government's Commodity Credit Corporation, senior economist at the President's Council of Economic Advisers, deputy assistant secretary of agriculture, and professor in the Division of Economics and Business at North Carolina State University. Mr. Sumner's academic research in agricultural economics focuses on the consequences of domestic and trade policies for agriculture and the economy. His research has appeared in numerous academic journal articles, books, and technical reports.

JULIAN M. ALSTON is a professor in the Department of Agricultural Economics of the University of California, Davis. He was the chief economist in the Department of Agriculture in Victoria, Australia, where he was involved in policy formulation and analysis of issues affecting rural Australians and in the management of agricultural research, extension, and regulation. Mr. Alston's research focuses on the economic analysis of agricultural markets and public policies concerning agricultural incomes, prices, trade, and agricultural research. He is the coauthor of *Science under Scarcity: Principles and Practice for Agricultural Research Evaluation and Priority Setting.*

JOHN M. ANTLE is a professor in the Department of Agricultural Economics and Economics at Montana State University. During 1989–1990 he was the senior economist for the President's Council of Economic Advisers, and he contributed to two chapters of the 1990 *Economic Report of the President*. Mr. Antle is a member of the National Research Council's Board on Agriculture and a university fellow at Resources for the Future. He was an economic consultant to the international agricultural research centers, the Rockefeller Foundation, and the Mexican agricultural research system. Mr. Antle's research focuses on the environmental impacts of agriculture, including production, health, and environmental consequences of pesticide use in rice production in the Philippines and potato production in Ecuador, links between economic growth and the environment across low- and high-income countries, and environmental effects of pesticide use in the United States.

PETER J. BARRY is professor of agricultural economics at the University of Illinois and director of the Center for Farm and Rural Business Finance. He is a past president of the American Agricultural Economics Association. His research activities include credit evaluation in agriculture, farm financial management, risk management, performance of financial markets for agriculture, asset-liability management, loan pricing by financial institutions, asset valuation, and investment analysis. Mr. Barry was the editor of the *American Journal of Agricultural Economics* and the *Western Journal of Agricultural Economics*. He was a faculty member at Texas A&M University and at the University of Guelph.

BRUCE L. GARDNER is a professor at the Department of Agricultural and Resource Economics, University of Maryland. He was the assistant secretary for economics at the U.S. Department of Agriculture, 1989–1991, and was the senior staff economist of the President's Council of Economic Advisers. Mr. Gardner's writings and research focus on agricultural commodity policy, food marketing, trade and environment, farm labor, population, crop insurance, and futures and commodity options in agriculture. He is the author of *The Economics of Agricultural Policies, The Governing of Agriculture,* and *Optimal Stockpiling of Grain.*

BARRY K. GOODWIN is an associate professor in the Department of Agricultural and Resource Economics at North Carolina State University. He was an associate professor in the Department of Agricultural Economics at Kansas State University. Mr. Goodwin's work emphasizes agricultural policy and price analysis, international trade, and applied econometrics. He has published more than forty articles, including papers in the *American Journal of Agricultural Economics, Journal of International Money and Finance, Land Economics,* and *Agricultural Economics.*

PHILIP G. PARDEY is a research fellow with the International Food Policy Research Institute. He is also an associate professor at the University of Minnesota, an associate editor of the *American Journal of Agricultural Economics,* and a former senior research officer at the International Service for National Agricultural Research. Mr. Pardey's research focuses on the economics of technical change, R&D policy, and economic development. He is the coauthor of *Science under Scarcity: Principles and Practice for Agricultural Research Evaluation and Priority Setting* and coedited *Agricultural Research Policy: International Quantitative Perspectives.*

VINCENT H. SMITH is an associate professor in the Department of Agricultural Economics and Economics at Montana State University. He was a consultant to the U.S. Environmental Protection Agency, consultant to the U.S. Agency for International Development and the government of Tanzania on the Consumption Effect of Agricultural Policy in Tanzania, and economist in the Energy and Environmental Research Division at the Department of Economics, Research Triangle Park Institute. Mr. Smith was on the faculties of Manchester University, North Carolina State University, Trinity College, and the University of Richmond. He is the author of several books, articles, and publications on agricultural and economic policy.

WALTER N. THURMAN is a professor in the Department of Agricultural and Resource Economics at North Carolina State University with an appointment in the Economics Department of the same institution. His work on the economic effects of agricultural policy has been published in the *American Journal of Agricultural Economics,* the *Journal of Law and Economics,* and the *Journal of Political Economy.* He is a senior associate editor of the *American Journal of Agricultural Economics.* He has also written on the economics of contracting in agriculture and on fisheries regulation.

BRIAN D. WRIGHT is professor of agricultural and resource economics at the University of California at Berkeley. He was on the faculty of Yale University. Mr. Wright is the co-author of *Storage and Commodity Markets,* and he has written more than forty academic papers. He is a reviewer for many economics journals and the National Science Foundation and is a consultant to the World Bank and other institutions. His research includes public economics, agricultural policy, trade, financial markets, research and development, market organization and behavior, and commodity market stabilization.

1
Introduction

Daniel A. Sumner

The government's role in agriculture has become a topic of growing interest throughout the world. For most of this century, the United States and other wealthy countries have applied intensive regulations to agricultural prices, production, and practices. In addition to regulation, these nations have pursued complex schemes of direct income subsidies for producers of selected crops. Recently, some progress toward more market orientation in agricultural policy has been made. While moderate at best, the continuing reforms are encouraging to those who believe that the world would benefit from less subsidy and regulation of agriculture. Although change has been slow and difficult, there is growing evidence that agricultural policy is responsive to well-developed empirical arguments that demonstrate the unwelcome consequences of current policy interventions and the benefits of specific reforms. For several decades, the American Enterprise Institute has helped create the analytical underpinning for many agricultural reform efforts. This book represents a continuation of that effort.

For the past decade, the federal budget deficit has focused attention on farm programs as a source of savings in federal outlays. This attention can be an impetus for positive policy change when it encourages scrutiny of broad public benefits from spending taxpayer dollars. Concern about the budget deficit, however, may also move policy toward more economic distortions when it encourages regulations and restrictions to substitute for the more visible costs of direct government subsidy. The recent emphasis on

1

the harm caused by unfunded mandates is thus a welcome development.

There is now an opportunity to build on momentum toward reform in some areas of agricultural policy. The 1985 and 1990 farm legislation, the North American Free Trade Agreement, and the Uruguay Round agreement under the General Agreement on Tariffs and Trade have all encouraged more attention to the market in setting farm policy. With this progress, now may be the time to initiate reforms in areas that have thus far been resistant. Of particular concern are those areas where the policy has recently been moving toward more intrusive regulation. In the past few years we have also witnessed new import subsidies, new export subsidies, new production subsidies, and expanded outlays that subsidize farmers for crop loss. All these areas deserve special attention in a general review of farm policy.

This book builds on a long tradition of the American Enterprise Institute by providing research information to guide policy on agricultural issues. For more than two decades, the periodic farm bills and associated legislation have been the main vehicles for policy changes specific to agriculture and related subjects. AEI published books of essays that surveyed farm policy information as a part of the 1977, 1981, and 1985 farm bill debates. The 1990 farm legislation will expire in 1995, and the policy debate associated with the new farm bill provides another significant opportunity to move agriculture toward market realities. To capitalize on the current opportunity and to facilitate the movement toward better public policy, AEI has sponsored a major research project on agriculture policy.

The AEI agricultural policy project includes a series of topical research studies prepared by experts and scholars who investigated the public rationale for the government's role with respect to several agricultural issues, developed evidence on the effects of recent policies, and analyzed alternatives. Most of the research was carried out in 1994; draft reports were discussed at a policy research workshop held in Washington on November 3–4, 1994. The workshop featured vigorous discussion and participation of analysts from the administration and congressional staffs as well as by scholars and other policy participants. The full research studies are being published as a series of individual monographs. The most important results and the core analyses comprise the following eight chapters.

Each of the eight chapters provides information useful for policy makers and stakeholders, including descriptions of empirical relationships and facts necessary for understanding the consequences of policy, critiques of recent policies, and analyses of specific policy alternatives. The research is addressed toward those who design policy in the various branches of government and those who influence policy from outside government, including farm and business representatives, academics, and analysts in policy research centers.

This book begins with a careful and unyielding examination of arguments that have been used to justify government's extensive involvement with agriculture for the past sixty years. Brian Wright, from the University of California at Berkeley, reviews these arguments one by one in the light of basic economic reasoning and recent history. He finds a lack of intellectual or empirical support for claims that the unique position of agriculture makes government programs more necessary or successful than in other parts of the economy. Wright's study challenges the current policies by providing a reasoned examination of their justification. He then reviews those parts of agricultural policy that deserve support for their contributions to efficiency or equity. He suggests alternatives or modifications without regard to their current political feasibility.

Bruce Gardner, from the University of Maryland, examines some specific consequences of the commodity programs under current farm legislation. He investigated potential modifications to policy operation that retain much of the basic structure. His study compares the projected effects of alternative policy changes; some changes may be considered in the continuing legislative debate. The study looks at various implications of current program options in a pro and con framework and discusses how to reduce the negative impacts while retaining some features that make the programs politically resilient. Gardner generally finds the current programs costly and inefficient and suggests innovative ideas that move agriculture to more of a market orientation. This study draws on Gardner's unique experience to analyze policy reform that may be feasible in the short term.

Gardner focuses on the domestic price and income support policies, but it is difficult to consider commodity policy in the United States without also considering the international context in which U.S. agriculture operates. Trade policies of the United States and most other countries facilitate and interact with domestic regulations and subsidies. Programs such as domestic peanut and sugar price supports could not operate without import barriers. Such important commodity industries as wheat and dairy have come to depend on a complex mixture of domestic subsidy programs, output regulations, import barriers, and export subsidies. Trade policies have themselves evolved rapidly since the 1990 farm legislation.

The fourth chapter of this book, which I prepared, reviews these recent changes along with the more fundamental questions. Beginning with the Canada-U.S. free trade negotiations and continuing with NAFTA and the Uruguay Round of GATT negotiations, the United States has been involved in major trade policy discussions for a decade. Chapter 4 considers the implications of recent and prospective multilateral trade agreements along with other farm trade programs and policies. The chapter devotes particular attention to export subsidies and new import barriers that run counter to the spirit of the recent trade agreements. This chapter suggests that U.S. agriculture and the economy as a whole would benefit if the United States pursued a consistent open market policy. Such a policy is best if accomplished multilaterally, but it is beneficial to the United States even if other countries do not reduce subsidies and barriers as quickly or thoroughly.

Many farm commodities are not covered by domestic

price supports, direct income support, export subsidies, or even significant import barriers. But almost all agriculture is affected by other policy. Closely connected to farm and trade policies that are specified on a commodity-by-commodity basis are issues of crop insurance and disaster aid, agricultural conservation and environmental programs, food safety regulations, farm credit programs, and policies related to agricultural research and extension. These are covered in the next five chapters of this book.

This book does not cover all issues. Several important policy areas that are not discussed have often been included in farm bills and are considered by the agricultural committees of the Congress. These include policies and programs that deal with national forests and other forestry issues, programs that subsidize domestic food consumption, and programs that subsidize rural communities. Each of these areas is important, and each affects agriculture. They have been set aside in this project only in order to focus on a smaller set of topics.

Chapter 5 considers policies that deal with the vagaries of nature. The Midwest flood of 1993 was the most recent of a long list of multistate disasters that seem to cause the administration and Congress to compete in seeming to be the most generous in subsidizing those with crop losses. Legislation enacted in the fall of 1994 was the latest in the attempt to reform crop insurance and disaster policy. The California floods of 1995 remind us that weather losses in agriculture will continue. Barry Goodwin, from North Carolina State University, and Vincent Smith, from Montana State University, consider the recent experience with crop insurance and disaster aid that led to the 1994 legislation. They also analyze more fundamental issues such as why the government provides crop insurance subsidy. They deal with the long-standing questions of why crop insurance does not provide the appropriate risk-management incentives and how to minimize problems of adverse selection and moral hazard. This study investigates policy options for disaster assistance and crop insurance by considering both basic changes and marginal modifications of the new programs.

Resource and environmental regulations and related subsidy programs play a large and increasing role in agricultural affairs and in the rural economy generally. In chapter 6 Walter Thurman, from North Carolina State University, deals with the implications of farm programs for the environment. The recognition that agriculture and farm programs have environmental consequences is not new. But this recognition and policies associated with it have become more widespread. In the past decade commodity subsidy programs have become less distortionary by reducing the artificial incentives to higher yields and by providing somewhat more flexibility in planting. These changes have reduced the negative environmental consequences of farm subsidies. Further, the receipt of subsidies has been made conditional on meeting environmental standards. Thurman explores these and other relationships between farm programs and environmental goals, and he considers the environmental consequences of alternatives to current farm programs. In addition to his analysis of commodity subsidies, Thurman analyzes the effects of long-term, paid land reserves and other programs directed toward limiting erosion, improving water quality, and preserving wetlands.

Food inspection, labeling, and other food safety and nutrition issues have been important issues since 1909. But becoming front-page news has spawned new regulations and increased government outlays. John Antle, from Montana State University, asks what economic principles should guide the regulation of food safety and what changes are needed in current policies. The various food inspection and safety regulations and agencies need to be modernized, streamlined, and consolidated. Besides the bureaucratic issues, Antle deals with the basic question of the appropriate role of government in food safety regulation. His research for the AEI project breaks new ground in the application of economics to food safety regulation.

Farm financial policy includes the Farmers Home Administration and the various institutions that form the Farm

Credit System. The costly farm financial regulations and subsidies of the 1980s led to major changes including the move toward credit guarantees rather than direct lending and a reorganization of the Farm Credit System. Despite these changes there remains the potential for significant federal outlays, and one may question the rationale for any government role in farm credit. Peter Barry, from the University of Illinois, examines the budget and nonbudget consequences of the whole array of farm financial programs and policies. He points out some serious problems and suggests remedies. Despite his measured tone, the improvements he suggests are important.

The final chapter is by Julian Alston, from the University of California, Davis, and Philip Pardey, from the University of Minnesota and the International Food Policy Research Institute. They discuss public-sector agricultural research and extension. There is substantial evidence that public agricultural research has greatly contributed to productivity growth in world agriculture. Further, a broad consensus supports government involvement in agricultural research. Alston and Pardey review the record and the rationales relating to government's role in the science of agriculture. They explain how alternative institutions and policies can enhance the net return on the billions of dollars per year spent on public agricultural research and extension. They do not argue for less involvement with or spending on research, but rather they provide information needed to spend our funds more effectively.

This final chapter on science policy helps clarify the federal government's significant and appropriate role in agriculture: to make agriculture more efficient and effective. Unfortunately, most agricultural policy in the United States does not accomplish that goal. In many ways the policies of the past six decades have been counterproductive and counter to productivity. By the last years of the twentieth century, the flaws of the policies developed decades ago are finally becoming so obvious that more close observers and participants are willing to consider gradually eliminating many traditional subsidies and regulations. Another round of minor fixes is clearly insufficient.

The 1995 farm bill season began differently from any other in recent memory. Those most central to the process, in Congress and elsewhere, seem willing to ask tough questions, and defenders of the status quo are truly on the defensive. How much is accomplished depends, however, on making available well-conceived analysis and carefully considered alternatives to the current programs. Even when the alternative is simply getting the government out of the way, understanding the consequences is not simple. The aim of this collection of studies and the research that underlies them is to provide some background information to make market-oriented reform of agricultural policy more feasible.

2
Goals and Realities for Farm Policy

Brian D. Wright

The greatest rate of progress in U.S. agriculture, in terms of increases in productivity, has occurred since the Great Depression—the inception of pervasive government involvement in agriculture. That is no coincidence. Government policies played a key role in helping farmers emerge from the depression and in fostering the high rate of productivity growth ever since.

The sustained fast pace of growth of agriculture over the past sixty years has completely transformed its role as an employer and generator of income and product in the U.S. economy. Yet the broad goals of current American agricultural policy are essentially those embraced under the New Deal in the 1930s. Does this imply their enduring social justification despite changed circumstances? Or has inertia in analysis and in policy making kept those goals from reflecting the transformation of the agricultural sector?

The bulk of the quinquennial review of the farm bill, *The 1995 Farm Bill Policy Options and Consequences*, is quite reasonably oriented toward modifications of existing programs. Such modifications are, in the main, the most likely outcome of the farm bill, whether or not they are what economists would choose.

I am grateful for the exceptional research assistance of Rachael Goodhue in preparing this study, and for information and comments provided by Warren Johnston, Dan Sumner, Tim Wallace, and Marguerite Wright.

9

My task in this review is quite different, however. I address the question, What agricultural policies should the U.S. government write on a clean policy slate? I can ignore any constraints imposed by the nature of existing policies. Given the current state of the agricultural sector, I consider the appropriate structure of a new agricultural policy regime—agricultural policy as it might be constructed from the ground up.

In such a radical reassessment it makes sense to start with the ends rather than the means of agricultural policy. We should consider only policy goals that are currently feasible and relevant. That rule sounds elementary, but it is mostly honored in the breach.

Economists obfuscate the analysis of existing agricultural programs when they look at a highly stylized policy objective to justify current programs or some variation of them. The demand for coherent economic models to evaluate marginal reform encourages that tendency. Like a contestant on *Jeopardy*, the economist produces a question to which price supports or crop insurance, to take two examples, is the answer. Thus, economists fail to investigate whether farmers' actual needs for government intervention match the stylized objectives that policy models assume.

Here I focus my attention on the ends rather than the means. To organize the analysis, I place the actual or potential goals of U.S. agricultural policy in five classes. The first category comprises feasible, achieved, and now obsolete goals. The second class includes popular or desirable but infeasible goals. In contrast, the third category comprises popular, desirable goals that are efficiently achievable without public assistance. The fourth class includes relevant goals that are achievable only with public intervention but are inappropriate social objectives. The final category comprises feasible, relevant goals that are appropriate as social objectives.

Only the final class of goals can justify public agricultural policy measures. Distinctions between the fourth and final categories obviously incorporate strong normative judgments. But I believe the general classification of goals is otherwise relatively uncontroversial, given the available facts and a modest exposure to economic reasoning.

The advantage of organizing my economic analysis around goals is that I can eliminate policies motivated by goals in the first four categories from the new policy set without considering the means themselves in any detail. That I do in the next four sections. Using rational economic principles, in the sixth section I recommend policy measures that might help satisfy feasible, relevant, and socially appropriate agricultural goals. Conclusions follow in the final section.

Feasible, Achieved, and Now Obsolete Goals

Truly successful social policies make themselves irrelevant. That has happened to the following venerable list of objectives, which comprises some of the greatest achievements of U.S. economic development.

Achieving Income Parity between Farmers and Nonfarmers. Persuasive evidence that U.S. agricultural policy has achieved income parity between farmers and nonfarmers is the complete elimination of any deficiency in the income of farm operator households. In 1990 the average income for farm operators was $39,007; the average income for all U.S. households was $1,600 less (Ray 1994).

Policy makers might like to attribute that achievement to price supports and other policy-induced transfers. But some countries, in particular Australia and New Zealand, have achieved a similar income parity without large transfers per farmer from consumers or taxpayers. Eliminating the rural income gap signifies integration of the farm sector into the rest of the economy, not closer ties between farming and government.

Historically, the dynamic equilibration of on-farm and off-farm incomes depended on migration from the land as farm productivity rose and prices declined (Kislev and Peterson 1982). In 1900, 38 percent of the labor force was in agricultural employment and 44 percent of the population

11

was rural. The figures are now less than 3 percent and about 26 percent, respectively. Migration is now most important in the rural areas with low population density. That process is often misconstrued. Fisher et al. (1994, emphasis added) note, for example:

> Income levels for many Great Plains counties are greater than or equal to the median for nonmetropolitan counties. *However*, due to a lack of employment alternatives, this region is experiencing the highest rate of out migration of any rural region in the United States.

Although the connection may not be obvious to all observers, the high rate of migration from the region undoubtedly plays a key role in maintaining high incomes in the Great Plains. In areas with a larger nonfarm economy, rural infrastructure in the form of roads, transport facilities, and communications has rendered off-farm jobs widely compatible with on-farm residence. A novel phenomenon in recent decades is the extent to which farm households have become engaged in the nonfarm economy *while still living on the farm*. The cost of migration no longer prevents most farms from moving part or all of their family labor off the farm. I anticipate that telecommuting technology, which can facilitate the performance of off-farm work within the farm residence, will enhance that integration.

U.S. Department of Agriculture figures indicate that the average farm household mentioned above received only $5,742 from farming in 1990 (Ray 1994). Although the precision of farm income data is questionable, clearly a large share of the average farm family's resources is employed elsewhere. Thus, returns to farm capital and labor are determined by what they can receive in the much larger nonfarm economy.

Providing Adequate Rural Credit for Agriculture. Farming is a highly capital-intensive business, and nearly three-quarters of that capital is in farm real estate. Access to land is the entry ticket to farm operation. The price of land and the conditions of credit supply set the terms for becoming a farm owner.

The price of land reflects expectations regarding the future stream of profits from farming and the long-term cost of capital. Young farmers with little capital have difficulty acquiring land. When the outlook is for increasing profits (from either market forces or an increasing trend in price supports), the land price tends to be high relative to current profits. Therefore, debt service is a challenge in the early years, even if optimistic expectations are generally fulfilled (Melichar 1979). Similarly, an upward adjustment in land prices tends to offset the benefits of low or subsidized interest rates. If, however, current conditions are good but the outlook is bleak, land costs are lower—but so are the prospective rewards from farming.

Apart from long-term expectations about profits and interest cost, other determinants of the price and availability of land include transaction costs, inheritance laws, the tax treatment of capital gains, and the influence of inflation on the effective tax rate. Luckily, one does not need a full model to know that the total area farmed is virtually independent of agricultural credit policy. But credit policy can favor some groups relative to others in the competition for land and working capital. The Farmers Home Administration, for example, has as a matter of policy channeled its direct loans toward otherwise noncreditworthy farmers. Indeed, its history of high loan losses relative to other lenders attests to its success in identifying those who truly are unworthy of credit.

The origins of the Farmers Home Administration lie in the Great Depression of the 1930s, when there was a natural concern with the operation of bank credit and other sources of finance for agriculture and for the economy as a whole. Since then, government has heavily intervened in farm lending.

Given the recent history of the savings and loans, it is not comforting to observe that both formal and presumptive credit risk guarantees are the means used by the other major instruments of agricultural credit policy—the Farm

Credit System and its independent entity, the Federal Agricultural Mortgage Corporation (Farmer Mac). The Farm Credit System operates as a borrower-controlled banking system with a market cost of capital reduced by its status as a government agency. Lenders apparently perceive its debts to be government-guaranteed. Since that guarantee is only implicit, however, it does not appear in accounts of anticipated government expense of the system, which is usually characterized as private. Farmer Mac, which guarantees secondary market sales of real estate loans, also has the advantage of agency status (Boehlje, Duncan, and Lins 1994).

Problems with private rural credit are now insignificant relative to the situation in the 1930s. The special-purpose banks for farmers are not in any way essential today. They will not help young farmers much. Yet they continue to expose the public budget to unwarranted risk through explicit and implicit credit risk guarantees, which recent experience has shown can be extremely costly.

One or more of the above goals might still be relevant in other countries. But in the United States, policy makers should feel free to declare victory and move on to focus on other objectives.

Popular, Desirable, but Infeasible Goals

Popular, desirable, but infeasible goals tend to be standbys for political sloganeers, for whom they have two great attractions. They are inherently appealing to the electorate, and they can never be made obsolete by being fulfilled.

Making Farming Permanently More Attractive to the Young. Making farming permanently more attractive to the young by means of price supports, deficiency payments, or market quotas positively related to production capacity is a goal that appears to be embodied explicitly or implicitly in farm policies of most developed economies, and it is often part of the rhetoric in support of policy legislation. Regardless of the merits of the objective, it is not achievable by the means listed above. Nor are the means consistent with common notions of equity among farmers or in the economy as a whole. Such conclusions are not matters of opinion or expressions of value judgments; they are implications of the workings of a competitive market economy.

In a competitive market, land rents adjust in response to changes in profits from farming. Once market participants recognize the prospect of future transfers that are related to farm size, land prices also increase. When there is a competitive market for land, farmers who own land when such policies become recognized have a capital gain. If, for example, the interest rate is 5 percent, a permanent policy that transfers $10 per acre per year to farmers causes a jump of $200 per acre in the land price—the value of a perpetuity of $10 per year. The fact that their land is worth more on the market does not make continuing to farm it any more or less attractive to landowners, except insofar as their increased wealth changes their attitude toward work.[1] New entrants to farming will find that the increase in the land price ($200 per acre) more or less offsets any anticipated future benefits from government transfers.

Many agricultural economists and farmers may not recognize that the scope of the implications of capitalization is so wide as to render the goals of equalizing the distribution of income and of stabilizing farm income infeasible as well.

Equalizing the Distribution of Income by Measures Related to Landholdings. Currently, major means of agricultural income redistribution include price supports, deficiency payments, or other measures whose value is related to landholdings. Assume for now that those measures change farmers' incomes in proportion to their effects on current farm receipts. The families running those farms generally have incomes above the average for farm and non-

---

1. If it does, the effect is likely to be negative with respect to the goal under consideration, encouraging them to leave farming for an easier urban life.

farm families alike. Most of the program benefits go to a minority of large farms (Browne et al. 1992). Since removing all agricultural transfers would bring the income of the major recipients closer to the national nonfarm average, the goal of equalizing farm and nonfarm income does not justify current policies.

Furthermore, it is obvious that such transfers are not in harmony with reasonable equity goals within the agricultural sector. Within farming, landholdings, output, and transfers to farmers are all highly skewed toward those with high income from farming.[2] What is not so obvious is the fact that capitalization means that the inequity of transfers related to production applies only to the owners of farmland at the time when policy changes first become known to the market. Given competitive land markets, buyers of land after the policy change will pay the full capitalized value of the transfers. They do not gain significantly from the transfer program; the transfers are just about enough to pay the increased cost of the land.

Even if the revenue flows are permanently skewed toward large farms, no significant inequity from a policy change persists to the next generation of farm families other than by way of effects on bequests from their forebears. Buyers of large farms have large, government-subsidized revenues because they are wealthy. They are not wealthy because their revenues were enhanced by policies in place when they bought their land.

Capitalization of transfers into the value of land (and other fixed assets) means that the widespread perception that policy skews wealth toward large landowning farmers is true only for those who are lucky enough to own land during unanticipated policy shifts. But capitalization also means that the gains of those particular landowners are huge relative to the effects on annual farm revenues. Permanent policy shifts have one-shot wealth effects, which farmers may or may not share with their heirs, who may or may

---

2. Payment limitations are probably relatively ineffective owing to well-known loopholes.

not choose to be farmers. Later entrants into farming and annual renters of land get no benefits.

Thus, beside ensuring that policy cannot make farming attractive for all future generations, capitalization also means that policy changes induce large but barely perceived inequities between generations of farmers. The size of the intergenerational bias in favor of current as distinct from future landowners is, paradoxically, larger if the policies are perceived to be permanent rather than temporary.

Stabilizing Farm Incomes. If all farmers find farms with more stable revenue streams more desirable, they will bid up the price of buying or renting such farms so that the higher value of land more or less completely offsets the anticipated advantages of stabilization. Those who value stabilization more than others might be somewhat favored in the bidding process in that they pay a little less for stability than what it is worth to them. But their gain comes at the expense of their less risk-averse competitors in the land market.

Achieving Rural Development. The foundations of achieving rural development with price supports and subsidies were laid in the Great Depression when the nonmetropolitan community was principally a farming community. Now less than 10 percent of the nonmetropolitan labor force works in farming. Most of the rest are employees; services, manufacturing, and government all employ more nonmetropolitan workers than the number in farming (Browne et al. 1992). To put that another way, 93 percent of the *nonmetropolitan* population resides in counties that have less than 20 percent of their labor force employed in agriculture. Assuming that agricultural policy could make farmers (already a relatively high-income rural group) more prosperous, how can we expect to tackle rural development in general by manipulating the welfare of a small, generally relatively wealthy minority of the population?

Indeed, to ask what agricultural policy can do for rural development is to get the big question backward. With most farm families earning most of their income off the farm and most of the rural labor force employed in other sectors, the real issue is what rural development policy can do for farmers (Luloff and Swanson 1990).

If rural development means rural but nonfarm job creation to maintain population numbers, it is important to note that economic theory and empirical evidence do point to government's substantial role in developing agricultural and more generally rural communities. But government's role consists principally of providing public goods and related infrastructure, activities beyond the scope of what is normally called agricultural policy.

Popular, Desirable Goals That Are Efficiently Achievable Privately

Saving Family Farming. One urban myth in America is that family farming is fast disappearing, being swallowed up by impersonal corporations run by city dwellers or, even worse, by foreigners. That is almost completely untrue. Despite the industrial and postindustrial revolutions and the revolution in agricultural production technologies, the managerial structure of agriculture in the United States is typically a family with some part of a person-year of hired labor supplying a total of about one and one-half person-years per farm. Even more remarkable, those numbers have remained virtually unchanged for the whole of the past century.

Non–family-owned corporations operate less than one-third of 1 percent of U.S. farms, and foreigners own only 1.3 percent of all farmland (Browne et al. 1992). Even of the largest farm size category, 89 percent is operated personally by owners. Farmers do, of course, rent a great deal of land, although the numbers to some extent reflect accounting adjustments in response to government limitations on price support payments. But families who own much if not most of their land operate the vast majority of farms.

It is no coincidence that a family farm, with between one and two full-time adult workers or their equivalent, is the operational rule in countries without much agricultural policy intervention, like New Zealand, and others with totally different agricultural policies, endowments, and technologies, like India. The typical farm, spread over a significant amount of land and subject to unanticipated disturbances from weather, pests, and other aspects of the environment, places a premium on workers with intimate local knowledge who are sufficiently self-motivated to need no close supervision (Nerlove 1994). The farm family member fits such a job description.

Like all myths, that of the disappearance of family farming has a grain of truth at its core. The number of family farms is continually falling because almost all farms are family farms and the total number of farms is falling. Indeed, over the past sixty years, the majority of family farms has disappeared, usually because the operator retires or dies without being replaced by an heir interested in and capable of taking over the farm. But family farmers still till the land and raise hogs and calves. Each farm family now works with much more land, however, and many small farmers are now mostly, in terms of labor allocation, not principally farmers at all.

In the future the rapidly advancing technology for communication, supervision, and real-time access to advice and information systems by spatially dispersed workers may shift the nature of the typical operational structure in primary agriculture and replace family operation with some other dominant mode.

Conversely, the advantages of family operation may actually increase. Most nonfamily operations specialize in a single commodity. Family organizations may be particularly well equipped to respond to the complexities of complying with green regulations or of producing environmental amenities along with agricultural commodities. Environmental demands placed on farmers are bound to become more important in the years ahead.

Nor is it necessarily true that farm size, in terms of land area operated, will continually increase. As more stringent controls are placed on chemical inputs, for example, it is likely that demand for managerial skill and attention will intensify and increase the inherent managerial advantages of family operation and perhaps reduce optimal farm size. Private demands for hunting and other environmental services from farmers may have a similar effect.

Recent evidence suggests that modifying farm policies can reduce farm size, not by increasing government intervention, but rather by radically deregulating. New Zealand is the only example of a country that has almost completely dismantled a complex system of agricultural subsidies in the postwar period.[3] In New Zealand the average farm size decreased from 277 hectares in 1984, when a policy revolution began, to 217 hectares in 1993, and the number of farms increased by 4 percent (Johnston and Frengley 1994). The number of full-time permanent employees also increased slightly. The high unemployment in the nonagricultural economy may explain part of that phenomenon.[4] But observers also point to diversification of farmers into new products in the new free-market environment, including labor-intensive specialty horticulture, as well as conversion of formerly subsidized sheep farms to smaller dairy farms.

With current technology, no policy can produce an agricultural sector of peasant-sized, full-time family farms with operators earning incomes that are not peasant-sized but comparable to those of typical modern urban families. Those twin goals are incompatible: as a package they belong in the "infeasible" category discussed above.

Providing Farm-specific Consulting on Technical or Managerial Issues. In the United States the Cooperative Extension Service has historically offered farms free consulting service on technical or managerial issues. Recently, however, the trend has been to cede that type of service to the private sector. Only if the service provides significant bene-

---

3. See Sandrey and Reynolds (1990) for an overview of the New Zealand experience.

4. U.S. history shows that a depression might increase the number of farmers.

fits that a fee-paying client would not capture is public provision indicated.

Supporting Applied Research on Fully Marketable Innovations. The government has an indisputable role in making applied research possible by enforcing proprietary rights through the legal system including the patent system and protection of trade secrets. Expanded patent protection and improved technological means of identifying infringements have allowed the private sector to take over and indeed greatly expand the production of novel final genetic material for most varieties of plants. Having successfully developed the scientific foundations and also the appropriate legal protections, the government can now gracefully withdraw from much of the commercial seed production business.

Relevant, Socially Inappropriate Goals Achievable with Public Intervention

Having eliminated those goals that are infeasible as objects of agricultural policy, obsolete in the United States, or achievable without public policy measures, we now turn to consider goals that are relevant and plausibly feasible but require public intervention for their implementation. We can justify intervention on two broad grounds. First, goals might involve distribution between individuals beyond voluntary transfers—redivision of the economic pie. Whether that redistribution is appropriate clearly depends on value judgments. Second, if some distortion of the private market induces it to fail to allocate resources efficiently, government policy might in principle at least partially remove the distortion—increase the size of the pie.

In this section I consider those objectives that do not merit public pursuit at this time in the United States. I leave development of a menu of appropriate objectives to the following section.

Increasing Price Supports, Deficiency Payments, or Other

Transfers to Make Current Farmers More Wealthy. There is a crucial distinction between the goal of making current farmers better off and the goal in the preceding section of making farming permanently more attractive to the young. It is quite feasible for policy to make *current* farmers better off by unexpectedly *increasing* transfers to farmers above what they expected to get. The more permanent the increase is perceived to be, the greater the immediate boost in landowners' wealth due to capitalization of future benefits. As time goes by, farmers sell their land and exit from farming. The majority of supporters of existing transfer policies changes from those who are trying to retain the benefits they received to those who never benefited in the first place. But the latter will desperately fight to protect themselves from policy reforms that would cause the value of their investments to fall. Does that help explain why today's agricultural policies look so much like those of the 1930s?

In the special circumstances of the Great Depression, perhaps it made sense to try to boost the fortunes of a particularly unlucky cohort of farmers, even at the expense of subsequent generations. A similar rationale could be offered for the initiation of pay-as-you-go social security, also established during the Great Depression. But transfers proportional to land or production are not egalitarian *within* the initial cohort—the cohort of true beneficiaries. That problem, in contrast to the intercohort inequity, is widely recognized. Agricultural payments of that general type currently predominate in the United States. A minority of larger farmers gets most of the benefits. Most farm program payments do not aid the poorest farm households, let alone the poorest rural households. Appalachia, the region with the lowest farm household incomes, received the lowest share of farm household income from government payments.

If we assume that the type of inequitable redistribution just described is what is wanted, supports that are decoupled from the recipient's own production and investment decisions are, all else being equal, preferable to payments that vary directly with production. Decoupling prevents the program from inducing distortions in the mix of inputs farmers choose. For example, price supports (especially if combined with acreage controls) tend to encourage substi tution of other inputs, such as fertilizer, for land, while deficiency payments paid on a program yield per acre, independent of actual production, do not induce comparable distortions because the future program yield is not responsive to current output.

The skewed nature of the distribution of farm price supports among current farmers leads many commentators to advocate direct transfers to farm operators, independent of the assets they own or the size of their productive capacity. Would they be better?

Providing Egalitarian Direct Transfers to Farmers. From an equity standpoint, transfers totally independent of assets, output, and output capacity have two great advantages. First, they can be completely egalitarian within a cohort of farmers, or even skewed toward those with lower incomes. Second, since they are not capitalized in fixed assets, they do not cause intercohort inequity by front-loading the discounted stream of benefits on the first cohort of recipients.

But payments to farmers *for being farmers* would be a disaster. What criteria would identify farmers: a rural lifestyle? location on a farm? a certain percentage of time spent on agricultural labor?

Were any of the above criteria adopted, it is a good bet that the supply response of the number of farmers to a meaningful level of redistributive transfers would be impressive. That would in turn imply that a large proportion of recipients would not have been members of the originally targeted farm population. The cost of the transfer per dollar to the originally targeted population could be correspondingly higher. Most seriously, the beginnings of a permanent, unproductive class of government-dependent, rent-seeking peasantry would be created, with its members being diverted from more gainful occupations or more appropriate residential locations. For a current example of that type of problem, consult the recent history of Pacific islands that are "beneficiaries" of U.S. welfare programs. Whatever the shortcomings of U.S. agricultural policy, it has avoided that policy catastrophe.

Protecting Producers against Risk. The most pervasive rationale for interventionist agricultural policy in developed economies, and the one economists give greatest respectability, is that farmers need government protection against risk to produce efficiently. That argument is distinct from its distributional counterpart, risk protection to make farmers better off, which is an infeasible long-run objective, as discussed above.

The efficiency argument for risk protection has great persuasive power. We all know that agriculture is subject to unusually large production disturbances, from weather fluctuations, pest infestations, and the like. Given the inelastic response of consumption to price that is typical of agricultural products, marketwide production disturbances translate into much greater price fluctuations. Since agricultural production takes time, the farmer has to make financial commitments to input choices for crop or animal production well before he knows output prices and yields. The result is that net income from most agricultural production activities is highly risky. Can government make farmers more efficient on average by reducing their reluctance to take production risks?

Private insurance usually is not available to remove all income risk and in many cases is not observed at all. Its absence lends credibility to the economic case for public intervention to create that "missing market" and ease the "capital rationing" that arises because of risk aversion.

Variants of the above argument are the main intellectual defense of major existing U.S. agricultural policies, including price floors, nonrecourse loans, deficiency payments, crop insurance, and marketing orders. The recent Iowa Farm Bill Study Team's plan (1994) and other revenue insurance proposals appeal to that rationale.

Economists realize that most of the above programs

tend to raise incomes rather than to stabilize them. But economists continue to give the risk-reduction argument inordinate weight by using an analytical approach that greatly overstates the value to farmers of reducing the risk of their income flows from farming. Economists generally use expected utility theory, the dominant approach to the economics of risk, in policy analysis of risk taking, market stabilization, and insurance. But agriculturally oriented studies tend to assume that a farmer's consumption tracks his farm income, which means that consumption fluctuates just as wildly as farm income. Those studies generally ignore all private means of smoothing the effects of farm income on consumption.

Accordingly, economists overestimate the risk premium, a measure of the gain from smoothing consumption around a given mean. The true premium increases roughly proportionally to the variance in consumption. So if the farmer smoothed half of each deviation in net income relative to the mean income, the remaining cost of risk would be only one-quarter of the unsmoothed value that the economist assumed.

In fact, without any special government intervention, farmers are extremely capable of smoothing their consumption flows relative to their unusually variable farm income stream. The methods they use include diversification of income sources, saving, and borrowing. Since analysts frequently ignore those methods, they bear some elaboration.

Diversifying. By incorporating fields with different soil types, farming bottom land and hillsides, or even exploiting local differences in rainfall patterns or soil water-holding capacity, a farmer can in many cases considerably reduce exposure to weather-related risk.

Single-field observations of risk can greatly overestimate the farm-level cost of risk. For example, in the International Crops Research Institute for the Semi-Arid Tropics' Experiment Station in a semiarid area of India, correlation of July rainfall between two ends of the 1,400-hectare station is only around .6 (Walker and Jodha 1986). Diversification of a peasant's small plots within the area around a local village can obviously reduce yield variation substantially (McCloskey 1976).

Diversification might come in the form of a mix of crops such as corn and soybeans. Diversification across crops and livestock, as in corn-hog or corn-beef operations, is a natural way of combining activities with countervailing sensitivities to the vagaries of the animal feed market; when the price of corn is low, meat production is cheaper, and vice versa. But even if two activities have unrelated, rather than offsetting, sources of income fluctuations, a great consumption-smoothing advantage lies in diversifying across the two, rather than in specializing. If both activities have equal mean and variance of incomes, farmers can reduce the cost of consumption fluctuations in terms of risk premium by one-half by giving each an equal share in the farm operation, rather than by specializing in one or the other.

The above on-farm diversification strategies are most pertinent for the minority of farm families that specialize in farming. But most U.S. farmers, as noted above, receive much more of their income from off-farm employment than from farming. We know that most farmers live in counties where most of the income is not related to agriculture. Unless off-farm income is highly correlated with the farmer's on-farm income, that diversification will very substantially dampen the general relative variability of the farmer's consumption.

If, as is likely, off-farm income is steadier than on-farm income, and the two are approximately independent, then the typical farmer can diversify most of the risk cost of farm income fluctuations by finding off-farm employment. To take a simple example, a farmer with one-third of family income from a certain type of farming would obtain only about one-ninth the benefit from complete stabilization of farm income, relative to another farmer with the same mean income who was totally specialized in the same type of farming.

Adjusting savings and borrowing. Another extremely important means of consumption smoothing is adjusting savings or borrowing. Even in developing countries with neither the diverse financial markets seen in the United States nor the off-farm income diversification nor the extensive agricultural price supports, it appears that savings or formal or informal loans buffer much if not all of farmers' short-run income shocks (Paxson 1992; Alderman and Paxson 1992).

A tough test of farm families' ability to handle shocks is the extent to which severe fluctuations in income associated with an abrupt cutoff of large agricultural subsidies translate into movements in consumption. The recent experience of New Zealand provides an example. In 1984 the newly elected Labor government of New Zealand abruptly reformed economic policy by placing it on a free-market path. The agricultural sector experienced the rapid dismantling of a system of large subsidies on products and inputs including fertilizer and capital. In addition, the government sold the rural bank to the private sector. Agriculture was also affected by tariff reductions, an abrupt devaluation and subsequent revaluation of the currency, and a rapid escalation in interest rates. Total measured government assistance of all kinds, including infrastructure, plummeted between 1984 and 1986, except that debt forgiveness continued to be important for a few more years.

Figure 2–1 shows the effects of that experience on a measure of disposable income of the average beef-sheep farmer. Real disposable income fluctuated wildly, but adjustments in saving or changes in debt buffered most of the year-to-year variation. Consumption remained remarkably steady. Those observations are averages from a large survey that might hide the true experience of many distressed farms. One would naturally expect that high-debt farms would have the least flexibility for that type of adjustment. But in that group, with more debt than equity and thus most likely to be credit rationed, real consumption is again relatively insensitive to fluctuations in disposable income because it is buffered by changes in net debt (Wright 1995).

I use foreign sources for my empirical analysis of risk

FIGURE 2–1

USE OF SAVINGS AND BORROWING FOR CONSUMPTION
SMOOTHING BY NEW ZEALAND SHEEP AND BEEF FARMERS,
1983–1992

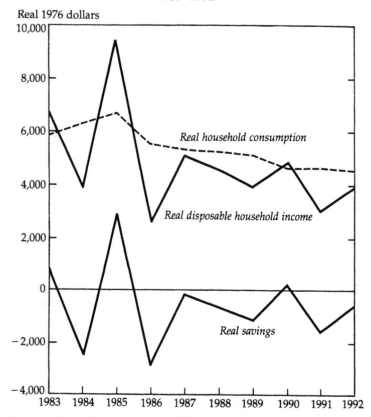

SOURCES: Frengley and Johnston (1992), table 2, p. 18; Johnston and
Frengley (1994), table 6; and unpublished data from New Zealand
Meat and Wool Board's Economic Service.

management because, despite the prominence of risk reduction in deductive arguments and theoretical analysis
supporting U.S. policies and despite the large expenditures
at stake, analysts have collected little empirical evidence in
the United States regarding either the economic need for
protecting farmers' risk or the risk-protection value offered

28

BRIAN D. WRIGHT

by current or proposed policies. Why has the agricultural economics profession been so incurious about the empirical validity of its theories, especially when they are used to give credibility to policies with such large budgetary implications?

The best U.S. evidence I know on the response of farmers' consumption to income fluctuations is data on eighteen Illinois farmers from 1979 through 1986 that Langemeier and Patrick (1990) analyzed. Using various conventional models, they find a marginal propensity to consume from current income of less than .03: a dollar of income fluctuation translates into a change in consumption of less than three cents.

Although the models used are subject to theoretical challenges, figure 2–2 tells the main story. In a period of wild fluctuations in family income—as well as in interest rates, credit availability, and net worth—consumption is remarkably steady relative to income.[5] Note that those income fluctuations constitute the variation that remains *after* the stabilizing effects of commodity policies like target prices, nonrecourse loans, and crop insurance. Clearly, those programs do not achieve a smooth income stream for farmers, but farm families nevertheless quite successfully smooth consumption.[6] Those data suggest that any analysis that assumes that income equals consumption, year by year, is radically misspecified and will vastly overestimate the effect of policies designed to reduce risk.

Farmers' own alternatives for reducing risk. Even if farmers' alternatives for private risk management are effective, they could still be sufficiently costly that farmers would welcome opportunities to smooth consumption by public programs that stabilize their incomes and make their production plans more predictable. One way to explore that possibility is to observe farmers' own choices when pre-

---

5. Its standard deviation is only one-tenth that of income in this sample.
6. Consumption may reflect the stabilizing effects of access to publicly provided or guaranteed loans.

FIGURE 2–2
INCOME AND CONSUMPTION OF EIGHTEEN ILLINOIS FARM FAMILIES,
1979–1986

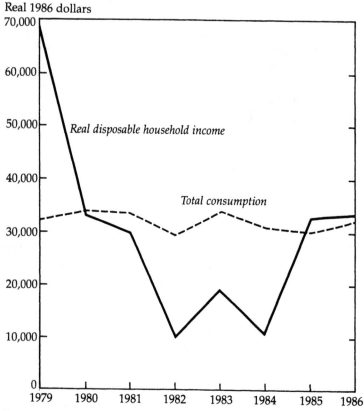

SOURCE: Langemeier and Patrick (1990), table 1.

sented with opportunities to reduce risk. The available evidence is instructive.

None of the many crop insurance schemes tried by governments in developing and developed countries over many years has attracted the participation of the majority of farmers without a substantial government subsidy (Wright and Hewitt, 1994; Goodwin and Smith 1995). A common-sense conclusion is that farmers do not have a high enough risk premium to make participation on an actuarially fair basis covering reasonable administrative costs sufficiently attractive, given their other alternatives to smooth consumption.

After a sufficiently high-powered education, most economists are more attracted to interesting and clever rationales involving moral hazard and adverse selection, discussed in a little greater detail in Wright (1995). Essentially, difficulties in identifying the nature of the insured's risk and in observing the insured's actions may make private insurance too expensive to be practical.

The evidence favors the common-sense conclusion. In the high-risk, low-rainfall Mallee wheat-growing area of Australia, the government took the unusually sensible step of asking farmers whether they would be willing to buy an insurance contract before implementing the insurance program.[7] The proposed contract had payouts conditioned on local rainfall measurements, and the price was actuarially fair and covered standard administrative costs. That contract had no problems of adverse selection or farmer moral hazard. But the majority did not wish to purchase rainfall insurance. Such survey evidence supports the simple hypothesis advanced above, that crop insurance is a money-losing proposition because it is simply of insufficient value to farmers.

Additional evidence against the standard economic argument for public insurance comes from the province of Saskatchewan, Canada, where the federal and provincial governments jointly implemented the Government Revenue Insurance Program in 1991 as comprehensive insurance against income risk due to fluctuations in price or yield. If farmers are risk averse according to the standard theoretical model of insurance, they should prefer income insurance to price or yield insurance.

---

7. Governments usually try crop insurance programs that end up losing millions if not billions of dollars without ever seriously considering research to see whether the program is needed, or why it is not working. Despite the billions of dollars lost on those programs every year, I know of no research in any country that examines the influence of crop insurance on farmers' consumption patterns.

But the Saskatchewan farmers successfully lobbied for a separation of the price and yield insurance aspects the following year, apparently on the grounds that they preferred payouts on price shortfalls, even if income were unusually high, given large yields, and vice versa. The farmers' behavior is consistent with the hypothesis that they are not sufficiently risk averse to value crop insurance highly.

In the United States comprehensive production contracts have been spreading from products like broilers and processed vegetables into other product lines including pork production. Those contracts generally fix input and output prices and offer various degrees of access to technical assistance. Apart from any concerns about monopsony or monopoly, farmers frequently object to those contracts on the grounds that they do not allow contract farmers to participate in price increases. Farmers usually ignore the fact that the contract equally protects against price decreases. It appears, then, that contractors who make that complaint actually prefer price risk.

That should not be excessively surprising. If producers can respond to price variations and their yield disturbances are small or independent of prices, their average profits are higher when their input and output prices are variable than when they are stable at their mean values. Preference for nonstabilized prices over contractually fixed prices indicates that risk aversion is not the dominant determinant of those producers' attitudes toward price stabilization by private contract. Why would they favor similar stabilization by the government in the absence of a sweetener in the form of a rise in mean price?

Policies to Write on a Clean Slate

In general, government interventions to improve efficiency come under the headings of either providing public goods or of correcting externalities and other market failures. Public goods are goods or services that the private sector cannot provide efficiently. If supplied to one person, they can be made available to others at no extra cost. Thus, one person's consumption does not reduce the availability of public goods to other people. The policy of charging each consumer the marginal cost of consumption is generally efficient in covering costs for private goods, but it fails for public goods for two reasons. First, marginal cost, the cost of providing another unit of (joint) consumption, is less than the average cost of production, so to price at marginal cost is to run a deficit. Second, it is economically undesirable to enforce a higher payment by the marginal consumer because to do so is to prevent some consumption that is more valuable to consumers than what it cost to produce. Both characteristics are obvious in the "pure" example of radio market reports or a new production technique, where the cost of one more farmer's acquiring the use is zero and it is not possible to charge a fee. Less pure cases might still merit public provision if the private alternative is less efficient.

An externality is a related phenomenon wherein one party's production or consumption activity affects the profits or utility of another in the absence of any market transaction between the two. A classic example is the positive interaction between beekeeping and clover production. Other types of market failure include cases in which a market for a good or service is distorted, as in conventional (nondiscriminatory) monopoly, or is missing altogether.

Recent econometric analysis of the agricultural sector in developing countries suggests that, while agricultural supply generally responds to price incentives, the provision of certain types of public goods can be much more important for the growth of agriculture. Among those are roads, communication systems, health services, and general education, all of which are already available in the United States and hardly come within the range of what is called agricultural policy in this country. Other public goods are crucial elements of U.S. agricultural policy, including agricultural research, environmental services, domestic food assistance, and food security.

Conducting Agricultural Research to Produce Externalities. In the United States the history of increasing yields and sustained productivity growth matches, with perhaps a thirty-year lag, the period of heavy public involvement in the agricultural sciences. If there was ever a truly successful industrial policy, it is U.S. agricultural research policy.

The agriculture-related sciences, in particular the biological sciences, are changing with the revolution in genetic engineering. In many disciplines the path from the basic science to the usable agricultural innovation appears to be shortening, and traditional product-related specialization is becoming obsolete. Paradoxically, precisely when Washington would love to find a vehicle for applying industrial policy, it is cutting back on support for the only industrial policy with a worldwide, sixty-year record of great success. And just when applied researchers need to be closer than ever to their mother academic discipline, the tendency nationwide has been toward funding special-purpose applied research centers concentrated on a particular crop or issue.

Modern public agricultural research should build on its history of success by emphasizing close links with the rapidly advancing mother disciplines. That research should be sufficiently flexible to take advantage of opportunities for applications as and where they arise.[8] Although research results are often transferable across regions or countries, local research is often needed for successful adaptation to local conditions. Countries or regions that attempt to take a free ride on research tend to get left at the starting gate.

With recent expansion in the patenting of life forms, stronger enforcement by courts, and the more effective policing afforded by genetic fingerprinting technology, the private sector is taking up more of the final developmental research. The government can withdraw some resources from that developmental work and reallocate them to the more basic agricultural sciences to enable the agricultural

---

8. For more on research administration, see Just and Huffman (1992).

sector to provide modern environmental and ecological services to society at large.

Providing Environmental Services Not Privately Capturable. Concern with environmental degradation in agriculture existed at the beginnings of current agricultural policy in the depression years of the Dust Bowl. Until recently, the major concern has been the correction of externalities acting *within* agriculture. Control of wind and water erosion protected productive topsoil.

Until recently, then, conservation has meant conservation *for* agriculture *by* agriculture. Now, however, society is becoming increasingly aware of the off-farm environmental consequences of farming, including not just erosion but also water pollution, flooding, air pollution, and the release of toxic or ozone-depleting substances.

Inputs can be regulated or taxed if they cause harmful externalities. Countries with the highest farm price supports—including Japan, South Korea, and those in the European Union—have the highest levels of input use. Within the latter, the Netherlands is already taxing fertilizer use as an environmental policy. For fertilizer control in such countries, a simpler alternative is to remove the nonmarket incentives. Removal of subsidies on farm inputs and outputs in New Zealand resulted in a dramatic drop in fertilizer use, along with an increase in farm numbers and conversion of some farmlands to private forests (Johnston and Frengley 1994). Beyond limiting pollution, farmers are increasingly being asked to play host to predators they had previously eradicated from their localities, such as wolves, coyotes, or mountain lions, and to previously insignificant animals and plants now decorated with the title endangered. Farmers are being pressured to meet new standards of respect for animal rights, often by people with questionable familiarity with the habits or needs of the animals in question. In short, the public is starting to demand that farmers produce not merely food and fiber but also a host of environmental amenities, some more quantifiable than others.

Current attempts to extract services by using coercive regulation to "take" profits are likely to fail. Experience with species such as the black-footed ferret suggests what should be quite obvious. To demand that any farmer who finds a black-footed ferret on his property obey expensive constraints on the operation of the farm is to ensure that no farmer will report ferrets, and the chance that visitors will get to see any is likely to be slim. Conversely, bounties to farmers for high counts of live endangered species could have a totally different effect on their numbers.

It is clear that agricultural policy with respect to environmental issues will move well beyond the existing Conservation Reserve Program in the future. We can expect policy to be more accurately targeted toward environmental goals, as distinct from reduction of farm output. Achieving a multiplicity of environmental goals through agricultural policy is likely to be a daunting task. The challenge is to design policies that include an incentive structure that preserves the remarkable benefits of an efficiently decentralized farming system while filling those new demands.

Assisting Disadvantaged Consumers. In the absence of historical precedent and political logrolling, it is dubious whether food stamps, the Special Supplemental Program for Women, Infants, and Children (WIC), subsidized school lunches, and similar measures would be classified as agricultural policies at all. But as it is, their cost of $34 billion (Kinsey and Ranney 1994) constitutes a major part of agricultural expenditures, more than the federal cost of all farm programs.

From the farmer's viewpoint, the crucial question is whether those programs increase demand for farm products in excess of what an equivalent income transfer would achieve. The conventional view is "not by much." But the reported market price discount of fifty cents on the dollar for food stamps suggests that they are not just treated like extra income, as many economists assume. I understand that analysis of the WIC program shows great cost effectiveness by reducing later social expenditures for the mother and child.

A crucial issue is whether and how those in-kind transfers affect the distribution of access to resources among family members. Different models suggest different outcomes. It would be interesting to know whether the means of transfer (stamps versus school lunches versus money) can increase the welfare of the more disadvantaged members of households by changing their bargaining power, especially in the chaotic environments often seen in the poorest families.

A downside of transfer programs like food stamps is that they can also be viewed as programs that increase the already high tax rate on poor people struggling to escape poverty. On the other hand, that is a characteristic of any program targeted at the currently poor. If society continues to support transfers of that magnitude to the poor, food stamps and particularly the WIC program are good means of making the transfer.

Providing Food Security. In the United States and indeed the entire Western world, the vast majority of the population has never experienced a serious interruption of its food supply. Nevertheless, food security should remain an important objective of agricultural policy. We cannot be sure that the world's food supply for the next generation will be as stable as it has been for the previous generation.

We should not expect the private sector to provide adequate protection against shortages. Contracts that guarantee resource supply might be effectively repudiated when prices rise unexpectedly. Moreover, anticipated government actions in an emergency dampen the incentive to provide private emergency supplies. Experience in the energy crises of the 1970s indicates that in a commodity shortage the government will interfere with private storage, pricing, and trade to prevent hoarding and price gouging. Unfortunately, the government is probably incapable of committing itself to refrain from such actions (Wright 1992).

Given the constraints on private-sector incentives, what

is the appropriate public food security policy? That question is difficult to answer, in part because it depends on the probability distribution function of world food harvests. We have enough data on the latter to have some confidence that the past few decades have furnished an unusually stable food supply, but we have too small a sample of observations to be confident about the frequency of global shortages of various degrees of severity.

Another problem that we should address is the possibility of disruption of the domestic food supply system after the harvest. The same functional and regional specialization that improves productivity also tends to make the population more susceptible to interruptions in domestic flows of food, by wars, terrorism, sabotage, earthquakes, and large-scale natural disasters. The possible short-run disruption of food distribution within the specialized economy of the United States may or may not be a problem; surely it deserves at least a modicum of research attention to decide whether it is.

For the longer-term problem of a possible shortfall in the global food harvest due, for example, to a multiyear drought in an important producing region, parts of an acreage reserve—perhaps the successor to the current Conservation Reserve—could furnish relatively low-cost reserve productive capacity to respond, with about a year's lag, to the crisis. Public or private stocks held in different countries could furnish a more immediate response. The arrangements of the International Energy Agency for international coordination of supplies from stocks in a petroleum supply emergency might be a useful first reference for a study of food supply arrangements in a global food emergency.

Protecting against Monopoly or Monopsony. Individual producers of most agricultural commodities are numerous and competitive; they have no ability to control the prices of their inputs and outputs. Economies of large size are much more significant in the industries that provide inputs and process and market agricultural outputs. For commodities with large transport costs, a farmer might have only one or two feasible input suppliers or output purchasers. In such a situation, farmers—especially those who must make long-term commitments to crop-specific investments, as in the case of tree crops or dairies—cannot ignore the possibility that their market might be distorted by the exercise of market power on the input or output side.

The usual antitrust protections are of little relevance, and encouraging entry is inefficient because it increases average cost. Because of a mismatch in the optimal size of the managerial unit, the alternative solution of vertical integration is also inefficient.

Other approaches to alleviating the problem include direct public control, as in state marketing boards such as the Canadian Wheat Board, or the formation of growers' cooperatives. In the United States antitrust exemptions and tax advantages encourage the latter. Although cooperatives and marketing boards have efficiency problems of their own, the case for some public encouragement of farmer cooperatives as protection against monopolization of farmers deserves consideration in formulating a new agricultural policy.

Collecting and Disseminating Information. Farmers, input suppliers, and processors need information on markets, regulations, and technology. Governments need information to execute their programs. Consumers benefit from being well informed about the price and quality of the goods they buy. Taxpayers and voters need information to know where their money should be and is being spent and what effect the spending is having.

In the language of economists, information is a public good. Any new agricultural program should include the public provision—perhaps using private contractors in some cases—of relevant information for producers and consumers. Dissemination of the information to farm households by computer will likely become so cheap that use of a private on-line service for communication of that information will be quite efficient.

I also propose that a new farm bill require the recipient

of government support to provide any data necessary for assessing the effects of that support. And no public program should be approved without provision for independent assessment—outside the Department of Agriculture—using modern economic theory, statistics, and econometrics as appropriate, of the program's effectiveness with respect to explicitly stated goals. The appropriateness of the goals should also be subject to the kind of critical assessment I have attempted here. Those assessments should themselves be available as public information. Institutions to promote "transparency" of policy have been important in encouraging trade policy reforms; they can help keep agricultural policy in line with the public interest.

Protecting Health, Safety, and Quality. The protection of health, safety, and quality covers animals, foods, feeds, workers, and consumers. Experience shows that industries have difficulties in policing themselves, hence the role for public assurance of performance. A related study in this volume, by John M. Antle, addresses that issue.

Conclusion

A farm bill, written on a clean slate unconstrained by previous policy and aimed at efficiency and fairness, would depart radically from the current policy structure. The huge and expensive programs for price supports, market stabilization, and credit provision that dominate current farm policy would have no place. They have no adequate justification on commonly accepted grounds of efficiency and equity. Because of capitalization, income transfers via price supports or subsidies cannot significantly improve the attractiveness of farming in the long run, and they are also inequitable within and between generations of farmers. Because farmers' consumption has been observed to be quite effectively buffered against income fluctuations by savings, borrowing, and various types of diversification, public crop insurance and market stabilization policies are unnecessary. Indeed, crop insurance is not popular in the absence of substantial subsidies. Farm credit is available on competitive terms from private sources; no public program would be needed in a new policy structure, beyond perhaps the services of Farmer Mac as a parallel to Ginnie Mae and Fannie Mae.

A farm bill written anew should closely target conservation measures to emerging environmental requirements. In anticipation of the further evolution of environmental demands on farmers, some experiments with positive decentralized incentives rather than coercive regulation for certain activities such as species preservation would seem appropriate as a prelude to more extensive measures in later farm bills.

Although this policy structure would be new, the farm sector would look familiar. Chemical inputs would be lower, the crop mix might be a bit more diverse, productivity would be higher, and government expenditure would be substantially lower. Family farming would remain the overwhelmingly dominant managerial form, and policy would be on the road to adapting to evolving environmental demands.

In this *de novo* legislation, government would still play an indispensable role in the U.S. agricultural sector. An important part of its contribution would continue to consist of providing general infrastructure including roads, waterways, irrigation facilities, legal structures, and communications. Furthermore, it would likely contain sector-specific measures recognizably similar to important parts of the current policy structure. Those include support for agricultural research, protection of farmers from anticompetitive exploitation, protection of health and safety, the provision of relevant information, assistance for domestic food consumption by poor children and their mothers, food security measures including grain stocks, and encouragement of the holding of reserve production capacity.

What I have sketched here is by no means a sneak preview of the 1995 farm bill. The 1995 farm bill will have much more in common with the 1990 bill than with the structure outlined here. Why? Partly because the infeasibility, redundance, or irrelevance of some of the most popular goals of agricultural policy is not widely perceived. And partly because the dead hand of past policies lies heavy on the process. Farmers would suffer a capital loss if policies were brought in line with the kind of policy goals that farmers and the rest of the public might otherwise recognize as equitable and efficient.

This does not mean that piecemeal and gradual improvement is not possible, as recent negotiations on the General Agreement on Tariffs and Trade have demonstrated. And, given sufficient public comprehension of the issues, an unanticipated opportunity for wholesale reform just might arise, as the New Zealand experience shows.

References

Alderman, H., and Christina H. Paxson. "Do the Poor Insure? A Synthesis of the Literature on Risk-Bearing Institutions in Developing Countries." Memorandum. Washington, D.C.: World Bank, 1992.

Antle, John M. "Choice, Efficiency, and Food Safety Policy." Paper presented at the conference "Future Directions in Agricultural Policy," sponsored by the American Enterprise Institute for Public Policy Research, Washington, D.C., November 3–4, 1994.

Boehlje, Michael, Marvin Duncan, and David Lins. "Agricultural and Rural Finance Policy." In *The 1995 Farm Bill Policy Options and Consequences,* edited by Ronald D. Knutson. College Station: Texas Agricultural Extension Service, November 1994.

Browne, William P., Jerry R. Skees, Louis E. Swanson, Paul B. Thompson, and Laurian J. Unnevehr. *Sacred Cows and Hot Potatoes: Agrarian Myths in Agricultural Policy.* Boulder, Colo.: Westview Press, 1992.

Fisher, Dennis U., Robert R. Fletcher, Thomas R. Harris, and Adell Brown, Jr. "Rural Development Policy." In *The 1995 Farm Bill Policy Options and Consequences,* edited by Ronald D. Knutson. College Station: Texas Agricultural Extension Service, November 1994.

Goodwin, Barry K., and Vincent H. Smith. *Economics of Crop*

Insurance and Disaster Aid. Washington, D.C.: AEI Press, 1995.

Iowa Farm Bill Study Team. "The Findings of the 1995 Farm Bill Study Team." Unpublished manuscript, Iowa Farm Bureau, 1994.

Johnston, Warren E., and Gerald A. G. Frengley. "Economic Adjustments and Changes in Financial Viability of the Farming Sector: The New Zealand Experience." Paper presented at the American Agricultural Economics Association 1994 Annual Meeting, San Diego, August 9, 1994.

Just, Richard E., and Wallace E. Huffman. "Economic Principles and Incentives: Structure, Management, and Funding of Agricultural Research in the United States." *American Journal of Agricultural Economics* 74 (1992): 1101–08.

Kinsey, Jean, and Christine Ranney. "Food Assistance Policy." In *The 1995 Farm Bill Policy Options and Consequences,* edited by Ronald D. Knutson. College Station: Texas Agricultural Extension Service, November 1994.

Kislev, Yoav, and Willis Peterson. "Prices, Technology, and Farm Size." *Journal of Political Economy* 90 (1982): 578–95.

Langemeier, Michael R., and George F. Patrick. "Farmers' Marginal Propensity to Consume: An Application to Illinois Grain Farmers." *American Journal of Agricultural Economics* 72 (1990): 309–25.

Luloff, A. E., and Louis E. Swanson, eds. *American Rural Communities.* Boulder, Colo.: Westview Press, 1990.

McCloskey, Donald N. "English Open Fields as Behavior Towards Risk." In *Research in Economic History,* vol. 1, edited by P. Uselding. Greenwich: JAI Press, 1976.

Melichar, Emanuel. "Capital Gains versus Current Income in the Farming Sector." *American Journal of Agricultural Economics* 61 (1979): 1085–92.

Nerlove, Marc. "Reflections on the Economic Organization of Agriculture: Traditional, Modern, and Transitional." Report. College Park: University of Maryland, Department of Agricultural and Resource Economics, July 6, 1994.

Paxson, Christine H. "Using Weather Variability to Estimate the Response of Savings to Transitory Income in Thailand." *American Economic Review* 82 (1992): 15–33.

Ray, Daryll E. "The Economic Setting for U.S. Agriculture." In *The 1995 Farm Bill Policy Options and Consequences,* edited by Ronald D. Knutson. College Station: Texas Agricultural Extension Service, November 1994.

Sandrey, Ron, and Russell Reynolds, eds. *Farming without Subsidies: New Zealand's Recent Experience.* Wellington: New Zealand Ministry of Agriculture and Fisheries, 1990.

Walker, Thomas S., and N. S. Jodha. "How Small Farm Households Adapt to Risk." In *Crop Insurance for Agricultural Development: Issues and Experience,* edited by Peter Hazell, Carlos Pomareda, and Alberto Valdés. Baltimore: Johns Hopkins University Press, 1986.

Wright, Brian D. "Policy Regimes, Market Disturbances and Food Security." In *Improving Agricultural Trade Performance under the GATT,* edited by Tilman Becker, Richard Gray, and Andrew Schmitz. Kiel, Germany: Wissenschaftsverlag Vauk, 1992.

———. "Agricultural Policy from the Ground Up: Goals for a New Regime." In *Reforming Agricultural Commodity Policy,* by Brian D. Wright and Bruce L. Gardner. Washington, D.C.: AEI Press, 1995.

———, and Julie A. Hewitt. "All-Risk Crop Insurance: Lessons from Theory and Experience." In *Economics of Agricultural Crop Insurance: Theory and Evidence,* edited by Darrell L. Heuth and William H. Furtan. Norwell, Mass.: Kluwer Academic Publishers, 1994.

3
Practical Policy Alternatives for the 1995 Farm Bill

Bruce L. Gardner

U.S. farm commodity programs have existed for six decades, but they have from the beginning been viewed as experimental. Policy details have been changed significantly, and the legislation has typically carried expiration dates. The farm acts of 1985 and 1990 had five-year lives. Possibilities for significant modification in 1995 are especially intriguing because both President Clinton in 1993 and the Republican congressional majorities in 1995 have come into office understanding that they had a mandate for change.

What changes will occur in farm programs are, however, open to question because neither President Clinton nor the Republicans ran on any particular promises about farm policy. Both parties were careful not to cause concern to farm constituencies. Yet budgetary pressures and an evident desire for less governmental intervention generally suggest an opening for bipartisan reform of agricultural commodity programs. This chapter considers a number of options for such reforms. I outline and analyze the pros and cons of each option.

Current Policy Situation and Baseline for Policy Options

The data in table 3–1 on budget outlays for farm price and income support summarize the general picture of U.S. farm policy for the past twenty-five years. The level of spending to support agriculture rose to record highs (both nominal and real) from 1982 through 1988 and currently remains

45

TABLE 3–1
AGRICULTURAL BUDGET OUTLAYS AND IDLED CROPLAND,
1970–1994

Fiscal Year[a]	Agricultural Budget Outlays[b] ($ billions)	Real Agricultural Outlays ($ billions)[c]	Idled Acres (millions)
1970	4.6	13.0	57
1971	3.7	9.8	37
1972	4.6	11.7	62
1973	4.1	9.9	19
1974	1.5	3.2	3
1975	2.2	4.4	2
1976	2.2	4.3	2
1977	5.7	10.3	0
1978	10.2	17.0	16
1979	9.9	15.1	11
1980	7.4	10.4	0
1981	9.8	12.4	0
1982	14.3	17.1	12
1983	21.3	24.5	77
1984	11.9	13.1	27
1985	23.8	25.2	31
1986	29.6	30.6	48
1987	24.7	24.7	76
1988	15.2	14.7	62
1989	14.8	13.7	58
1990	9.8	8.6	58
1991	12.9	11.0	49
1992	12.5	10.3	50[d]
1993	18.9	15.2	52[d]
1994	15.0	11.8	44[d]

a. Fiscal year 1994 runs from October 1, 1993, to September 30, 1994.
b. Subfunction 351, Farm Income Stabilization, in the budget of the United States.
c. Deflated by the implicit GDP deflator, 1987 = 100.
d. Author's estimates, including 36 million acres in the Conservation Reserve Program.
SOURCES: Budget of the United States; USDA.

above the levels from 1950 through 1970. Indeed, the level of spending during the New Deal farm programs never exceeded $4 billion (1987 dollars), compared with $13 billion to $14 billion from 1993 to 1994. From 1991 through 1994, spending on agriculture has been at about the 1970 through 1972 level in real terms.[1]

Some worried farm commodity interests wonder whether taxpayers will continue their willingness to pay up at those rates. On the other hand, the agriculture committees of Congress have reminded their colleagues that agriculture has taken a substantial budget cut in the Clinton and Bush budget reduction efforts, especially when the Omnibus Budget Reconciliation Act of 1990 introduced "mandatory flex" acreage (15 percent of each farmer's payment acreage on which the farmer could plant any program crop, or a few nonprogram crops, but on which no payments would be made). That and other provisions were scored as a $13 billion budget cut for agriculture over five years.

Those reductions have not materialized, and it is worth reviewing the reasons in detail. Congressional debate on proposed programs in agriculture typically is conducted with reference to a baseline. Each option's effects on budget outlays, commodity prices, farm income, and other variables are compared with budget outlays under a "current policy" baseline. Thus, currently legislated target prices, loan rates, and related policy instruments are continued. Specifying that baseline is fraught with difficulty, because program parameters, such as percentages of acreage required to be idled by program participants, vary annually

---

1. Real spending is higher currently if we include the Conservation Reserve Program, which is omitted from farm program spending in OMB's accounting. That program, which did not exist in the 1970s, cost about $1.8 billion annually in 1993 and 1994. A second indicator of government action to support farm income, but at the expense of food consumers rather than taxpayers, is the number of cropland acres held idle under farm programs. That indicator also climbed to record heights in the mid-1980s and has now returned roughly to 1970 through 1972 levels.

FIGURE 3–1

NET OUTLAYS, ACTUAL AND PROJECTED, OF THE COMMODITY CREDIT
CORPORATION, FISCAL YEARS 1988–1995

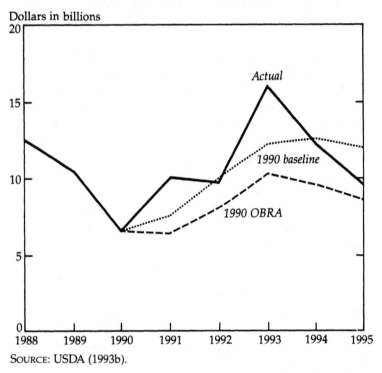

SOURCE: USDA (1993b).

according to market conditions, and future market conditions are inherently uncertain.

Figure 3–1 shows how savings were measured in 1990.
The fiscal year 1990 level of Commodity Credit Corporation
outlays (most but not all the spending shown in table 3–1)
was $6.5 billion. The 1990 Omnibus Budget Reconciliation
Act was not intended to reduce spending from that level.
Instead, savings were scored from the baseline spending
level shown as "1990 baseline" in figure 3–1. The policy
changes introduced generated the projected spending
shown as "1990 Omnibus Budget Reconciliation Act." Cu-
mulating the vertical distances between the 1990 baseline
and 1990 Omnibus Budget Reconciliation Act projections

48

TABLE 3-2
CBO PROJECTIONS OF CCC SPENDING, 1991–1995

	Fiscal Year ($ billions)					
	1991	1992	1993	1994	1995	1991–95
Pre-1990 OBRA (FY91 budget resolution baseline)	8.6	11.5	11.0	10.5	9.9	52
1990 OBRA and farm act	−1.6	−3.2	−2.3	−2.3	−2.5	−12
Post-OBRA baseline	7.0	8.3	8.7	8.2	7.4	40
Actual CCC outlays	10.1	9.7	16.0	10.3	10.5[a]	57
Factors accounting for excess of actual over projected outlays						
Post-1990 legislation[b]	0	0.9	0.8	2.8	−0.5	4
Accounting change[c]	0	−0.8	−0.8	−0.8	−0.8	−3
Remaining unexplained excess of spending over 1990 baseline	3.1	1.3	7.3	0.1	4.4	16

a. Author's estimate.
b. Crop disaster appropriations, 1993 OBRA, wool program and export program reduction in 1993 and 1994.
c. Administrative expenses of the Agricultural Stabilization and Conservation Service shifted out of CCC account.
SOURCE: Data from Senate Agriculture Committee, Republican staff.

from 1991 through 1995 yields the $13 billion savings claimed.

Actual spending and mid-1994 projections are shown as "actual" in figure 3–1. Not only did the Omnibus Budget Reconciliation Act savings not make it to the bank, but we have ended up spending more than the pre–Omnibus Budget Reconciliation Act baseline! The projections and data used in figure 3–1 are those of the U.S. Department of Agriculture and the Office of Management and Budget as reported in *Agricultural Outlook*. They are still not final for fiscal years 1994 and 1995. Also, Congressional Budget Office scoring differs in a few ways. Table 3–2 presents CBO data on 1990 Omnibus Budget Reconciliation Act savings and also an accounting for effects of some policy changes since 1990. Actual Commodity Credit Corporation outlays exceed the post–1990 Omnibus Budget Reconciliation Act baseline by $17 billion from 1991 through 1995. That performance is even worse than the USDA and OMB data indicate.

Table 3–2 also includes two items to help understand why outlays exceeded the baseline. First, policy changes caused part of the increase. From 1991 through 1995, Congress made $5.8 billion in appropriations for crop disaster assistance that were not in the baseline. Those more than offset additional savings made in the 1993 Omnibus Budget Reconciliation Act and other appropriations reductions in 1993 and 1994. Second, an accounting change was made. Starting in 1992 the administrative expenses such as payroll and equipment of the Agricultural Stabilization and Conservation Service were shifted from the Commodity Credit Corporation budget. Those expenses amount to $780 million per year (about $2,500 per U.S. commercial farmer). That, of course, is not a "saving" at all and means that the gap between expected and actual outlays from 1991 through 1995 is really about $3 billion higher than the earlier calculations indicate.

To see more specifically the linkages between commodity program parameters and government outlays, consider the recent history and current projections for corn. The target price for corn, after rising about 30 percent between 1978 and 1984, was cut in the 1985 farm act from $3.03 to $2.75 per bushel, starting in 1988. The 1990 legislation introduced a provision by which 15 percent of each farmer's acreage base would receive no payments.

With a six billion bushel payment base, cutting the target price from $3.03 to $2.75 reduces annual government outlays by $1.68 billion. The 1985 act's changes thus were not trivial. The 1990 reductions are more difficult to quantify because they depend on the market price. In 1990 analysts expected market prices for the early 1990s to average about $2.15 per bushel, indicating payments of $3.6 billion. A 15 percent reduction of the six billion bushels to 5.1 billion bushels would therefore save $540 million in annual outlays. In addition, the 1990 act changed the market price used in calculating deficiency payments from a five-month to a twelve-month basis in such a way that deficiency payments will be reduced by seven cents per bushel (and not more or less) from the five-month approach in effect through 1992. That change saved an additional $36 million annually. Taken together, the corn policy changes since 1985 reduce deficiency payments by about $2.6 billion annually.

So why did corn deficiency payments in 1993 go up to $5.1 billion (accounting for much of the excess over the baseline shown in figure 3–1 for that year)? The most important reason is that the price of corn in 1992 and 1993 was about twenty cents per bushel below the baseline level. That added about $1 billion in outlays. A similar result is likely in 1995. The main causes are the record large corn production in 1992 and again in 1994. On the other hand, the 1993 corn price was above the baseline level because of the short crop caused by extraordinarily wet weather in the Midwest, so outlays were below the baseline in 1994.

For all the feed grains, wheat, rice, and cotton, it is worth noting the escalation in already overly complex laws and regulatory provisions that occurred in the 1985 and 1990 acts. The complexities were induced by the combined desires for increased flexibility for farmers, budgetary savings, and environmental sensitivity—all to be achieved at the least possible cost to farm income and with special attention to formerly neglected crops such as minor oilseeds and raw materials for "new uses" of farm commodities.

An example is the USDA's description of how it would determine deficiency payments for the 1994 wheat crop:

> If the national weighted-average market price received by producers during the first *five* months of the marketing year (June 1994 through October 1994) plus 10 cents is below the *target price*, eligible producers will receive deficiency payments in December 1994, less any advance, equal to the difference between the target level and the higher of the five-month price plus 10 cents and the *basic* (statutory) loan rate—$2.72 per bushel. If the national

weighted-average price received by producers during the first *twelve* months of the marketing year (June 1994 through May 1995) is less than the five-month price plus 10 cents, an additional payment will be made in July 1995, equal to the difference between the five-month price plus 10 cents and the higher of the 12-month price and the *basic* loan rate.

Additional "Findley" payments, if they are earned, will be paid to eligible producers in July 1995, less any advances, equal to the difference between the basic loan rate and the higher of the 12-month price and the *announced* national average loan rate ($2.58).

Producers may elect, at sign-up time, to receive a minimum of 75 percent of any projected additional "Findley" deficiency payment on December 1, 1994, based on a December 1, 1994, estimate of the season average market price.

Payments will be determined by multiplying the payment rate times the farm payment acreage times the farm program payment yield.

The 1994 farm program payment yield remains at the 1993 level. However, if a farm has had both irrigated and nonirrigated payment yields for a crop, the 1994 payment yield will reflect the history of irrigating and not whether the payment acreage is actually irrigated in 1994.

If the payment yield for a crop is less than 90 percent of the equivalent yield in 1985, producers will be compensated to ensure they receive the same return as if the yield had not been reduced by more than 10 percent.

For the 1994 crop and subsequent years, irrigated yields will not be established on any acreage not having an irrigated yield prior to the 1986 crop year.

Deficiency payment acreage is the lower of the acreage actually planted to wheat or the maximum payment acreage [85 percent of the farm's wheat base]. However, producers may underplant their maximum payment acreage and still, under some conditions, receive deficiency payments. Wheat producers may devote all or a portion of the maximum payment acreage to Conserving Uses (CU), and receive minimum guaranteed deficiency payments on the acres designated in excess of required nonpayment acres. The payment rate will be the higher of the projected or actual deficiency rate for the wheat program crop.

Required nonpayment acres normally are 15 percent of maximum payment acreage. Exceptions for wheat which allow producers to reduce their required nonpayment acres below 15 percent of maximum payment acreage are provided to producers who designate acreage exceeding 8 percent of the maximum payment acreage to minor oilseeds, industrial and other crops, or when the acreage of the crop was prevented from being planted or failed and was subsequently devoted to conserving uses for payment.

Note that "minor" oilseeds such as sunflower seed, safflower, canola, rapeseed, flaxseed or mustard seed, may be planted on the [wheat] land and qualify for payments. However, if payments are received, the oilseed crop becomes ineligible for price support loan for all of that oilseed produced on the farm.

Soybeans may be planted on wheat acres following a minor oilseed crop. The producer must have a history of double-cropping soybeans following any other crop on the farm in three of the previous five years. Other restrictions may apply.

Dry peas and lentils may be planted on up to 20 percent of the wheat acreage base and receive planted and considered planted credit. No deficiency payments will be paid on acreage devoted to these crops.

The wheat acreage base is the average of planted and considered planted for the five year period (1989–1993).

Producers who choose not to participate in any annual program and certify that no acreage on the farm was planted to the crop have two options for protecting their planted history: (1) the "zero certification" option allows them to have their entire program crop acreage base considered as planted for base retention purposes. However, they must certify that any fruits or vegetables planted on the farm were not in excess of normal plantings.

Haying and grazing will be permitted on the [set-aside] acreage and on the conserving uses for payment (including the 15 percent of qualifying acres), except during a consecutive five-month period between April 1 through October 31 (USDA 1994b, 4–5; emphasis in original, brackets added).

In addition, by January 1, 1995, all producers of program crops must have fully applied an approved conservation plan if they plant any agricultural crop on highly erodible land. Producers who do not have a USDA-approved plan or have not fully applied it by the deadline remain ineligible for USDA commodity programs until the USDA's Soil Conservation Service certifies that an approved plan is fully applied. Also, any person who plants a crop on a wetland converted to cropland after December 23, 1985, or who converted a wetland after November 28, 1990, is ineligible for USDA benefits. And, of course, program participants must comply with acreage reduction program requirements and stay within payment limits.

Many of those provisions have caused confusion and consternation and have created many difficulties in implementation, appeals, and resolution of disputed cases. Neither Congress nor the political decision makers in the executive branch have a clear idea of what they have done. The regulations for each crop are fully understood only by a few USDA specialists, congressional committee staff, and industry experts. It is doubtful that anyone in the universe has a complete grip on all the regulations for every commodity.

The main reasons why alternatives to current policies may be viable in 1995 include: changes in the political situation; changes in the economic situation of agriculture and in the general economy; lessons learned from implementing the 1990 farm act and subsequent legislation, and new information about the effects of continuing policies; and development of new policy ideas.

Two key political facts are that voters elected a Democratic administration in 1992 and a Republican Congress in 1994. Under the Clinton administration, the USDA has become more heavily weighted with proponents of keeping market prices up. But another political fact underlying the 1994 Republican victory is that public mistrust of government and desire for less taxation and spending remain strong and probably have increased. Those facts suggest further intense scrutiny of the farm income support budget.

An additional political fact is that the Clinton administration entered office to a persistent beat of environmental tom-toms. That, together with the fact that existing Conservation Reserve Program contracts will almost all expire from 1996 through 1999, has created a potential for change in the conservation and environmental aspects of commodity programs. That fact also gives oxygen to an agenda for subsidized technology in "sustainable" agriculture and a general increase in regulation (as in ethanol-use mandates) and public investment that can be summarized under the heading of "industrial" policy for agriculture. The 1994 election results are widely seen as damaging to environmental interests, but the effect on the broader industrial policy agenda, notably promotion of new uses for farm products, is less clear.

Furthermore, the international policy situation has changed with the NAFTA and GATT trade agreements. Some U.S. policy decisions may look different under the light of those agreements.

The foggiest political fact is that rural representation in Congress, particularly in the House of Representatives, has continued to evolve and perhaps to weaken. On that subject concrete evidence is not yet in place. The *New York Times* opened its season of reporting on the 1995 farm bill with a boost for hopes of radical change; the paper stated that "in recent years Federal money for subsidies has dropped precipitously, a measure of the long, slow erosion of farmers' political clout in Washington" (July 25, 1994, p. 1). But the reporter has not looked at the data shown in table 3–1, which indicate that agriculture has more support now than it did twenty-five years ago.

With respect to the economic situation, there are no compelling sources of policy changes. The most notable development in 1994 was the end of a period of exceptionally profitable livestock prices, especially for hogs. But there are no price support programs for meats, except relatively minor and sporadic export subsidies and import restrictions. Despite a record-large corn crop in 1994, the major program crops are not far from the economic conditions that were expected when the 1990 farm bill was debated. Evidence for that is that events have transpired much as projected in the USDA and Food and Agricultural Policy Research Institute baselines used at that time. The biggest departure from 1990 expectations has been in dairy. In 1990 analysts expected milk prices to remain near the $10.10 support level from 1991 through 1995 and to require substantial Commodity Credit Corporation purchases to maintain that level. Congress was inclined to impose supply controls to support milk prices, but industry disagreements and Bush administration opposition apparently tipped the balance to only a study of supply control measures in 1990 that would lead to possible new policy in 1991 or 1992. That never happened. Yet, milk prices turned out higher and Commodity Credit Corporation purchases less than had been predicted. Dairy policy is still unsettled as compared with policy for the major crops.

Commodity Policy Options for 1995

Areas of policy alternatives that must be considered include adjustments in market support prices (loan rates), changes in requirements placed on farmers for program eligibility (flexibility), changes in supply management programs, reductions in government outlays for commodity programs, and "industrial" policy for agriculture.

Options in each of those areas move either toward or

away from market orientation and increase or decrease support for farmers. I have selected options that seem to have the greatest economic significance and political backing. For each option I provide a list of pros and cons before analyzing the option.

Raising Loan Rates for Grains. In February 1994 the USDA increased the wheat loan rate to $2.58 per bushel and corn to $1.89 per bushel for the 1994 crops. Secretary Mike Espy stated that this "demonstrates the commitment of this Administration to increase farm income which, in turn, will have a positive effect on rural areas" (USDA 1994a). The issue is how to follow up in 1995 and beyond. The government can either keep loan rates low enough that Commodity Credit Corporation stock acquisition due to loan forfeitures is nil or raise loan rates further—for purposes of analysis by 5 percent.

The advantages of raising loan rates are that farmers will get larger nine-month Commodity Credit Corporation loans at favorable interest rates and will face less financial pressure to sell at harvest. In addition, farmers can sell at harvest for higher prices in large-crop years. Moreover, Commodity Credit Corporation stocks added in large-crop years will contribute to price stability through later Commodity Credit Corporation sales.

Those gains, as usual, are not costless. Holding prices up during the harvest season reduces seasonal consumption, for example, of feed wheat in summer, that helps utilize surplus production without government stockholding. In addition, for every additional dollar farmers receive for their grain, buyers pay a dollar more. Finally, Commodity Credit Corporation stocks are quite costly to hold and tend to overhang the market in subsequent periods.

With respect to farm income resulting from higher market prices for farmers—besides being offset by consumer costs—the effects are likely to be minor. The larger worry is the hundreds of millions of dollars that have been spent in the past holding and disposing of Commodity Credit Corporation stocks. Both the government and farmers appeared happier, and with reason, when the Commodity Credit Corporation stocks accumulated in the mid-1980s were finally drawn down in the early 1990s.

What are the chances that increases in loan rates from current levels would generate substantial Commodity Credit Corporation stocks? Suppose that the loan rates for 1995 were increased 5 percent from $2.58 to $2.71 for wheat and from $1.89 to $1.98 for corn. That would be 10 percent below the five-year average farm price for wheat and 14 percent below that average for corn. Surely that would be harmless? The answer turns on the probability that we might end up with surplus stocks at the loan levels in 1995. One way to get an idea of the risk in monetary terms is to exploit the fact that the right to sell at the Commodity Credit Corporation loan rate is equivalent, from the producer's viewpoint, to being given a put option—an option to sell the crop at a strike price equal to the loan rate. The Chicago corn price equivalent to a $1.98 price at the average farm level is about $2.20. Therefore, the premium on a put option expiring in December with a $2.20 strike price indicates roughly the value to farmers of a $1.98 loan rate for corn. As of mid-September 1994, the futures price for December 1995 corn was $2.40 to $2.45 per bushel, equivalent to a U.S. average farm-level price of about $2.20. Therefore, a $1.98 loan level for 1995 corn is equivalent to a put option twenty-two cents per bushel out of the money that expires in fifteen months. Corn put options with so long to expiration are not currently traded, but the premiums on puts similarly out of the money that expire in six and eight months can be extrapolated to indicate that December 1995 puts with a $1.98 strike price would be worth about ten cents per bushel under current market expectations. With the output of program participants at about eight billion bushels, the value of a $1.98 loan rate is $800 million. Thus, a seemingly innocuous increase of 5 percent in the corn loan rate gives a price floor that provides a considerable expected cost to the Treasury.

For wheat, put options corresponding to a $2.71 loan rate are further out of the money. But the U.S. wheat price has been at or below the *current* loan rate for three of the past ten years. So the probability that a 5 percent wheat loan rate increase would cause Commodity Credit Corporation acquisitions and market distortions is far from negligible—probably about one in three years.

In short, raising Commodity Credit Corporation loan rates would do little to solve farmers' problems, while opening the door to significant costs and market distortions.

Production Flexibility and Supply Management. *Flexibility.* The "flex" provisions of the 1990 legislation pertain to a farmer's use of the payment base acreage for each crop. Flex acres are important not only because of the lack of deficiency payments on the 15 percent "normal" flex acres, but also because on that acreage plus an additional 10 percent "optional" flex acres, producers may plant any crop other than fruits, vegetables, nuts, peanuts, or tobacco, or leave the acreage idle, while maintaining the payment base for future years. Thus, on 15 percent of their acreage base producers are free to decide which program crop to plant on the basis of expected market prices rather than target prices. Moreover, a producer through "zero certification" can drop out of all deficiency payment programs and grow any crop desired while maintaining payment bases.

The main limitations on a farmer's flexibility to respond to market conditions are the loss of deficiency payments if another crop is planted on optional flex acres, the upper limit of flex acres to 25 percent of base acres, and the exclusion of fruits and vegetables from planting on flex acres. Removing those three limitations would make the deficiency payment program almost completely a program of lump-sum (nondistorting) payments with respect to output reductions. A farm would receive payments based on program yield and program acres, neither of which would be reduced or increased if the farmer switched to another crop in part or in full or if he changed the use of purchased inputs such as fertilizer.

With respect to output increases, however, producers

could respond to increased market prices for a program crop only to the extent that they have flex acres in other program crops. These programs, even with zero acreage reduction required, preclude a participating farmer from expanding acreage of any program crop beyond the sum of acreage bases for the farm.

Market orientation would be promoted by a flexibility package that retains deficiency payments for a crop, even if its flex acres are planted to another crop or idled. That package should expand flex acres from 25 percent to 100 percent of the crop acreage base. In addition, that package should allow any crop to be grown on flex acres and should allow producers to plant more than the farm's acreage base of a crop (without building the payment base) if its acreage reduction program is zero. Finally, that package should repeal payment limitations.

One advantage of a flexibility package that retains deficiency payments for a crop is that it results in crop acreage determined by market conditions, not target prices, and thus increases the efficiency of agriculture. Second, such a package eliminates costs and paperwork that hinder larger operations.

A disadvantage of such a package is that nonprogram crops, notably fruits and vegetables, have to compete with subsidized farms. In addition, more payments will go to large farms at the expense of taxpayers (or if outlays are held constant, at the expense of smaller farms).

This issue centers on the trade-off between efficiency, in the sense of allocating resources to their best use as measured by market signals, and equity or fairness to producers of different crops. The list of changes would improve efficiency; but the cons are driven largely by views of fairness.

There is, however, an efficiency aspect of the first disadvantage. If permitting fruits and vegetables on flex acres would cause fruits and vegetables to be produced more than under a complete absence of programs, then there is also an efficiency argument against that extent of flexibility. Why would that occur?

One argument is that deficiency payments would support the incomes of grain and cotton producers on the acres where they produce fruits and vegetables, so the program crop producers have an advantage *in producing fruits and vegetables* that the growers without payment bases do not have. But that would be equally true if program payments were converted to an annual lump-sum payment to historical program crop producers.

A second argument is that deficiency payments are not fully decoupled from production, even under full flexibility as defined above, because payments do depend on the farm's remaining in production. Farmland is regularly converted to tree growing or nonagricultural activities, and even fully flexible payments would be lost when that occurs; so the payments do keep more land in production than would be the case with no programs. Under full flexibility, that would drive down the prices of all crops (program and nonprogram) roughly proportionately. But only the owners of program crop payment bases are cushioned by deficiency payments.

Supply management in grains. Reforms to increase flexibility may be viewed as inconsequential tinkering as long as fifty to sixty million acres of cropland are being held out of production under acreage reduction programs and the Conservation Reserve Program. To obtain real flexibility the items just discussed would be supplemented with an end to acreage reduction programs and not reauthorizing the Conservation Reserve Program.

One advantage of such a policy is that it ends the social waste—the biggest component of dead-weight losses under current programs—caused by idling productive land. In addition, ending acreage reduction programs may increase farm income if demand is elastic. Finally, the policy takes better advantage of increased trade opportunities under the GATT.

A disadvantage of ending acreage reduction programs is that it increases government outlays because prices fall when output increases. Moreover, ending the Conservation Reserve Program payments reduces farm income. Finally, annual acreage reduction programs have become the government's primary tool for year-to-year commodity market stabilization; ending acreage reduction programs would make prices more variable.

The costs and benefits of acreage reduction programs and the Conservation Reserve Program can be estimated in several ways. All are conjectural as they require judgment of what producers would do in the absence of acreage reduction programs. Fortunately, the experience of zero acreage reduction programs for all the grains in 1994 provides some direct evidence. Consider what the wheat markets would look like in 1996 if zero acreage reduction programs were continued.[2]

The mid-1994 Food and Agricultural Policy Research Institute baseline acreage reduction program for a continuation of current policy is 5 percent for 1996 (indeed for each crop from 1995 through 2002). Moving to a zero acreage reduction program would add three million acres to crop production. Under flexibility that acreage may not all go back to wheat, but for maximum effect suppose that it does. At 90 percent (because acreage reduction program land should not be the best land) of U.S. baseline yield, those acres would produce 105 million bushels of wheat. That constitutes 4.1 percent of baseline consumption. With an elasticity of demand for all wheat (domestic use and export) of -1.1, the market price of wheat would fall by 3.7 percent, or eleven cents per bushel.

The effects of a 3.7 percent decline in the price of wheat at baseline quantities include the government costs of higher payments—$200 million on 1,800 million payment bushels and $80 million on formerly idled acres. In addition, the government savings on export sales (the export enhancement program equivalent)[3] are $138 million on 1,250

2. Large amounts of Conservation Reserve Program acreage would not be returned to production until 1997 in any case.

3. The reduction in price of exported wheat is scored as a savings of government expenditures because about $1 billion annually is now spent on export enhancement program subsidies to sell wheat at lower prices abroad. Relaxing acreage reduction programs means that

million bushels of exports. The consumer savings from lower prices on 1,250 million bushels of domestic consumption are $138 million. Farm incomes suffer a $275 million loss on production. Farmers do, however, receive an extra payment on base production of $200 million and an $85 per acre return over variable cost on three million acres of $255 million. Thus, the farmers gain $180 million. In total, the United States gains $135 million from the 3.7 decline in the price of wheat at baseline quantities.

Over the longer term, if we similarly analyze bringing 10.6 million acres of wheat base out of the Conservation Reserve Program, we would have 371 million additional bushels. Ending both the Conservation Reserve Program and 5 percent wheat acreage reduction programs would increase U.S. wheat available by 14 percent (using the Food and Agricultural Policy Research Institute's [1994] baseline values for 1998). With a longer-term elasticity of demand for wheat of −2, the market price would fall 7 percent or twenty cents per bushel. In that case the costs and benefits include saved Conservation Reserve Program payments of $480 million, higher deficiency payments of −$360 million, the export enhancement program equivalent of $260 million, and farm income of $115 million, for a total gain of $775 million.

The net benefits to farmers, consumers, the government budget, and to the nation as a whole are greater in the longer run because of the higher elasticity of demand. That reflects the point, made by many in discussions of acreage reduction programs, that over the longer term their main effect is to give away export markets to foreign producers.

Those calculations omit the pervasive uncertainty in grain markets. What weight shall we give to the disadvantage that ending acreage reduction programs destabilizes prices? The consumer benefit arises when, as occurred following the short crop of 1993, the corn or wheat acreage

export enhancement can be accomplished without government costs. Of course, if we were analyzing the elimination of both acreage reduction programs *and* the export enhancement program, we could not count that gain. (See also chapter 4, below.)

idled is decreased when corn stocks become low enough. In that respect acreage reduction programs are a substitute for larger carryover stocks. In the absence of acreage reduction programs triggered by stock levels, there would be a greater incentive for private grain merchants and farmers to hold stocks in lean years. In 1993 the market let stocks decline in part because everyone knew that lower acreage reduction programs in 1994 would increase 1994 production. If acreage reduction programs had already been zero in 1993, there would have been more reason to hold carryover stocks against the chance of another short crop in 1994. In short, it is not clear that the acreage program is a better way to stabilize price than relying on stockholding. And, if private stockholding provides insufficient price stabilization, it is likely to be more efficient to subsidize stockholding through the farmer-owned reserve program than to manipulate acreage reduction programs.

Supply management in dairy. Governmental attempts to control milk production have been less systematic than for the grains and are still unsettled. In the 1990 farm act Congress expressed a general sense that dairy supplies should be controlled through new policy measures. But, reflecting disagreements within the dairy industry, no plan was adopted beyond assessments of about 1 percent of the price of milk on producers who expand milk production. Instead, the secretary of agriculture was instructed to submit recommendations by August 1, 1991—eight months after the 1990 act became law—for policies that would limit USDA purchases to 6 billion pounds annually. In 1991 Secretary Edward R. Madigan sent Congress his report but found no desirable supply control program. With the dairy industry still unable to agree, Congress did nothing in 1991, and supply management remains an open issue.

The dairy industry has remained largely convinced that some supply management scheme is needed. Led by the National Milk Producers' Federation, a coalition of cooperatives and producer groups has endorsed a "self-help" approach to manage supplies (Barr 1993). That would combine elements of previous programs, notably assessments on producers to finance a range of price-enhancing activities. An industry board would make key decisions about the program. Analytically, the proposal would establish a governmentally sanctioned cartel for dairy products. The powers of the board vary in alternative self-help proposals. As described in Barr (1993) the dairy stabilization board would have the following features and powers. It would be authorized to intervene in dairy product markets at prices higher than the Commodity Credit Corporation's support prices. It would be funded by assessments of up to twenty cents per hundredweight on milk sold by producers. That funding is intended to be sufficient to buy up to 2 billion pounds of milk equivalent, in years when Commodity Credit Corporation removals, absent the board's purchases, are projected to be between 5 and 7 billion pounds of milk equivalent (as is the case for 1995). The board's purchased products would be sold in domestic or foreign markets chosen by the board to be least competitive with normal commercial outlets. If Commodity Credit Corporation removals are projected to exceed 7 billion pounds, producer assessments, as under current law, would be used to make further purchases by the board. If the price of manufacturing milk fell to within fifty cents per hundredweight of the support price for two consecutive months, a further "excess marketings" assessment would be collected to control production.

One advantage of such a proposal is that it supports dairy producers without increasing federal budget outlays. Second, it gives producers a role in shaping their own program.

A disadvantage of the program is that it is costly to consumers of dairy products. In addition, the program places the burden of adjustment on producers who would otherwise increase production and who tend to be lower-cost producers.

The self-help cartel would be difficult to implement because of the divergence of interests among producers, which indeed has so far scuttled industrywide agreement on any plan. An underlying problem is that, in the West and Southeast particularly, some producers can profitably expand at current prices. But others, particularly in the upper Midwest and Northeast, are economically pressed and need higher prices for long-term survival. Those disagreements probably preclude any plan that would be very costly to consumers or beneficial to producers.

There is a more fundamental problem with the approach. The proposed program is not just accelerating socialism when it is elsewhere in retreat; it is socialism that hands over the relevant governmental monopoly powers and agencies to a private industry. It is hard to imagine a worse precedent for economic policy making.

Budget Savings Options. I shall consider two broad approaches to cutting commodity outlays: means-testing payments and across-the-board cuts.

Means-testing payments. Current law limits deficiency payments to $50,000, continuing a practice that was introduced along with the target price approach in the Agricultural Act of 1970. Subsequent farm bills have specified separate payment limits for disaster programs ($100,000), loan deficiency payments ($75,000), Conservation Reserve payments ($50,000), and combined deficiency, disaster, and other payments ($250,000) and have tightened the definition of who qualifies as a person for payment purposes and restricted the number of payment-receiving enterprises in which a farmer may participate. Current limitations have been estimated to reduce payments by $70 million annually (as of 1989) compared with the situation with no payment limits.

In the 1990 farm bill debate, urban representatives introduced amendments to restrict payments further by not permitting any payments to farmers who, for example, had more than $1 million annually in sales. The amendment of that type that received the widest publicity and was debated in the full House was one that would have prohibited payments to anyone who had off-farm income of more than $100,000. The idea was to get a wedge in the door of payment reform by excluding doctors, lawyers, and wealthy business people. But about 60 percent of the House voted against that amendment.

In its budget submissions to Congress, the Clinton administration has followed the Bush administration in endorsing the general idea of means testing. The Bush administration's 1992 budget submission claimed that "deficiency payments have gone to more than 10,000 individuals whose annual adjusted gross income from nonfarming sources has exceeded $125,000" and estimated that they received about $90 million in payments. The administration suggested a means test to make those people ineligible for farm program payments (U.S. Budget 1992, 139). The Clinton administration included a broader proposal in its 1993 budget to make anyone with more than $100,000 in adjusted gross income from all sources on his tax returns ineligible for payments. That was estimated to save $140 million annually when fully implemented. The CBO (1994, 215), however, estimates that such a measure would save $60 million annually.

Considering either the $100,000 adjusted gross income test or the $1 million sales test as a policy option, the advantages and disadvantages are similar. The advantages of the means test are that it saves government outlays, that losers do not need the payments, and that it opens the door politically for further reform. The disadvantages are that such a test induces resource expenditure to avoid losing payments, penalizes farming enterprises that may be relatively efficient, and reduces the ability of acreage reduction programs to control production.

We can expect the actual savings from means testing to be much smaller than the estimates above would suggest because it is too easy to convert payments into roughly equivalent market returns. The lawyer who owns a farm only has to rent the cropland out to a "real" farmer, who will then be the farmer of record for USDA purposes. The market rental value of the farm will include the value of payments that the renter can expect to receive, so that the lawyer can retain the value of the payments by, in effect, selling them to someone else. It is costly to make those arrangements, which are revealed as not preferred by the lawyer since by hypothesis they were not made until induced by the means test. The cost has to be counted as a deadweight loss of the means test.

The penalty for relatively efficient farmers could be important, particularly for means testing based on sales. The USDA estimates that 16,000 farms, 0.8 percent of all U.S. farms, sold products valued at $1,000,000 or more in 1991. Those farms received $443 million in government payments, which was 5.4 percent of all payments in 1991. Those farms received an average of $27,000 and had an average net cash income of $1.2 million as estimated by the USDA (USDA 1993a, 69).[4] Thus, the USDA could hope to reduce its outlays by 5 percent, if that is required in total budget reduction efforts, just by denying payments to farms with over $1 million in sales. The owners typically are well-off. Moreover, the payments average only about 2 percent of their $1 million or higher net incomes.

Such a scheme has problems, however. First, the USDA is not well equipped to determine, when a farmer signs up for program participation, what the farm's sales are. The USDA could require income tax returns if legislation permitted, but a USDA farm is not the unit of account for income tax purposes, so it is not clear that the data provided would still apply. In addition, such a scheme will induce the indirect capture of payments through rental or other contracting, as discussed above. Note also that while the farms with $1 million in sales get 5.4 percent of all payments, they sell 10.5 percent of commodities receiving payments. For all farms the government paid $8.2 billion on $28.4 billion of payment-receiving commodities in 1991; payments were 29 percent of the value of those commodities (grains and cotton). But for the farms with $1 million in sales, the government paid $443 million on $3.0 billion of payment-receiving commodities; payments on the large farms were 15 percent of the value of the commodities.

---

4. IRS adjusted gross income would be less.

Thus, the large farms have already been driven out of programs to a substantial extent by existing payment limits, or else they have already found ways to capture payments indirectly.

Suppose that existing payment limits really have been effective and that farms with $1 million in sales have been driven out of programs to the extent indicated. That would mean that those farms get 20 percent less for program crops than smaller farms do. Removing payments completely from the largest farms would mean that their effective price for program crops is about 35 percent less than the price farms with less than $250,000 in sales receive. Since the number of large farms is growing and smaller ones shrinking, it is likely that the large ones are lower-cost producers. A strict limitation on program benefits to larger farms thus subsidizes high-cost relative to low-cost producers by causing large farms to receive perhaps 20 percent less per unit of output than small farms. Means tests may have appeal if we see farm programs as welfare programs, but they are perverse for farm programs as industrial policy.

Across-the-board cuts. Across-the-board reductions will have to come predominantly from deficiency payments, since that is where most of the spending is. The main alternatives are cuts in target prices, as in the 1985 act, or reductions in payment acreage, as in 1990. Which of those approaches is preferable? If payments were strictly lump sum—determined by a payment rate and quantity on which payments were absolutely fixed—then the choice would not matter. With respect to the chief way in which current law does affect producer behavior—imperfect flexibility among crops—cutbacks in payment acreage reduce the distortive effects more. That increases planting flexibility by increasing normal flex acres. But cutting target prices helps, too, by reducing the incentive to make acreage decisions based on expected deficiency payments.

Consider cutting target prices by 15 percent and payment acres by 10 percent over five years. Starting in 1996, target prices would be cut by 3 percent each year and payment acreage by 2 percent. One advantage of such a policy is that it would substantially reduce government spending. Another advantage is that farmers would gear production more to market realities. The disadvantage is that farm income would decline.

That policy option involves a classic trade-off between the general public and a producer interest group. The chief economic question is how much the general public will gain relative to what farmers lose—the recoverable dead-weight losses caused by current policies.

Consider such an option for wheat after full implementation in the year 2000. The target price will be $3.40 and payment acres about 50 million. Averaging USDA and Food and Agricultural Policy Research Institute baselines, the expected market price of wheat is about $3.10 per bushel in 2000 (USDA 1993b). Keeping payment yields at 34 bushels per acre, deficiency payments would be $510 million, compared with about $1.7 billion under current law. That cuts outlays by $1.2 billion or 70 percent from the current-law baseline.

The question can be raised whether the wheat price would remain at the $3.10 baseline price under the deficiency payment cuts. The Food and Agricultural Policy Research Institute baseline assumes a 5 percent wheat acreage reduction program in 2000, although the USDA baseline has a zero acreage reduction program. Supposing the 5 percent estimate is correct, one needs to consider whether program participation pays when deficiency payments have been reduced so far. If producers drop out to produce on acreage reduction program land, their added output will depress market prices.

For all commodities, payments by the year 2000 would be reduced from baseline levels by $1.2 billion for wheat, $2.2 billion for corn (to which we should add $.4 billion for other feed grains), and $.3 billion each for cotton and rice. The annual budget savings would total $4.4 billion for the deficiency-payment crops. That constitutes a reduction of two-thirds from the $6.6 billion current-law baseline that this analysis uses for those crops.

The objection to that policy option is the loss of payments by the farmers who would otherwise receive them. In the political arena in which the 1995 farm bill will be determined, that loss may well count for more than the taxpayers' $6.0 billion gains.[5]

It is dangerous for farmers and costly to the economy, however, to have the matter turn simply on political clout. And many farmers do not want farm programs as just a variety of welfare payment. An issue economists might helpfully address is how to structure agricultural policy in such a way as to assist agriculture while making the economy more efficient rather than creating dead-weight losses. Such a consideration leads to a broader set of policy options that I shall discuss under the heading of industrial policy.

Industrial Policy for Agriculture. The analytical approach to policy options that go beyond redistributing income is to consider areas in which government action can plausibly improve on the workings of the market. Those areas include environmental externalities, price stabilization, public good aspects of new knowledge and information, and dealing with other nations whose policies affect U.S. exports. The 1995 farm bill will consider a wide range of programs of public investment in research, environmental improvement, and promotion of new uses for agricultural products. Environmental and conservation options and research options are the subject of other chapters. I shall only briefly discuss public spending on research and promotion. I shall

---

5. The difference between the farmers' loss and the taxpayers' gain, the marginal dead-weight loss of the deficiency payment programs, is actually greater than the $920 million cited. The reason is that reducing outlays by $4.4 billion is worth more than $4.4 billion because of dead-weight losses involved in taxation to raise those funds. Alston and Hurd (1990) argue for a range whose midpoint is thirty-five cents per dollar raised. Then the total gains to the U.S. economy of the $4.4 billion cuts would be $2.5 billion. Producers give up $3.5 billion and the rest of the economy gains $6.0 billion. In addition, such accounting omits administrative costs of the program, currently about $800 million annually for the Commodity Credit Corporation programs.

state the policy option in the spirit of the pay-as-you-go requirement of the 1990 and 1993 budget agreements.

Reallocating government spending from commodity price support to research and promotion of new uses for farm products. The advantages of such an option are that it confers benefits on consumers and the environment as well as on farmers and that it generates less dead-weight loss since instead of idling land, it creates uses for the products of it. One disadvantage of the public investment option is that farmers may not gain so much from a given level of spending on research and promotion as they do from commodity programs such as deficiency payments. In addition, such a policy option generates more dead-weight losses due to "pork" in research and promotion programs.

The argument in favor of the public investment approach is essentially that it does better than commodity programs in a benefit-cost test. Indeed, a large body of literature estimates that the social rate of return to research is greater than the rate of return to investment in the economy generally. Some have questioned that finding. But while the evidence is not incontrovertible, the weight of it today indicates that research has increased agricultural productivity sufficiently to more than repay the costs.

What is much less clear is whether farmers gain as much from, say, $1 billion in research as compared with $1 billion in deficiency payments. In neither case will farmers get all the benefits, because of dead-weight losses and sharing the gains with other interested parties such as farm input suppliers and marketing firms. For the wheat and corn programs from 1984 through 1987, Lin (1989, 16) estimates that producers gained about seventy cents per dollar spent by the federal government.

Estimates are lacking of farmers' benefits from federal research spending. For state level research and research in smaller countries like New Zealand and Australia, one can more convincingly make the case that farmers gain. The reason is that benefits from reductions in production costs must largely go to producers because international or national markets set product prices. But for a large country like the United States, increases in output at reduced costs are likely to benefit consumers more than producers and may not benefit producers at all if product demand is inelastic. Thus, some U.S. milk producers are suspicious of the growth hormone BST. Over the long term and given the importance of world markets even for U.S. farm products, however, it seems likely that farmers benefit. Urban and rural interests are more likely to agree on public investment in research than in commodity programs because research generates gains to society as a whole.

The discussion so far has not involved industrial policy in the sense of governmental direction of research spending details. The 1990 farm act moved in that direction. The alternative is to let the scientific community, traditionally through the land-grant universities and the USDA's Agricultural Research Service, decide how to allocate research efforts. The argument for more congressional micromanagement is that the USDA and the universities are not sufficiently interested in practical, profit-generating research, but instead are too much focused on scientific disciplinary research with little commercial value. The argument against congressional industrial policy is that Congress does not know what the promising lines of research are, in terms of either pure science or commercial prospects, and will end up mainly distributing pork to the scientific enterprises whose snouts are most deeply in the trough.

With respect to federal spending on commodity promotion, the arguments are weaker for both the benefits of the programs and the desirability of detailed industrial policy from Congress. Such evidence as exists for benefits of promotion programs usually indicates that the programs generate returns for producers that cover their costs. But there is doubt about the persistence of demand increases, and generally the evidence is even weaker than for research programs.

Some might also consider the Conservation Reserve Program a part of industrial policy that generates farm income benefits at relatively low dead-weight loss, while providing environmental benefits. The cost effectiveness of the Conservation Reserve Program has also been questioned, however. Walter Thurman's chapter provides further discussion.

Analysts properly consider several agricultural trade policy options as elements of industrial policy. The most costly items are export subsidy programs for wheat, dairy products, and other commodities. More attuned to the regulatory and "picking winners" aspects of industrial policy are the market promotion program with an emphasis on high-value exports and policies like the "circle of poison" restrictions on pesticide exports. Columnist George Will called a recent budget reduction in the market promotion program "a 13.6 percent cut in a program that is 100 percent indefensible" and called its supplements to advertising activities abroad "ineffective welfare payments to corporations" (*Washington Post,* July 11, 1993). Is the criticism fair? A policy step that would have trivial costs but could contribute greatly to sensible industrial policy is establishing a continuing unit for benefit-cost assessment of regulatory proposals and public investments affecting agriculture. Such assessments would likely recommend completely eliminating the export subsidy and promotion programs and would help forestall wasteful regulation aimed at wildlife protection and other environmental objectives. But one cannot be sure without much more thorough benefit-cost analysis than has been carried out to date.

Market stabilization. A traditional purpose of governmental intervention in commodity markets is price stabilization. A policy option for focusing commodity programs on stabilization would be to increase the market orientation of the farmer-owned-reserve program by giving farmers complete freedom to decide when to store or to withdraw commodities and to widen the program beyond grains but keep strict upper limits on quantities permitted to receive storage or interest-rate subsidies. The main element of such an option would be to convert the deficiency payment, dairy, and other programs to strictly stabilization purposes.

The program would have several other features. Target prices for grain and cotton would be set for three-year periods, at the baseline market price for that period, with payment bases updated to 85 percent of 1992 through 1994 average output. In addition, loan rates would remain at current levels. The milk support price and Commodity Credit Corporation purchases would be replaced by a deficiency payment scheme with the target price initially at $10.10 and the grains procedure adopted after three years; the payment quantity would be frozen at 85 percent of actual 1993 through 1994 average sales. The oilseed, sugar, peanut, and tobacco programs would be converted to a similar approach. Finally, all acreage reduction programs, marketing loans, advance deficiency payments, and payment limits would end.

The baseline prices used would be the same as those now used in budget scoring. But because agreement on baseline prices would become even more important, an institutional arrangement would be established in which the CBO and the General Accounting Office would collaborate with the OMB and the USDA in developing the baseline.

To see how the program would work, consider corn for the period 1996 through 1998. Suppose that the baseline corn price arrived at was $2.05 for that period.[6] Then the target price would be $2.05. Suppose that the season-average price of corn turned out to be $2.00. The U.S. payment base would be about 7.5 billion bushels (85 percent of 1992 through 1994 U.S. production). Deficiency payments would be $375 million.

If the season-average price were above $2.05, there would be no payments. By construction, payments at baseline prices would be zero. With budget scoring that uses baseline prices, that program would be scored to have zero outlays.

---

6. That is ten cents lower than current USDA or Food and Agricultural Policy Research Institute baselines, because for purposes of this program, which has no acreage reduction programs, we need a zero acreage reduction program baseline, while current-policy baselines have 5 to 10 percent acreage reduction programs.

The spirit of that program is similar to the 1994 crop disaster insurance program, which automatically pays indemnities to program-crop producers whose yields fall below 50 percent of average and are in a county where the yield is below 65 percent of its average. (See the chapter by Barry Goodwin and Vincent Smith.) But the "price insurance" has no individual-farm trigger, has no deductible (payments accrue for any shortfall below the baseline price), and involves no fee from producers.

A more drastic version of such a reform would have a deductible and would charge a fee. For example, payments might be made only if the market price falls below 90 percent of the baseline price, and a fee, say $5 per acre, might be charged. That version of the program would be equivalent to the government's selling put options with a strike price at 90 percent of the baseline price. That highlights a parallel to the pilot programs using commodity options that have been carried out under the 1985 and 1990 farm acts. The pilot programs involved highly subsidized puts that are far in the money, for example, guaranteeing a sale of corn at $2.75 when the expected market price is $2.20. The new "put options" considered here would have a smaller subsidy of the premium on an out-of-the-money put.

While such a stabilization option would be scored at zero budget outlays, expected outlays would not, of course, be zero. Prices are sure to be below the baseline in many years for many commodities and thus would trigger payments, while prices above baseline prices would not trigger savings. Scoring conventions have been modified to give budget costs to disaster programs, and it would make sense to undertake probabilistic or statistical scoring for the stabilization option also. The CBO is said to be considering such an approach even for existing price support programs. Implementation would be a formidable task, but probably easier than environmental benefit-cost scoring that will have to be undertaken at some stage. The costs of ignoring the issue are too large to do nothing.

The advantages of the stabilization option are that it

eliminates the dead-weight losses from acreage idling and the distortions of farmers' production choices and that it affords budget savings of about $9 billion annually. In addition, that option stabilizes markets more predictably and uniformly across producers.

One disadvantage of the stabilization option is that farmers give up about $9 billion annually in payments, and farm income declines (but by much less than $9 billion). In addition, payment-base asset values decline—a loss to landowners. Finally, such sweeping changes raise major implementation issues.

Such a stabilization option is a more substantial revision of programs than any of the others considered earlier. The details require a lot of working out, especially for the nondeficiency payment commodities. The option could be implemented for deficiency payment commodities only, but there is an important equity issue in leaving untouched the commodities—sugar, peanuts, and tobacco—that get their support directly from the pockets of consumers rather than through government payments.

The basic idea of such an option is that it could accomplish more for taxpayers and consumers than the earlier across-the-board target price cuts, while at the same time costing farmers less. The reason is that target price cuts would still leave the structure of current programs intact and would retain the distortions and inefficiencies that are especially burdensome for those commodities without a deficiency-payment program. The stabilization option, which removes existing constraints, would fit well with shifting the federal government's efforts toward industrial policies that meet a benefit-cost test for investment in environmental improvement, research and information, technological developments in new uses of farm products, and market stabilization. The international economic environment that will emerge under the new GATT agreement, NAFTA, and free-trade negotiations yet to come is better suited to a prosperous agriculture under the industrial policy option than under current farm programs.

Recommendations

Recommendations on policy options require overarching criteria by which they may be judged. That is to say, what do we want farm programs for anyway? What is their purpose? Even with agreement on basic purposes, many of the most contentious issues involve trade-offs among economic interests—program participants versus taxpayers who pay for the programs, equity in program benefits among producers of different commodities. Those trade-offs are ultimately a political matter to which economists have little to contribute beyond pointing out that dead-weight losses of economic distortions make it inevitable that the gainers will gain less than the losers will lose from government intervention. But unless one is willing to make judgments about the value of transferring a dollar from, say, an average taxpayer to an average wheat grower, one cannot make the call on how the pros and cons of wheat policy alternatives add up.

A key overarching economic issue for farm policy choice in 1995 is whether we (as a society represented by Congress) want our farm policy to be welfare policy or industrial policy. Farm policy as welfare policy involves redistributing income from one group of people to another. Farm policy as industrial policy involves efforts to make the farm economy, and hence the U.S. economy, work better, through investment in public goods, improvement of the environment, or correction of other market failures.

I believe that experience with farm programs indicates that we ought to move away from farm policy as welfare policy. The reason is that majority support for welfare policy requires that the beneficiaries be needy and deserving— having suffered harm not their fault. But while rural areas have needy people, they are not the beneficiaries of farm commodity programs. They do not produce enough that even high prices would solve their problems. On the other hand, commercial-scale farmers on average have income and wealth well above the U.S. average. And the minority of farms at risk of business failure through large debts and low returns are not plausibly assisted through price supports that provide windfalls to the majority of farmers, bid up land values, and engender commodity surpluses. Those farms need individual financial attention, after which they should be reinvigorated or placed under new management.

The rejection of farm policy as welfare leaves us with the industrial policy issues. Impartial observers indeed have found social goods for agricultural legislation to address: market stabilization, research, food safety, and environmental improvement. Again, however, experience shows us that the sixty-year vigorous pursuit of interest-group agendas has largely coopted the social goods hoped for. By now it is widely accepted that farm policy, whatever its public-interest wrappings, generates market-distorting intervention that predictably yields results counterproductive to the well-being of the nation as a whole.

It is this situation that has led me to consider successively less marginal and more radical options for the 1995 farm bill and finally to endorse the relatively modest intervention of the pure stabilization option, supplemented with limited public investment in environmental, food safety, informational, and research activities, and continuing government efforts to open markets for U.S. farm products abroad. Each of those areas, however, requires careful assessment on its own terms. That is what the legislative hearing process for the 1995 farm bill should be all about.

References

Alston, Julian M., and Brian H. Hurd. "Some Neglected Social Costs of Government Spending in Farm Programs." *American Journal of Agricultural Economics* 72 (February 1990): 149–56.

Barr, James C. Testimony on H.R. 2664: The Milk Producers Self-Help Program. House Committee on Agriculture, Subcommittee on Livestock, July 21, 1993.

Congressional Budget Office. "Reducing the Deficit: Spending and Revenue Options." Washington, D.C.: Government Printing Office, March 1994.

Food and Agricultural Policy Research Institute. *FAPRI 1994*

International Agricultural Outlook. Staff Report 2-94. Iowa State University and University of Missouri, May 1994.

Lin, William. "Aggregate Effects of Commodity Programs." USDA-ERS mimeo. Washington, D.C.: U.S. Department of Agriculture, 1989.

U.S. Department of Agriculture. *National Financial Summary, 1991.* Economic Research Service, ECIFS-11-1, January 1993a.

―――. "Long-term Agricultural Baseline Projections." World Agricultural Outlook Board, WAOB-93-1, October 1993b.

―――. *News.* Release 0149.94, February 25, 1994a.

―――. *Wheat: Commodity Fact Sheet.* Farm Service Agency, November 1994b.

U.S. Executive Office of the President. *Budget of the United States Government: Fiscal Year 1992.* Washington, D.C.: Government Printing Office (undated).

4

Agricultural Trade Policy Reform

Daniel A. Sumner

This chapter investigates U.S. agricultural trade policies and considers reforms in three areas: (1) policies that create barriers to agricultural imports, (2) programs that directly or indirectly subsidize agricultural exports, and (3) policies that facilitate the expansion and extension of international trade agreements. The recently completed Uruguay Round agreement negotiated as a reform of the General Agreement on Tariffs and Trade (GATT) provides the background for the analysis of agricultural trade policies to be considered as a part of the 1995 farm bill.

Implementation of the Uruguay Round agreement began in January 1995. It provides for some immediate and some gradual changes in agricultural trade policy on a global basis (USDA 1994b). But this agreement does not imply that further changes in U.S. agricultural trade policy would not be useful. In fact the completion of the Uruguay Round creates new incentives and opportunities for trade policy reform.

This study takes a conventional economic approach to agricultural trade policy reform. The analysis is based on

I wish to thank the following individuals for assistance and comments on the research underlying this chapter: Julian Alston, Colin Carter, Bruce Gardner, Roger Hitcher, D. Gale Johnson, Julius Katz, Hyunok Lee, Christine McCracken, Jeffrey McDonald, Andy Morton, David Orden, John Quilkey, Christopher Wolf, and additional participants in a workshop held at the American Enterprise Institute on November 3–4, 1994.

standard economic models, with implications that movement toward less government intervention in international trade would be a wise course in most cases (Baldwin 1992). Often U.S. agricultural trade policy has been rationalized as necessary to facilitate domestic farm programs or to overcome problems created by those programs. But as domestic programs continue to be reformed, the rationale for maintaining the associated trade policies weakens further.

The topics considered here have been issues for many years. For example, D. Gale Johnson's 1950 book, *Trade and Agriculture: A Study of Inconsistent Policies,* written just after the GATT was created, analyzed such continuing U.S. policies as section 22 import quotas and subsidies for wheat exports. The present analysis covers some of the same ground and takes a policy perspective much like that in Johnson's 1973 book, *World Agriculture in Disarray.*

This essay is based on a more extensive work, *Agricultural Trade Policy: Letting Markets Work* (Sumner, 1995), one of a series of agricultural policy monographs published by the American Enterprise Institute. This chapter makes no attempt to review and comment on the massive literature on agricultural trade policy; only a few references are made in passing to work that is particularly relevant. In general, sources available from the Department of Agriculture (USDA) provide detailed and accurate descriptions of the policies and programs mentioned below, and academic and similar sources provide some detailed analysis of stylized policies.

Current Agricultural Trade Patterns

We now take for granted that the United States is a net exporter of agricultural products. This was not the case, however, in the middle part of this century. Except for the years during and immediately after World War II, the United States was a minor exporter of agricultural goods and often imported more than it exported. The value of U.S. agricultural exports exceeded the value of imports for only two years in the 1950s.

TABLE 4-1

U.S. EXPORTS AND IMPORTS OF AGRICULTURAL COMMODITIES,
1941–1995

(billions of dollars)

Year[a]	Total Exports	Total Imports	Agricultural Trade Balance
1941	0.7	1.7	−1.0
1951	4.0	5.2	−1.1
1961	5.0	3.7	1.3
1971	7.7	5.8	1.9
1981	43.4	16.8	26.6
1993	42.5	24.5	18.0
1994	43.5	26.4	17.1
1995 (forecast)	48.5	28.5	20.0

a. Calendar years for 1941–1971, fiscal years for 1981–1995.
SOURCES: *President's Council of Economic Advisers* (1993); USDA (1994 c and d).

The growth of agricultural trade has not been constant (table 4–1). Imports actually declined in the 1950s. They expanded rapidly in nominal terms in the 1970s but did not keep up with the rapid expansion in agricultural exports. During the 1980s, while U.S. agricultural exports declined and then gradually approached the prior level, imports continued to expand. In 1981 exports reached a peak that is exceeded only by 1994 and 1995. But at more than 25 percent of total gross farm revenue for the year, 1981 exports were a more important source of demand than exports in 1995 will be, even if forecasts hold.

Besides documenting the importance of trade to current agricultural supply and demand, recent international trends suggest that trade can become even more important. Economic growth, especially in Asia and Latin America, indicates the potential for expanding exports so long as market access is available. Further, if access can be improved, even regions with relatively static demands for food and fiber can provide new markets for trade.

Trade in itself, however, should not be the issue. The mercantilist logic (or illogic) that encourages some to think

83

that imports are bad for the economy also causes some to infer mistakenly that more exports are good for the economy no matter what the source. The importance of trade to the U.S. agricultural economy should not be misinterpreted or overstated. Domestic markets matter too, and using higher taxes or higher domestic consumer prices to "buy" more exports does not contribute to the health of the economy.

The next three sections discuss agricultural trade policies and programs in the wake of the Uruguay Round agreement. Space constraints do not allow providing details of the agreement, but the needed information is provided for each topic, beginning with policies related to agricultural imports.

Import Policy

Several import policy issues are discussed. Commodities are dealt with separately, on the basis of the principal access instrument that is applied.

The Conversion of Nontariff Barriers to Tariffs. Nontariff barriers have often been used to provide trade barriers for U.S. agriculture. This was particularly true for commodities with a history of price and income support programs. Section 22 of the Agricultural Adjustment Act of 1933 (as amended) made specific provisions for import quotas for these commodities.

The North American Free Trade Agreement and the Uruguay Round agreement each required that nontariff barriers be converted to tariffs (tariffication) and these and all other tariffs gradually reduced. This procedure has already occurred (or is scheduled to occur) for imports from Mexico. The multilateral conversion of nontariff barriers to tariffs required by the Uruguay Round agreement will have a much more pervasive impact on trade policy in the United States than has the tariffication required by NAFTA. Under the Uruguay Round agreement the United States will apply tariff-rate quotas rather than strict quotas to potential im-

TABLE 4-2
SELECTED TARIFF-RATE QUOTAS IN THE URUGUAY ROUND
AGREEMENT, 1995 AND 2000

	1995		2000	
Product[a]	Quota (tons)	Over-quota tariff	Quota (tons)	Over-quota tariff
Beef and veal	656,621	31.1%	656,621	26.4%
Cotton	51,927	$0.37/kg	86,545	$0.31/kg
Peanuts	33,770		56,283	
In-shell		192.7%		163.8%
Shelled		155.0%		131.8%
Peanut butter	19,150	155.0%	20,000	131.8%
Dairy products				
Cheese	110,999	$1.443/kg	141,991	$1.227/kg
Butter		$1.813/kg		$1.541/kg
Powder		$1.018/kg		$0.865/kg

a. New tariff rate quotas are also provided for sugar and sugar-containing products.
SOURCE: USDA (1994a).

ports from all nations that are signatories to the agreement. Table 4-2 provides the new schedule of tariff-rate quota quantities and import duties.

The United States agreed to recompute the tariff-rate quota for sugar even though sugar imports have been restricted by a tariff-rate quota established in 1990 in response to a GATT panel finding. The new tariffication of the sugar program, at a new higher tariff of 17 cents per pound, applies to all potential imports above 1.14 million metric tons. In addition, section 22 quotas on selected sugar-containing products are being converted to tariffs.

U.S. sugar policy has long exemplified a trade-distorting policy with substantial costs to consumers. The Uruguay Round agreement failed to reduce significantly the excess costs of sugar to domestic consumers or the excess resource cost of producing sugar in the United States when it could be imported at roughly half the cost. The price of sugar available on the world market varies but has remained in the range of about 10 cents per pound compared with a little more than 20 cents per pound in the United States. If more import access were allowed, the domestic price would decline, and the import price might rise slightly. The benefit of an expanded quantity of low-tariff imports of, say, 0.5 million tons of sugar would be a direct gain of about $100 million to consumers in lower outlays. The costs to growers and those who own sugar-producing land or other resources would be less than these gains to consumers because much of this sugar is produced at high cost on land that is environmentally fragile or better suited to other uses.

For beef and veal, the Meat Import Law provided for a quota that varied each year according to a formula incorporating indicators of the domestic supply and demand situation. The law, however, also provided that no quota would be imposed unless projected imports were more than 10 percent above the quota. Thus exporting nations had an incentive to restrict imports "voluntarily" to just below the "trigger" quantity. Implementation of the Uruguay Round agreement replaces this system with a tariff-rate quota set roughly equal to the earlier quota amount. The agreement provides that import access be maintained or improved from the preagreement conditions, but this does not seem to have been maintained for beef in other than legalistic terms.

Beef tariffs also show how the agreement was interpreted to maintain protection. In the late 1980s and early 1990s, at the Organization for Economic Cooperation and Development, exporting nations wanted to show that the U.S. Meat Import Law provided substantial support to the U.S. beef industry. At the GATT tariffication negotiations, however, the United States adopted a variant of the OECD approach to calculate tariff equivalents in the 30 to 40 percent range. Now, in a role reversal, the Australian and New Zealand negotiators tried to insist on comparing beef of similar grade and quality with appropriate adjustments for transport and other associated costs. The final result is a tariff equivalent of 31 percent, even though objective measurements might suggest a tariff equivalent of less than 10 percent.

More protection, not less, resulted from the Uruguay Round agreement for beef imports. The quota amount allowed at the low tariff is smaller than previous imports in most years, and the tariff applied for the second tier is clearly excessive. The cost to consumers remains hundreds of millions of dollars per year.

Dairy products are among the section 22 commodities with the most economic importance and political sensitivity. The Uruguay Round agreement provided that for commodities with almost no imports prior to the agreement, import access would be provided for at least 3 percent of domestic consumption. For dairy products, minimum-access tariff-rate quotas raise a number of complications. Often, domestically produced goods do not exist in the form imported, and domestic consumption data are never available at the level of disaggregation in the tariff schedules. The dairy product tariff-rate quotas are among the most important and complex of the U.S. agricultural policy adjustments to the Uruguay Round agreement.

More dairy products will be imported as a consequence of the Uruguay Round agreement, but the quantities are limited at most. In addition, the over-quota tariff levels are much higher than could be derived from objective data on prices of potential imports and domestic sales. Remaining import barriers for manufactured dairy products help to keep domestic prices well above those of potential imports. Most of the U.S. domestic dairy industry could compete quite well on international markets, but the combinations of domestic price policy and import barriers make the domestic market and U.S. prices much more attractive than exports at international market prices. Some regions, especially New Zealand and a limited part of Australia, can produce tradable dairy products at lower cost than the United States. But the capacity of these regions is limited compared with the size of the world market. Therefore the appropriate long-term strategy for both consumers and producers of dairy products is to open the United States and other markets and to ban the use of dairy export subsidies. Such action would cause higher international prices for dairy products, would allow U.S. producers to compete in a non-subsidized export market, and would allow U.S. consumers access to additional low-cost dairy products.

Rucker, Thurman, and Borges (forthcoming) have summarized the effect of the Uruguay Round for the U.S. peanut industry. U.S. peanuts are exported into the world market at competitive prices, but until implementation of the Uruguay Round agreement, an import quota (set near zero) allowed the domestic marketing quota to determine a domestic price well above the export price. In its final and complete form, the Uruguay Round agreement did provide some additional access for peanuts, but at the same time it added barriers for processed peanut products (especially peanut butter from Canada). Therefore, under the new policy it is not clear that import access will actually increase significantly for peanuts and processed products taken together. An indication that access did not increase is that the U.S. peanut industry, which had vigorously opposed the Uruguay Round agreement until the final weeks of the negotiations, supported the agreement in its final form.

Cotton is another major commodity that has had section 22 quotas. In this case, however, no additional imports are expected from the conversion to a tariff-rate quota because the current quota was not binding and the United States is a major cotton exporter of a wide variety of cotton qualities.

Tariffs. The Uruguay Round agreement simply requires that each agricultural tariff be reduced by at least 15 percent over the next six years and that the reductions average at least 36 percent across all tariff lines. Tariff reductions in the Uruguay Round agreement and NAFTA were controversial for several commodities in the United States that are protected solely by bound tariffs. Of particular political sensitivity were concentrated orange juice, fresh limes, and a few additional horticultural items. The tariff reductions negotiated are especially gradual; substantial consumer costs will remain for a decade or more even if the schedule of cuts in the Uruguay Round agreement is continued after the initial six years.

A New Tobacco Barrier. The implications of the Uruguay Round for tobacco became more complicated in the months leading up to the final agreement because U.S. trade policy for tobacco changed. In fall 1993, a few months before the December 15, 1993, completion of negotiations for the Uruguay Round, the United States approved a new nontariff import barrier for tobacco. In 1994, cigarettes manufactured in the United States were not allowed to contain more than 25 percent imported tobacco. Zaini, Beghin, and Brown (1994) describe the policy and consider incentives for cigarette manufacturers to comply. (See also Sumner [forthcoming].)

HR 5110, the implementing legislation for the Uruguay Round agreement, contained several provisions to revise import barriers for tobacco. Section 421 grants authority to raise import barriers under GATT article 28: in the tobacco case, negotiations to create new trade barriers and compensation for exporters can proceed. Section 422 modifies importer assessments along with domestic tobacco marketing assessments and allows the president to waive the domestic content law if it violates any U.S. trade agreement (that is, GATT, NAFTA, or the new Uruguay Round agreement). The section also modifies the duty drawbacks for tobacco exports to make them more protectionist and to make them conform with the tariff-rate quotas likely to be created under the article 28 negotiations. These provisions in section 422 take effect with "the Presidential proclamation, authorized under section 421, establishing a tariff-rate quota pursuant to Article XXVIII."

A preliminary paper by Zaini (1994) uses an equilibrium displacement model and parameters from earlier work to evaluate the effects of the content restriction on U.S. tobacco demand, supply, price, and income of producers. For its chosen parameters, Zaini's model indicates that the content law would raise the use of domestic tobacco and benefit U.S. tobacco producers. The substitution of domestic tobacco for imports would outweigh the reduction in tobacco use. Plausible supply and demand parameters imply a gain in domestic leaf price and quantity of about 4 percent. Domestic use of tobacco increases by about 11.5 percent, and exports fall by about 9 percent.

The Zaini analysis may overstate the long-term benefit to U.S. leaf tobacco producers because its parameters tend to minimize the impact of the import barrier on the location of cigarette manufacturing and on the export market for U.S. leaf. Importers of U.S. leaf may view the new U.S. trade barrier as a violation of the U.S. commitment to freer trade and may respond with more trade barriers. Further, the domestic content regulation, or the new import barriers that replace it, add constraints to U.S. cigarette manufacturers that may encourage a shift offshore as the domestic market shrinks and export market retaliation by foreign countries becomes more important.

Even if the domestic leaf industry gains from the content restriction, clearly the economies in tobacco growing and cigarette manufacturing regions lose. Even with an increase of 4 percent in domestic leaf use, the quantity of cigarettes manufactured falls by about 0.5 percent, with less employment and revenue in the tobacco industry. In addition, tobacco leaf exports and cigarette exports both fall significantly.

The inconsistency implied by the United States instituting a nontariff barrier for a major export industry just when other such barriers in the United States and elsewhere are being dismantled (in part because of U.S. insistence) is particularly ironic given that the U.S. tobacco industry has operated a successful cartel and that its future depends on exports. This new domestic content law caused trade friction, and the new barriers under article 28 will not undo that damage to the tobacco industry or the effectiveness of the United States in negotiations for more open market in other countries.

A New Trade Barrier for Wheat. After the Uruguay Round

was settled but before implementing legislation was completed, the United States and Canada temporarily resolved a continuing wheat trade dispute by agreeing to a voluntary export restraint agreement. Under this agreement the United States promised to impose no temporary unilateral barriers (under section 22) and to suspend seeking a permanent new wheat tariff under article 28 of the GATT if Canada would agree to restrict wheat exports to the United States "voluntarily" for the year August 1994 to July 1995. Canada agreed that any shipments above the separate quota quantities for durum and other wheat would be subject to high and likely prohibitive tariff rates per ton. Thus, this "voluntary" restraint takes the form of a tariff-rate quota and is officially not a nontariff barrier.

The United States undertook a section 22 proceeding to block wheat imports in early 1994. The U.S. implementing legislation for the Uruguay Round agreement amends section 22 so that it no longer applies to commodities produced by countries that are members of the World Trade Organization. Section 22 ends when the WTO agreement goes into force except that for wheat the effective date for ending section 22 is delayed until September 12, 1995. Thus the United States has maintained its domestic legal authority to apply unilateral barriers on Canadian wheat imports for several additional months.

There is little puzzle why imports of wheat have increased in recent years. The real questions are why imports from Canada have not risen by even more and why wheat imports from Argentina and other suppliers have not occurred. The U.S. export subsidy provides $40 per ton or more as an added incentive to ship U.S. wheat offshore. This subsidy depresses the price in these international markets and raises the U.S. domestic market price. Imports of grain from Canada have been surprisingly moderate given the differential between the price in the U.S. market and other export markets used by Canada (Alston, Carter, Gray, and Sumner 1994).

The U.S. wheat market is closely connected to other markets in the world mainly because the United States is the world's largest wheat exporter. Canada is also a major wheat exporter to international markets, where U.S. and Canadian wheat compete directly. Lower U.S. imports mean more supplies from Canada to international markets and consequently more competition for U.S. exports. The U.S. domestic market price is higher than the effective export price from the United States because the Export Enhancement Program (EEP) provides per unit subsidies to make up the difference between the domestic price that exporters must pay to acquire wheat in the United States and what the wheat can sell for in the export market.

The implications of restricting wheat imports into the United States depend on the important role of the United States in the world wheat market and on the fact that restricting imports from Canada diverts that wheat and causes a slightly weaker market for U.S. exports. Restricting imports in the current setting would imply (1) increased pasta imports; (2) only slightly increased production; (3) lower U.S. exports especially for durum, for which imports are most important; (4) slightly higher U.S. market prices with the largest impact on durum; and (5) an average price received by producers that is only marginally higher so that outlays on farm payments would be only marginally lower (Alston, Gray, and Sumner 1994).

The issue for the 1995 farm bill is how to deal with import pressure without reverting to new protectionist measures. One obvious answer is to reduce the export subsidies that generate the price wedge between the U.S. domestic and export markets. Lower export subsidies by the European Union (EU), and by Canada in the form of reduced transport subsidies, are expected to provide higher export prices for wheat and other grains as the Uruguay Round takes effect. The 1995 farm bill could enhance those export price increases by reducing EEP quantities and bonus levels more rapidly than required by the Uruguay Round agreement. A multilateral agreement for accelerated implementation of the reduction commitments negotiated during the Uruguay Round would mean even greater price increases.

Export Policy

This section focuses on the consequences of export price subsidies, credit subsidies, marketing subsidies, and food aid. All these policies and programs act to increase exports by using government assistance; they differ in the form of the aid or the international markets that they target.

Explicit Export Price Subsidies. In 1985 the United States introduced a new round of export subsidies under the Export Enhancement Program. The EEP began operation under the continuing charter authority of the Commodity Credit Corporation (CCC). It was subsequently authorized under the 1985 Farm Security Act. (See Ackerman and Smith [1990] and Gardner [1993] for a history of the EEP program.)

The EEP covers a number of commodities but in practice has been used most for wheat and flour. The Dairy Export Incentive Program (DEIP) was also authorized under the 1985 act to provide bonuses to exporters of dairy products. Subsequent to the 1985 act several commodity-specific export subsidy programs were introduced. The Sunflower-seed Oil Assistance Program (SOAP) was authorized in 1988, and the Cottonseed Oil Assistance Program (COAP) began in 1989.

The importance of export subsidies varies widely even among the applicable commodities. Only a tiny share of rice, beef, or pork is exported under EEP. But recently almost all barley and more than half the egg, vegetable oil, and wheat are exported under the relevant export subsidy programs.

Several characteristics of the export subsidy programs should be taken into account in any discussion of reform. First, the subsidies are targeted to a subset of the total export market. In particular the subsidies have not been provided to Japan, Korea, Taiwan, the EU, or much of Latin America. Second, the subsidies are no longer provided in kind from government stocks. They are provided in cash to the U.S. export firms. Third, the EEP process within the

93

government first requires that individual national markets be judged eligible and per unit price subsidies to eligible markets vary by transaction. Export firms deal with export buyers directly to determine the export subsidy required to complete a sale. Finally, the proposed per unit subsidy is evaluated to determine if it is the minimum necessary for the given transaction in the eligible market.

Programs that apply direct export price subsidies are subject to the disciplines on export subsidies of the Uruguay Round agreement. For each commodity, subsidized export quantities in the year 2000 must be 21 percent below the average during the 1986–1990 base period. In addition the value of export subsidies must be reduced by 36 percent compared with the base period values for each commodity. The schedule of reduction requires that export subsidies be cut in equal installments from either the 1986–1990 base or from the 1991 levels if export subsidies in that year were higher than in the base period. The commitments for each commodity are noted in table 4–3.

The size of the implied reductions compared with current exports or the 1995 commitment depends on the quantity of subsidized exports and the value of the export subsidy for that commodity in the base period. The wheat commitment on a tonnage basis, for example, requires a reduction of about 30 percent by the year 2000 from recent quantities subsidized and a reduction of more than 50 percent in the value of export subsidies for wheat from 1993 EEP outlays for wheat. The quantity of wheat subsidized averaged about 18 million metric tons in the base period, and the average per unit bonuses were below those experienced more recently. Therefore the cuts in quantities, especially in total outlays, are substantially larger than 21 and 36 percent when calculated on the basis of current program levels. This issue is seen much more dramatically for commodities such as rice and milk products, for which there was relatively little use of export subsidy programs from 1986 to 1990.

Export price subsidies have been the subject of a vigorous academic and political debate in recent years. (See, for

TABLE 4-3

U.S. URUGUAY ROUND COMMITMENTS FOR EXPORT SUBSIDIES,
1995 AND 2000

Commodity	Annual Quantity (metric tons)		Annual Outlay ($1,000)	
	1995	2000	1995	2000
Wheat	20,238,000	14,522,000	765,490	363,815
Coarse grains	1,906,000	1,561,000	67,735	46,118
Rice	272,000	39,000	15,706	2,369
Vegetable oil	587,538	141,299	52,960	14,083
Butter, butter oil	42,989	21,097	44,793	30,497
Skim milk	108,227	68,201	121,119	82,464
Cheese	3,829	3,030	5,340	3,636
Other milk	12,456	34	14,374	21
Beef	21,486	17,589	33,520	22,822
Pork	483	395	730	497
Poultry	34,196	27,994	21,377	14,555
Eggs	30,262	6,920	7,588	1,604

SOURCE: USDA (1994a).

example, Abbott, Paarlberg, and Sharples [1987]; Alston, Carter, and Smith [1993]; Anania, Bohman, and Carter [1992]; and Dutton [1990].) Almost all the analysis to date has focused on the EEP, especially the effects of the EEP for wheat. The export subsidies for other commodities are similar, and the same conceptual issues apply to them.

Any evaluation of a complex commodity policy such as the EEP hinges on what other policies and market conditions are expected to hold independently of the policy evaluated. In particular, with the EEP one must decide how the income and price support programs respond to EEP funding and operation.

Several conceptual arguments show that targeted export subsidy programs can increase national income. These theories should be evaluated carefully for the case at hand. One such argument relates to more favorable terms of trade in the nonsubsidized export market. An export subsidy to only part of the market can be used to raise total quantity

95

demanded and to raise the export price in the nonsubsidized part of the market. Then the additional profits from this higher price offset at least some costs of the original subsidy.

A second argument relates to the ability of export subsidies to reduce the total budget cost of all program subsidies by reducing the budget costs of direct payment programs or price support policies. By shifting out total demand, a targeted export subsidy raises the domestic price to producers. When this price is also used to calculate the domestic farm program payments, part of the potential gain to producers is transferred instead back to taxpayers as lower outlays for the domestic subsidy. In theory the domestic price effect could be large enough that the savings in domestic program costs more than offset the expenditures on the export subsidies. Then if the dead-weight cost of taxation is large enough, the export subsidy can actually increase national welfare.

A third argument for export subsidies relates to mitigating the economic resource cost of the domestic farm payment scheme rather than the budget costs. In particular the amount of land required to be idled under the farm program may be reduced in response to an increase in demand caused by the export subsidy. In that case the national welfare losses associated with land idling are smaller, and this improvement may offset some of the economic cost of the export subsidy.

Figure 4–1 illustrates simultaneous operation of targeted export subsidies and decoupled deficiency payment programs. Price support policies are not included in the figure to simplify the illustration and because price supports have become relatively unimportant in U.S. farm programs in recent years. The figure allows examination of some key features of the U.S. export subsidy policy operating in the context of a deficiency payment program. Based on the acreage flexibility features of the 1990 farm act and the frozen payment yields of the 1985 act, the program may be treated as roughly decoupled. The amount of government payments has relatively little effect on production,

FIGURE 4–1
Targeted Export Subsidy with Decoupled Domestic Deficiency Payments and Constant ARP

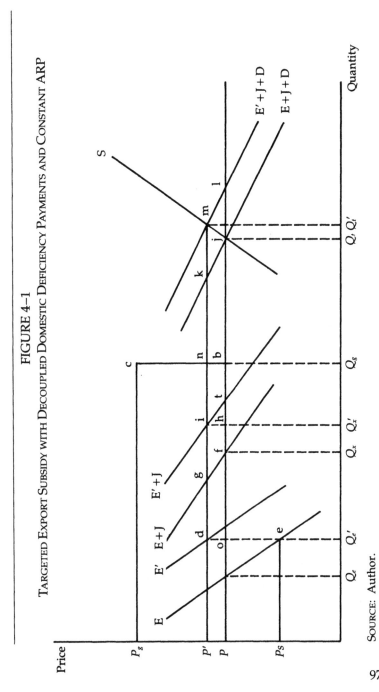

SOURCE: Author.

97

and the quantity of production does not affect the quantity eligible for payment.

In figure 4–1 the market price that applies without an export subsidy program is shown as P. At this price the market clears at quantity Q_t. The market supply curve, S, crosses the total demand curve, labeled $(E + J + D)$, at this price and quantity. Supply responds to a higher market price along the relatively inelastic market supply function. Figure 4–1 illustrates the case in which the Acreage Reduction Program (ARP) is constant so the supply curve does not shift in response to the export subsidy program. Three demand curves indicate three distinct markets for U.S. wheat. Demand curve E represents the export market to which the export subsidy is applied. The demand with an export subsidy available in this market is illustrated as E', and the resulting per unit subsidy is measured by $P' - P_s$. The nonsubsidized export market is shown by the distance from E to $E + J$. (J is used to represent this market because Japan is the largest importer not provided with EEP subsidies.) The domestic market, D, is also not eligible for subsidies. The size of this market (about half the total demand) is shown by the difference between the curves labeled $(E + J + D)$ and $(E + J)$.

When the export subsidy is provided in market E, the resulting total demand is represented by $(E' + J + D)$, the new market clearing price is P', and the new total market quantity is Q'_t. We now use the figure to trace through the effects of the subsidy on the various market participants. Subsidized buyers pay P_s rather than their original price P or the new market price P'. They now buy quantity Q'_e so additional sales in this market (in proportionate terms) are $(Q'_e - Q_e)/Q_e$. The total expenditures on export subsidies are $(P' - P_s)(Q'_e)$ shown by area $(P'deP_s)$ in figure 4–1. The non-subsidized export quantity had been $(Q_x - Q_e)$ or the difference between demand curve $E + J$ and demand curve E. Total exports are indicated by quantity Q_x. Because the subsidy is not available for the J market, the horizontal quantity shift from $(E + J)$ to $(E' + J)$ is equal to the quantity shift from E to E'.

The quantity $(Q'_x - Q_x)$, however, is less than the quantity $(Q'_e - Q_e)$ because the J market demand curve is itself downward sloping. The $E + J$ demand curve (representing total exports) is flatter than the E demand curve. The J market receives no subsidy and so faces a price increase from P to P'. Therefore consumers in this market buy less. The total percentage increase in exports is $(Q'_x - Q_x)/Q_x$.

The domestic buyers also receive no subsidy, and they consume less because their price is higher. They lose consumer net benefits in the amount shown by the area (*tiel*). This is equal to (*fgkj*) because the demand curves $E + J$ and $E' + J$ are parallel (as are $E + J + D$ and $E' + J' + D$).

The government spends general tax revenue on the domestic farm income subsidy program as well as on export subsidies. The farm program for wheat is approximated here by an income transfer that provides a variable subsidy per ton on a fixed quantity of output, shown by Q_g. This quantity is approximately constant under changes in the export program and is treated as though it were fixed in this analysis. Initial farm program cost is $(P_g - P)(Q_g)$, shown by the rectangular area $(P_g cbP)$. After the market price rises to P', domestic program costs fall to $(P_g - P')Q_g$, shown by area $P_g cnP'$.

These domestic budget costs are also program transfers to wheat producers. Because the higher price that raises market returns to farmers reduces transfers to farmers by the same amount, the effects on farm incomes are offsetting. Producers' losses of program benefits are offset by market revenue gains. That is, the dollar amount $(P' - P)Q_g$ becomes sales revenue rather than deficiency payments. In addition producers gain producer surplus in the amount shown by the area (*bnmj*). But while taxpayers gain, domestic consumers lose from higher prices.

In the figure the export subsidy outlay is shown by area $(P'deP_s)$. The upper part of this rectangle $(P'doP)$ is offset by reduced deficiency payments; the new outlays are $(P - P_s)Q'_e$ shown by area $(PoeP_s)$. Whether the export program increases or reduces total government outlays depends on the calculation $[(P-P_s)Q_e'] - [(P'-P)(Q_g-Q_e')]$. In the figure we compare areas $(PoeP_s)$ with $(dnbo)$.

Government budget costs of farm programs are a particular concern for two reasons. First, from a practical view from the farm constituency, the total outlays available for farm subsidies may be limited. Therefore, if a combination of programs can accomplish added farmer benefit with the same or lower government outlays, it may be preferred by the agricultural constituency. Second, taxation itself has costs to the economy. If the outlay of tax money can be reduced for the same income transfer to farmers, the total economic benefit may be increased. Estimates of the deadweight costs of taxation (the excess burden) vary widely, but these costs are likely in the range of 10 to 30 percent. (See Alston and Hurd [1990]; Fullerton [1991].) With the deadweight cost of taxation, a targeted export subsidy could theoretically be devised to reduce deficiency payments by more than the amount of the export bonuses and benefit the whole U.S. economy. Unfortunately such a program does not seem likely under realistic market and program parameters. Sumner (1995) provides some sample calculations to show how unlikely it is for the EEP program to reduce total outlays.

A potential benefit of allowing the market price to rise when the subsidy is provided to only a part of the export market is that higher prices generate additional revenues to the domestic suppliers from the nonsubsidized export buyers. These revenues have already been included in the additional producer benefits or in the reduced deficiency payments. In the figure area $(ditr)$ shows the additional revenue earned from foreign buyers who do not benefit from the export subsidy. The reduced deficiency payment associated with this area is not included in the export subsidy outlay or in the lost domestic consumer outlays.

The terms of trade benefit of the targeted export subsidy may be indicated by comparing the export subsidy cost with the added export revenues from the nonsubsidized market. With plausible supply and demand elasticities, it is difficult to see how total revenue in the nonsubsidized market could rise by more than $200 million (at most $15 per ton on at most 13 million tons) compared with EEP outlays of more than $1,200 million. Even in this case, excess outlays on the EEP are larger than revenue gains in the nonsubsidized export market. Thus, the terms of trade gains are positive but limited.

Now let us turn to the case of more acreage and a constant domestic price. The Office of Management and Budget working for the executive branch has assumed that the budget costs of the EEP program were generally offset by lower deficiency payments because the farm price of wheat rose with the EEP. The Congressional Budget Office, however, has assumed that the acreage reduction programs are relaxed to accommodate increased export subsidies so that market price is constant and total budget costs rise when the EEP increases. If the acreage allowed to be planted under the wheat program increases when the export subsidy program expands export sales, the quantity produced may expand enough such that the market price is a constant. This is the polar opposite case from the previous illustration of no supply shift. With a constant domestic price, there are no budget savings in the domestic farm program to offset export subsidy costs, and in fact farm program payments increase because the production eligible for payments increases as the ARP is reduced. Nor are there terms of trade gains in the nonsubsidized export market.

When the farm price does not rise with more subsidized exports, U.S. consumers do not face higher prices, and farmers gain from a relaxation in the requirement to idle land and from additional direct government payments made on about two-thirds of the increased production. The national economy benefits when idled land is returned to production, but the economy loses when subsidies are paid to foreigners and when higher taxes or increased deficits are used to finance export subsidies and additional deficiency payments to farmers.

A few sample calculations suggest the magnitude of the value of the additional use of farmland. Assume first that the value per year of the idled acreage is about $40 per acre and that about 15 million acres would be returned to production. With those figures the value of the land returned to production would be approximately $600 million. The $40 per acre figure is based on an approximate average rental rate of wheat land that would be idled if the ARP were raised. The 15 million acres is based on the amount of land used to produce 16.4 million tons at slightly below average yield per acre.

For two major reasons, the $600 million figure is likely an overstatement of the value to the economy of keeping wheat land in production. First, it is difficult to see how 15 million added wheat acres could be attributed to the EEP program. This figure would imply that without the EEP there would have been a 20 to 25 percent wheat EEP in recent years. Second, the wheat land has some value when it is idled, and this land is naturally of lower than average productivity; therefore the $40 per acre rental value probably overstates the value of keeping idled land in production.

The foregoing analysis discussed the export subsidy programs and focused on the export enhancement program for wheat. The details of the analysis would differ for analysis of export subsidies for other commodities, but the policy conclusions would not differ. In fact, for a number of commodities to which the export subsidies are applied, there are no deficiency payments to be offset. Further, for some commodities almost all exports are shipped with subsidy, the United States is a relatively minor player in the world market, or exports play a minor role in total demand for the product. For these commodities, it is hard to derive any case under which export subsidies have even the potential to increase national income.

There is also an argument for export subsidies as strategic trade policy tools. It is often argued that the EEP may have contributed to the EU reform of the Common Agricultural Policy (CAP) and to the reduction of EU export subsidies through Uruguay Round commitments. The Food, Agriculture, Conservation and Trade Act of 1990 (FACT) explicitly required the use of the EEP and related programs to counter unfair trade practices. Further, the 1990 Omnibus Budget Reconciliation Act (OBRA) tied spending for export programs directly to progress in the Uruguay Round. The act required spending on export programs to increase when the round was not successfully concluded by June 1992. This threat failed.

Export subsidies now have even less potential to encourage international reforms. Further, they have other international policy consequences that should be considered. They almost surely affect nonsubsidizing nations that are generally trade allies of the United States. Countries such as Argentina in wheat trade or New Zealand in dairy product trade do not have the policy clout that comes with large domestic markets, but they do play significant roles in multilateral negotiations. These countries are in a strong position to emphasize the hypocrisy of U.S. agricultural trade policy, particularly if export subsidies are directed toward competing with them for markets that are otherwise not subsidized.

Export subsidies are counterproductive as trade policy for U.S. agriculture. Export subsidies may provide benefits to specific farm interests, but larger benefits could be derived from the same budget and economic cost to the U.S. economy by using direct domestic subsidies. Export subsidies could theoretically be part of a policy mixture that maximized benefits to the industries subsidized, but such a policy mixture is likely impossible to develop and maintain; export subsidies are more likely to be used for purely unproductive mercantilist ends.

Export Credit Subsidies. The current export credit programs began in 1980 with the Export Credit Guarantee Program (GSM-102), which provides CCC backing for commercial loans to importers for terms up to three years. In recent years this program has provided guarantees for about $5 billion of credit per year. The accompanying Intermediate Export Credit Guarantee Program (GSM-103) is similar but allows loans for three to ten years. This program has had an authorized limit of $1 billion per year (USDA

1994c). In recent years about 10 percent of all U.S. agricultural exports have been shipped under these credit programs. About 20 to 30 percent of grain and oilseed exports have been financed with credit guarantees, while less than 10 percent of exports of other commodities have used these programs.

U.S. export credit programs are operated as follows. The Department of Agriculture determines eligible countries based on assessments of creditworthiness and potential benefits by commodity. Buyers obtain credit from U.S. commercial banks or other financial institutions; the export shipper receives cash on shipment. If the foreign buyer fails to repay its loan on schedule, the CCC repays the U.S. financial institution and attempts to collect the repayment directly from the foreign buyer.

Unlike explicit price subsidies, credit programs that meet some basic international criteria are not subject to Uruguay Round GATT disciplines. Specific rules limiting the use of credit guarantees were to be worked out by the OECD in conjunction with the general credit rules for industrial exports. Several issues related to export credit programs are similar to those raised by explicit price subsidies (Vercammen and Barichello 1994). These include the effects of credit subsidies on the quantity of exports, on the export and domestic prices, and on the net government farm subsidy budget. In addition, credit subsidies, as implemented by the United States and by other major export competitors, are always targeted to particular buyers and therefore have the potential to facilitate price discrimination. Unlike explicit price subsidies, it may be difficult to measure the amount of subsidy provided by credit programs. Further, the value of the credit guarantee to the buyer may differ from the government cost of the guarantee.

The amount of implicit export subsidy may be assessed in several ways. One way is to use the budget costs associated with the credit guarantee. For fiscal year 1993, for example, the budget allocation cost originally assigned to GSM-102 and GSM-103 programs and the Emerging Democracies Program, with total program levels of $5.7 billion, was $158.5 million, or 2.78 percent. The 1993 rate, based on subsequent experiences, has been revised to 13.2 percent. A higher program level or a more risky portfolio of loans would imply a larger expected budget cost. Currently the executive branch uses an ex ante rate of about 7 percent, and the Congressional Budget Office uses an anticipated loss ratio rate of about 12 percent for agricultural credit guarantees.

The use of U.S. government credit guarantees may itself influence the probability of default. Some foreign governments may find it particularly costly to default on loans backed by the government of the United States. In these cases a credit guarantee by the U.S. government may be an important factor in the feasibility of exports into selected markets by making payment more likely. Conversely, the very fact that loans are backed by the U.S. government sometimes encourages default.

Other measures of the subsidy component of credit guarantees are assessing how much lower the interest rates for the credit extended would have been if the CCC had not provided the guarantees and measuring how much lower the price of the product would need to be if the sale were made on a cash basis.

Let us use the current ex ante estimate of 7 percent of the loaned funds as an approximation of the net value of the guarantees to compare these subsidies with the EEP. In 1993 the average EEP bonus was approximately $40 per ton for wheat. For purposes of comparison, consider the counterfactual experiment in which the credit guarantee program levels were all applied to grain, with an export price of $150 per ton. In this case the $5.7 billion would be spread over 38 million tons. The expected loss, at a rate of 7 percent of the guaranteed funds, is approximately $400 million, which amounts to an expected budget outlay of approximately $10.50 per ton.

The $10.50 per ton is not a fully accurate measure of the effect of the credit guarantees on the quantity or value of exports. If it were, one could simply apply the appropriate export demand elasticity to the price subsidy equivalent of credit guarantees to arrive at the impact on exports. A country that makes use of export credits, however, may have a particular interest in a subsidy in this form. Alternatively, when a credit guarantee is available, a country may use it even though its risk of default is low and it could have access to commercial credit at only slightly higher rates. That is, the value to the importer may be larger or smaller than the expected cost to the U.S. Treasury.

Credit subsidies may become an increasingly used export policy as direct price subsidies are phased down under the Uruguay Round agreement. As demonstrated above for direct export price subsidies, the net effect on national income is in general almost surely negative. In some limited cases, however, government-backed credit guarantees could add to the efficiency of international market transactions. In some cases export buyers are foreign governments that would be heavily influenced by the participation of the U.S. government to repay loans for which they might not otherwise qualify. In these limited cases some U.S. government participation in the credit process may be useful. This participation, however, could take the form of a legal commitment to help enforce contracts rather than a financial commitment to repay the loans.

Three policy changes regarding export credits would help rationalize the programs. First, more effort is needed to ensure that they not be used as development assistance or rewards to countries for being political allies of the United States. If there is a strong need for such programs, they should be authorized through the State Department, and the funds should be explicitly appropriated for those purposes. Second, vigilant oversight is required to ensure that accurate ex ante budget costs of credit guarantees are always recorded in the year in which the loans are issued. U.S. policy regarding credit guarantees improved greatly with the change in budget rules in 1990. What is needed now is a strong effort to ensure that potential losses are not systematically underestimated. If accurate estimates are used, considerable budget pressure will be brought to bear on the credit programs. Third, export credit guarantees and direct credit programs should be explicitly acknowledged as export subsidies. Then, with this acknowledgment, the United States should take the lead in including credit subsidies in export subsidy disciplines in multilateral trade agreements.

Market Promotion. Programs classified as market promotion involve subsidizing such activities as participation in trade shows and in store displays and some advertising. The headline case is the Market Promotion Program (MPP), which was renamed from the Targeted Export Assistance Program (TEA) in 1990. Other older but smaller USDA programs, such as the Foreign Market Development Program (FMD), also provide promotion funding and assistance for food and other agricultural exports. The MPP was originally funded at $200 million per year (the authorized maximum) to provide matching funds for overseas advertising and related promotion activities. After cuts in each of the previous two years as well, in the fiscal 1995 agriculture appropriations act MPP funding was further reduced to $85.5 million.

Under the MPP the USDA distributes funds to a spectrum of private firms and commodity organizations that complete a complex application process and are willing to submit to detailed program rules and oversight. This money has been used both for branded goods of large multinational firms and for generic promotions by industry organizations. Over the life of the MPP, a substantial share of the funding has been provided to organizations promoting fruits, vegetables, tree nuts, and other high value per unit and value-added products.

Plausible rationales for export promotion efforts are difficult to find; they seem to be simply handouts to politically favored constituents. Two related hypotheses, however, will be examined to explain how the use of taxpayers' funds for overseas promotion has a general public purpose. The first concerns some barrier or market failure that causes firms to underspend on advertising overseas. If marketing firms systematically fail to spend enough on promotion, the rate of return to such investments will remain high, and some encouragement for more spending may be appropriate. If firms already spend enough on overseas promotion such that the rate of return on additional promotion is no higher than for other investments, then subsidizing these activities will simply prompt promotion beyond an efficient amount.

An argument for some governmental role in agricultural promotion that has some prima facie plausibility relates to promotion that focuses on generic U.S. products. In this case the promotion, if successful, would improve the market for all U.S. exporters, and so no single firm would have the incentive to undertake such an effort. Generic advertising is common in domestic markets, and its payoff is subject to dispute, in part because it is often difficult to attribute significant gains in industry profitability to generic promotion. Even if such promotion is profitable, however, this argument suggests funding by an industry consortium, not by the general taxpayer.

The MPP distributes a substantial share of its funding to large firms that sell branded high-value products. Criticism of the program because it supports branded products or products of large firms seems based, however vaguely, on the notion that these firms and these products have sufficient incentives to provide their own advertising funds if the payoff is high enough. If the reason for the program is simply to increase the demand for U.S. farm output, however, supplementing the promotion budgets of large successful firms may be a reasonable course.

Attempts to provide support for the payoff to market promotion funds by the Foreign Agriculture Service indicate amazingly high returns to promotion, but this work suffers from methodological defects that render the results less than convincing (Dwyer 1994). The major problem with empirical estimates is isolating the effects of promotion from the myriad of other factors that affect sales. Therefore, it is difficult to show convincingly that export promotion programs have increased exports, let alone to justify the expenditures of taxpayers on these programs.

Subsidized promotion activities have characteristics similar to credit subsidies. Both amount to paying an export subsidy in the form of a specific input that is often tied to the primary product sales. Subsidized export promotion programs have not been dealt with comprehensively in international trade agreements, because most export competitors do not see such programs as much of a threat. Nonetheless, promotion aids are export subsidies, and the only rationale for not treating them as such in multilateral agreements is the complexity of designing rules to limit their use without banning them outright. Some may wish to exploit this loophole in the wake of the Uruguay Round, as was clear by administration commitments during efforts to pass the implementing legislation for the Uruguay Round agreement.

International Food Aid. The United States contributes about $2 billion in food aid each year under several programs. This amount provides more than half the world's supply of food aid and about 20 percent of the total U.S. international economic assistance. International food aid is authorized under three distinct titles of the Food for Peace, or PL-480, Program; under section 416 (b) of the Agricultural Act of 1949; and under the Food for Progress Program of the 1985 Farm Security Act. The 1990 FACT act made substantial changes to these programs.

Since 1990, title 1 of PL-480, operated by the USDA, provides mostly concessional aid to stimulate development and encourage the expansion of commercial markets. Title 2 provides humanitarian donations and other donations to stimulate economic reforms through private organizations and multilateral programs. Title 3 provides aid to the least developed nations based on criteria for relieving malnutrition. These latter two titles are administered by the Agency for International Development. Food aid under section 416 (b) relies on surplus commodities held by the CCC. The amount and form of these donations depend on what the CCC has in surplus stocks.

Food aid is not limited by Uruguay Round disciplines

on export subsidies. In fact, so long as it is accepted that shipments meet food aid criteria, the Uruguay Round does not restrict these shipments; rather, it encourages them as a part of the effort to ensure that the agreement does not harm developing countries. The U.S. food aid program clearly meets the criteria of the agreement and can continue to operate unencumbered.

Three arguments for food aid contribute to its use by the United States. The first is humanitarian: providing food to the hungry is the decent thing to do when people are in dire circumstances. The second argument is that food aid can be used as a part of long-term development assistance. Third, food aid provides a market for U.S. farm output.

Food aid has at best questionable value as development assistance. To be successful, it must contribute to longer-term income growth in developing countries. But food assistance almost surely reduces the returns to investment in agriculture by poor countries: such food aid tends to lower agriculture production growth as a share of total growth and to maintain a market for U.S. exports. It is certainly cynical and only marginally practical to support food aid on the basis that it reduces the long-term development of agriculture in poor countries and thereby reduces the rate of income growth of the poor. Further, such support is likely to be self-defeating. Aid in a form that lowers the potential for a beneficial impact on economic growth lowers the potential for longer-term demand for agricultural imports. Food aid furthers the long-term prospects of food exporters only if the bias against agriculture that it introduces in poor countries more than offsets its detrimental impact on total growth. The practical implication for policy is to shift food aid to purely humanitarian purposes. As development aid, food is an awkward instrument and reduces commercial sales.

One continuing controversy relates to the cargo preference rules that require that at least 75 percent of food aid be transported in U.S. vessels. The cost of shipping in U.S. vessels is more than double that of foreign competitors: the cargo preference adds substantially to the cost of food aid.

The quantity shipped might be significantly smaller than would otherwise be the case.

The Uruguay Round agreement on agriculture included no limits on bona fide food aid; it actually envisioned an increase in food aid to offset the anticipated increases in world market grain prices for poor, food-importing countries. The U.S. Uruguay Round implementing legislation, H.R. 5100, states, "The United States should increase its contribution of bona fide food assistance to developing countries consistent with the Agreement on Agriculture"; see section 411 (e) Food Aid (2) Sense of Congress subparagraph (B).

Summary on Export Policy. In response to the Uruguay Round agreement, the United States seems intent on treating negotiated maximum subsidy limits as the minimum for purposes of domestic policy. Oddly, at the same time that many have questioned the rationale and effectiveness of export market promotion and credit programs, spending for these may actually increase at least for the next few years in the context of implementation of the Uruguay Round agreement.

The implementing legislation for the Uruguay Round does not require additional export measures. The administration, however, has made public pledges that it will proceed along these lines. While the implementing legislation was being considered, the secretary of agriculture and the director of the Office of Management and Budget jointly stated in a letter on September 30, 1994, to the chairmen and ranking members of the House and Senate agriculture committees that export subsidies would be continued at the maximum allowable levels for the next six years. They further stated that the administration would propose increasing the funding for domestic and export market promotion programs by $600 million over five years.

Negotiation Policy

Agricultural trade policy involves more than unilateral reforms of agricultural policies. Particularly in the wake of the

111

Uruguay Round, the importance of a policy for negotiating continuations and extensions of the current agreements and perhaps new multilateral agreements is obvious. Expanding or deepening the liberalization in international trade agreements is likely to be a valuable enterprise. This activity, however, should be used not to substitute for appropriate unilateral reforms but rather to extend the scope of liberal trade policy.

There are three sorts of direct economic benefits for the United States from international agreements to liberalize trade policies. First, the United States benefits directly in the international export market when foreign countries have lower import barriers and devote less to subsidize exports. Second, the world economy grows more rapidly when there are liberalized trading rules. Freer trade is good for economic growth for a number of reasons related to expanded investment and more efficient capital flows as well as more rational production patterns in the world. Further, as models of Uruguay Round benefits indicate, the U.S. economy gains substantially when there is more economic growth among our trade partners. Finally, some trade policy reforms are more feasible politically when they are included in an international agreement than when they are proposed unilaterally. Therefore, international agreements may have an indirect policy benefit in the United States. And as the previous sections have documented, the U.S. economy gains when U.S. trade policies are liberalized.

Current trade negotiation policies for the United States include establishing positions on the extension of NAFTA and the continuation of the Uruguay Round policy reforms now under way. In addition new ideas for free trade areas such as in the Asian Pacific Rim are useful to explore. Finally, it is important to establish policies that make it easier rather than harder to negotiate trade agreements that remove barriers and reduce subsidies.

The United States could facilitate multilateral reform by supporting a continuation of agricultural tariff reductions at an accelerated pace after the current implementation period. With the goal of continuing to reduce trade agricultural tariffs toward zero, the specifics of the pace are less important than the clear signal that no slowing of progress is acceptable.

Two implications for export programs are important for the 1995 farm bill and continuing negotiations. First, the United States should begin the accelerated unilateral reduction in export price subsidies so that reducing subsidies multilaterally is easier. If the United States proceeds with subsidy cuts ahead of schedule, we will be in a strong position to demand that others follow. Second, the United States should take the lead in urging that nonprice export subsidies be included in WTO disciplines on export subsidies. The best way to do this is by continuing to reduce these programs unilaterally.

If U.S. export subsidy programs were ever important as trade policy weapons, that time is now past. The United States has substantial negotiating clout in multilateral negotiations because of the size of our economy. In most cases we can trade better market access for trade benefits without an export subsidy war that damages us more than our trade competitors.

International trade negotiations are important but are not a substitute for domestic trade policy reforms. Occasionally there are strategic arguments for undertaking policies to negotiate more successfully for multilateral reform. Such arguments, however, are more common as excuses for protectionism and for subsidies to be maintained for their own sake than as careful quantitative assessments of the national interest. Preparing for negotiations should not be used to avoid unilateral reform in the 1995 farm bill.

Implications and Conclusions

The major criterion for the trade provisions of the 1995 farm bill is that they facilitate continued movement toward multilateral liberalization consistent with the implementation of the Uruguay Round agreement. Using export subsidies and import barriers to provide income support for farm industries or to insulate domestic farm programs has a long

113

tradition in the United States (Benedict and Stine 1956; Johnson 1950). However, having turned the corner on multilateral agricultural trade rules with the Uruguay Round, there is an opportunity to make U.S. policy more consistent with our liberal trade rhetoric.

This essay has analyzed a variety of U.S. agricultural trade policies and suggested policy reforms. The general thrust has been in the direction of open and unsubsidized agricultural trade. These reforms were suggested as negotiating positions where progress is possible multilaterally and as unilateral reforms where multilateral implementation would be delayed.

The 1995 farm bill offers the opportunity to reform farm trade policy in the direction that the United States has long claimed was appropriate. That means reversing some recent policies and reinforcing movements toward liberalization where the momentum has stalled.

References

Abbott, P. C., P. L. Paarlberg, and J. A. Sharples. "Targeted Agricultural Export Subsidies and Social Welfare." *American Journal of Agricultural Economics* 69 (November 1987): 723–32.

Ackerman, K. Z., and M. E. Smith. *Agricultural Export Programs.* Washington, D.C. USDA/ERS, Staff Report AGES 9033, May 1990.

Alston, J. M., and B. H. Hurd. "Some Neglected Social Costs of Government Spending in Farm Programs." *American Journal of Agricultural Economics* 72 (February 1990): 149–56.

Alston, J. M., C. A. Carter, R. Gray, and D. A. Sumner. "Domestic Distortions and the Gains from Trade Liberalization: The Case of Canada-U.S. Durum Wheat Trade." Paper presented at the American Agricultural Economics Association annual meeting, San Diego, August 1994.

Alston, J. M., C. A. Carter, and V. H. Smith. "Rationalizing Agricultural Export Subsidies." *American Journal of Agricultural Economics* 75 (November 1993): 1000–1009.

Alston, J. M., R. Gray, and D. A. Sumner. "The Wheat War

of 1994." *Canadian Journal of Agricultural Economics* 42 (December 1994): 231–51.

Anania, G., M. Bohman, and C. Carter. "United States Export Subsidies in Wheat: Strategic Trade Policy or Expensive Beggar-Thy-Neighbor Tactic." *American Journal of Agricultural Economics* 74 (August 1992): 534–45.

Baldwin, Robert E. "Are Economists' Traditional Trade Policy Views Still Valid?" *Journal of Economic Literature* 30 (June 1992): 804–29.

Benedict, Murray R., and Oscar Stine. *The Agricultural Commodity Programs: Two Decades of Experience.* New York: Twentieth Century Fund, 1956.

Dutton, J. "Targeted Export Subsidies as an Exercise of Monopoly Power." *Canadian Journal of Economics* 23 (August 1990): 705–10.

Dwyer, Michael J. "Effectiveness of MPP in Promoting U.S. High Value Agricultural Exports." Paper presented at the annual meeting of the International Agricultural Trade Research Consortium, Washington, D.C., December 16, 1994.

Fullerton, D. "Reconciling Recent Estimates of the Marginal Welfare Cost of Taxation." *American Economic Review* 81 (March 1991): 302–8.

Gardner, B. L. "The Political Economy of U.S. Export Subsidies for Wheat." Working Paper 93-06, Department of Agricultural and Resource Economics, University of Maryland, 1993 (prepared for the National Bureau of Economic Research conference, February 3–4, 1994, Cambridge, Mass.).

Johnson, D. Gale. *Trade and Agriculture: A Study of Inconsistent Policies.* New York: John Wiley & Sons, Inc., 1950.

———. *World Agriculture in Disarray.* 2d ed. London: Macmillan, 1991.

Organization for Economic Cooperation and Development. *Agricultural Policies Markets and Trade.* Monitoring and Outlook. Paris, 1990.

President's Council of Economic Advisers. *Economic Report of the President.* Washington, D.C.: GPO, 1993.

Rucker, Randal R., Walter N. Thurman, and Robert B. Borges. "The Effects of the GATT on U.S. Peanut Markets." In *Supply Management in Transition toward the Twenty-first Century*, edited by Garth Coffin, Andrew Schmitz, and Ken Rosaasen. Boulder, Colo.: Westview Press, 1995.

Sumner, Daniel A. "Tobacco Supply Management with and without Import Barriers: Examples from Policy in the United States and Australia." In *Supply Management in Transition toward the Twenty-first Century*, edited by Garth Coffin, Andrew Schmitz, and Ken Rosaasen. Boulder, Colo.: Westview Press, 1995.

———. *Agricultural Trade Policy: Letting Markets Work*. Washington, D.C.: AEI Press, 1995.

U.S. Department of Agriculture, Foreign Agriculture Service. "GATT–Uruguay Round Fact Sheets." February 1994 (a).

———, Office of Economics. "Effects of the Uruguay Round Agreement on U.S. Agricultural Commodities." March 1, 1994 (b).

———, Economic Research Service. "Agricultural Export Situation and Outlook." November 29, 1994 (c).

———. "Agricultural Outlook." AO-217, March 1995.

Vercammen, James, and Richard Barichello. "Export Credit and Targeted Export Subsidies: Price Discrimination with and without Arbitrage." Working Paper, University of British Columbia, 1994.

Zaini, Hasyim. "Impact of Domestic Content Requirement on the U.S. Tobacco and Cigarette Industries." Seminar Paper, North Carolina State University, October 1994.

———, John Beghin, and Blake Brown. "Complying or Not with Domestic Content Policies? The Case of the U.S. Cigarette Industry." Working Paper, North Carolina State University, August 1994.

5

Crop Insurance and Disaster Policy

Barry K. Goodwin and Vincent H. Smith

Popular wisdom maintains that agriculture is subject to greater risk and uncertainty than most other sectors of the economy and therefore is more in need of government disaster assistance. The fundamental reason for this presumption is the random nature of agricultural production. Agricultural output is subject to unpredictable, random shocks caused by weather events, pest damages, and other natural disasters such as fire. The randomness of supply, coupled with inelastic demand for many agricultural products, leads to price and income movements perceived as more volatile for farm products than those commonly experienced in other sectors of the economy.

In addition, most farm enterprises are small firms operating with small asset bases and high fixed costs. Moreover, agricultural producers are often believed to be highly leveraged against their small asset bases even though, in fact, the average debt-to-asset ratio in the U.S. agricultural sector of less than 0.2 is low. Low asset bases and high debt levels would certainly create problems for the feasibility of self-insurance by farms against production risks. Many businesses with small asset bases in other sectors of the economy, however, also depend on borrowed capital, are highly leveraged, and face potentially ruinous shifts in prices, often as a result of volatility of demand.

Historically, policy makers have repeatedly justified a wide range of government programs providing farmers with income transfers, stable prices, and stable incomes on the basis of the instability of agricultural production and agricultural prices. Most programs are intended to support and stabilize agricultural prices and incomes. Two programs, however, federal crop insurance and legislated disaster relief payments, specifically target protection for producers against the risk of reduced yields and have played an increasingly important role in U.S. domestic agricultural policy.

In 1938 legislative efforts to protect producers against yield risks resulted in the Crop Insurance Act. The 1938 act provided protection against crop losses from any (multiple) risks. The program was briefly discontinued between 1943 and 1945 but has generally maintained many of its original features over the past fifty years. Over its entire history, the program has suffered from low participation and high losses. Under the current program, producers have the opportunity to insure their crops at guaranteed yield levels of 50 to 75 percent of their average yields. The insurance is marketed primarily through private insurance companies, although at times producers have also been able to purchase insurance through county U.S. Department of Agriculture offices of the Agricultural Stabilization and Conservation Service (ASCS). The private insurance companies are reimbursed for a share of their operating expenses and actuarial losses. To encourage participation, the government has offered significant premium subsidies to producers since 1980.

In addition to multiple-peril crop insurance, more recent initiatives have included ad hoc disaster relief payment programs. In 1949, Congress established the Farmers Home Administration emergency disaster loan program, which made low-interest loans available to agricultural producers who suffered significant yield losses. Agricultural disaster payments were initially established in the early 1970s. Producers who suffered catastrophic losses (typically, yields below 50 to 60 percent of normal) received reimbursements for their losses through direct government payments. Much of the impetus that led to the introduction and persistence of disaster relief programs is reflected in low participation rates for the concomitant crop insurance program. Producers had the option of insuring against catastrophic yield losses by purchasing protection through the Federal Crop Insurance Program. Most producers, however, chose not to buy federal crop insurance. When widespread losses occurred in the 1970s and 1980s, constituents from agricultural states, made up largely of uninsured producers, successfully lobbied their representatives for direct disaster payments. As disaster relief payments became institutionalized, the disaster program became analogous to free insurance. As a result, incentives to participate in the voluntary Federal Crop Insurance Program were further diminished.

Table 5–1 contains summary statistics for recent (1985–1993) U.S. crop insurance and disaster relief programs. In most years, about 50 million acres of U.S. crop acreage have been insured, while total insurable crop acreage has averaged about 250 million acres, corresponding to a typical participation rate of about 20 percent. Participation levels were relatively high in 1989 and 1990. Participation was mandatory, however, for recipients of disaster payments in the preceding years. An examination of indemnity payments and producer premiums shows that in every year indemnity outlays far exceeded premiums collected from farmers. When direct premium subsidies are included as part of indemnity payments, the annual average loss ratio (the ratio of outlays to funds collected) for the program is 2.04 over the nine-year period 1985–1993. Thus, on average, producers received $2.04 in indemnities for every $1 of premiums they paid.

Over the same period, nearly $9 billion were distributed in the form of ASCS ad hoc disaster relief payments. These payments do not include defaults on emergency loan payments of the Farmers Home Administration, which totaled nearly $11 billion over the same period. Thus, the sum of net taxpayer outlays for the three agricultural disaster assistance programs (crop insurance, emergency loans, and disaster relief payments) amounted to more than $25 billion between 1985 and 1993, at an annual average cost of about

TABLE 5–1
SUMMARY STATISTICS FOR U.S. DISASTER RELIEF AND CROP INSURANCE PROGRAMS, 1985–1993
(millions of dollars)

Year	Insured Acres (millions)	Total Premiums Paid	Government Subsidies Paid	Indemnities Paid	Net Outlays[a]	Implied Loss Ratio[b]	ASCS Disaster Payments	Disaster Payment Recipients (thousands)
1985	47.50	339.73	100.11	683.17	443.55	2.01	− 0.06	0.06
1986	47.82	291.65	88.10	615.70	412.15	2.11	1.87	7.72
1987	48.25	277.51	87.62	369.80	179.92	1.33	557.16	122.54
1988	54.68	328.40	107.99	1,067.56	847.15	3.25	1,319.08	249.51
1989	100.47	613.11	206.28	1,215.22	808.39	1.98	2,740.22	658.10
1990	101.31	618.48	214.39	971.05	566.96	1.57	849.94	255.78
1991	82.36	547.01	190.10	956.40	599.49	1.75	734.69	243.61
1992	83.08	561.96	196.67	921.36	556.07	1.64	1,112.66	461.03
1993	83.74	555.64	199.95	1,647.59	1,291.90	2.97	1,521.24	325.31
Average	72.14	459.28	154.58	938.65	633.95	2.04	981.87	257.48
Total	649.22	4,133.49	1,391.22	8,447.85	5,705.58	2.04	8,836.80	1,283.97

a. Outlays include government premium subsidies and indemnity payments.
b. Loss ratios are ratio of total outlays to premiums collected. The loss ratios thus include premium subsidies.
SOURCE: Environmental Working Group, Agricultural Disaster Assistance Database.

$3.1 billion. Most of these outlays were payments to compensate farmers for yield shortfalls.

One important question raised by such large transfers from taxpayers to agricultural producers is whether any economic efficiency rationale or equity argument justifies such welfare reallocations. Agriculture has received special protection on the grounds that the business of farming is riskier than other business enterprises. In addition, farmers have been assumed to be more dependent on borrowed funds, making them more vulnerable to random production shocks. Both these assumptions have some factual support. Crop yields are subject to a variety of natural hazards, and many farmers (especially new entrants) are highly leveraged.

Given this popular wisdom, a natural question is why private insurance markets have failed to develop comprehensive contracts to protect farmers against multiple perils. Extensive insurance markets exist for a wide range of risks in the private sector. Standard economic arguments for government intervention usually involve the proposition that some form of market failure exists. A primary function of private insurance markets is to spread nonsystemic risks among a pool of risk-averse agents. If risks are nonsystemic (uncorrelated among agents), then the insurance provider diversifies the risks of individual losses across the insurance pool. If risks are systemic such that insured agents suffer losses together, however, diversification of risks is impossible, and the insurance provider may be unable to cover losses in a given year.

In the case of multiple-peril or all-risk crop insurance, it is usually argued that the systemic risks of crop failures make diversification and risk pooling difficult on a scale feasible for most private insurance markets. This argument follows from the fact that large crop losses, triggered by drought, flooding, or other natural disaster, usually affect agricultural production over a large geographic area. Natural disasters that lead to crop failures are assumed to create loss exposures too large for standard private insurance companies to manage. Thus, the government has to accept the role of reinsurer of last resort on the basis of a general market failure (nondiversifiable systemic risk) that prohibits purely private insurance contracts.

Although a significant proportion of the risks of insuring crops may be systemic within the U.S. agricultural sector, these risks are not necessarily nondiversifiable. A larger array of reinsurance options exists in both national and international insurance markets. Such markets are easily able to permit enough diversification to spread risks that appear to be systemic to individual markets across a wider range of activities and markets.

Problems with identifying and measuring risks may be more fundamental to the prohibition of private insurance contracts than arguments that appeal to the lack of risk-pooling opportunities. In particular, insuring against multiple crop risks presents formidable challenges in the construction of insurance contracts and premium rates. The development of actuarially sound insurance contracts requires insurance providers to obtain accurate measures of risks of loss. If agents have more information about their risk of loss than do insurance providers, as is often the case, markets become distorted, and participation becomes skewed. This is the classic problem of *adverse selection*. In the absence of an accurate means for measuring individual risks, insurance providers may set rates according to some average, measurable level of risk. In this event, low-risk agents are overcharged for insurance, and high-risk agents are undercharged. Participation levels are skewed toward the riskier agents, the risk of the insurance pool rises, and indemnity payouts rise. In these circumstances, insurance contracts may fail if losses are sufficiently large.

A further problem facing insurance providers is the monitoring of individuals' actions. If insurance providers cannot monitor agents' actions and if agents alter their behavior after buying insurance to increase their likelihood of collecting indemnities, the problem of *moral hazard* may threaten the actuarial soundness of an insurance program.

Adverse selection and moral hazard present major obstacles to the formation of private crop insurance markets, especially all-risk contracts. Because of a general lack of producer-specific risk information, yield risk and agents' self-protection against losses may be particularly hard to measure. The historical experience of the Federal Crop Insurance Program has reflected these difficulties. Whether private, actuarially fair multiple-peril crop insurance markets would develop in the absence of the federal program is unclear. Such markets, however, would almost certainly have higher premium rates and thus much lower participation. Only if private markets were able to offer coverage at much lower rates (because of some unseen efficiency gains) would one expect participation to remain close to current levels. Given that the government currently subsidizes about half the indemnities paid to farmers, this seems unlikely.

Alternative views on the reasons for the protection of agriculture have emerged in the political economy literature in recent years. Becker's (1983) seminal work revealed that support was sensitive to factors related to the costs and efficiency of generating political influence. Less concentrated pressure groups cannot focus support and are less successful in generating government aid. In general, groups offer incentives in the form of campaign contributions or votes to politicians who supply policy-generated income transfers to ensure the continued political support of their constituency. Political considerations lead to a demand for support, while the economic costs of generating such support constrain the supply side. In this context, Gardner (1987) revealed that farm programs are mechanisms for efficiently redistributing welfare from taxpayers to agricultural producers. He found that government support for individual commodities was related to the amount of money spent to generate political pressure, including the size of the producer group and the geographic dispersion of production.

These concepts easily extend to a wider consideration of agriculture's role in the economy. For many commodities, the geographical concentration of production creates strong incentives for representatives to secure support. The number of agricultural producers relative to consumers of agricultural products is small. Hence, small taxes or distortions borne by consumers of agricultural products or taxpayers translate into large benefits for individual producers. As a result, agricultural protection is an efficient way for elected representatives from agricultural regions to secure support for their constituents.

According to the empirical evidence, the benefits of the Federal Crop Insurance Program and ASCS disaster relief are concentrated among a small number of producers. The Environmental Working Group's database (Hoffman et al. 1994) showed that, when districts are ranked by total indemnity and disaster relief payments, the top ten U.S. congressional districts accounted for over 46 percent of the total taxpayer losses suffered by the Federal Crop Insurance Program between 1985 and 1993. They also reported that the top five congressional districts (for each crop) accounted for roughly 67 percent of all wheat losses, 86 percent of all cotton losses, 41 percent of all corn losses, 97 percent of all peanut losses, and 35 percent of all soybean losses. Benefits from ASCS disaster relief programs have also been heavily concentrated in a small number of congressional districts; the top ten congressional districts accounted for 36 percent of all disaster assistance. Thus, the empirical evidence supports the view that programs that protect farmers against yield risk are mechanisms for redistributing economic welfare from taxpayers to agricultural producers to garner political support for politicians.

To determine whether the purpose of federal crop insurance and other disaster relief programs is to transfer income to farmers or to remedy some form of market failure, if such programs are politically viable, we must address a second fundamental issue: how disaster aid to farmers can be provided at the lowest possible economic cost to the rest of the economy. Both major issues raised in this discussion—is there any economic efficiency rationale or equity argument for disaster aid programs and which disaster aid program transfers income to farmers at the lowest possible economic cost—are central to any debate about these programs. As such, they form the core around which we focus our discussion.

Current Crop Insurance and Disaster Relief Programs

The current policy mixture of federal multiple-peril crop insurance (MPCI), area-yield insurance, and disaster relief programs is quite complex. The passage and implementation of the 1994 Crop Insurance Reform Act (CIRA) further complicate the policy environment. Under the 1994 Federal Crop Insurance Program for most field crops, producers are able to select from three guaranteed yield levels (50, 65, or 75 percent of their insurable yield) and from a range of guaranteed price levels. Price election levels are determined by the Federal Crop Insurance Corporation (FCIC) forecasts of expected prices. The top price election level is set at 90–100 percent of the expected price. Before 1994, three levels were available for most crops. Recent program changes under the 1994 Crop Insurance Reform Act now allow price elections between 50 and 100 percent of the top level. If the producer's yield falls below the elected coverage level, the producer receives an indemnity payment equal to the product of the price coverage level and the yield shortfall.

The per acre premium is determined by the product of the price guarantee, the yield guarantee, the FCIC's estimate of the farm's yield, and the premium rate. Under the 1980 act, subsidies were introduced to encourage participation in the program. There was a 30 percent subsidy on the 50 and 65 percent yield guarantees. The subsidy for the 75 percent yield guarantee was equal to the dollar amount of the 65 percent guarantee level. The premium subsidy has averaged 25 percent since 1985. Because insurance companies are reimbursed for administrative and delivery costs, however, implicit subsidies are somewhat higher. Federal crop insurance is currently available for about fifty different crops.

Accurate determination of the insurable yields of individual farms has been a major obstacle to avoiding adverse

125

selection. Before 1985, insurable yields for a particular farm were determined by average yields in the farm's geographic area. As Skees and Reed (1986) noted, this method exacerbated adverse selection, as farmers with risks of loss above the area averages composed an ever-increasing proportion of the insured pool. In an attempt to address this problem, the FCIC revised its determination of insurable yields in 1985 and now uses the actual production history of the farm to determine insurable yields. To qualify for actual production history yields, the producer must have continuous, verifiable production records for the relevant (four to ten) years. If no actual production data are available, producers' insurable yields are determined by transition yields calculated from ASCS area yields. Some have argued that the use of a ten-year average to calculate insurable yields may understate actual expected yields because yields have generally increased.

Many view adverse selection as the most significant problem affecting the actuarial soundness of the Federal Crop Insurance Program (Miranda 1991). The presence (or absence) of adverse selection is directly related to the extent to which insurance premiums accurately reflect the likelihood of losses. The FCIC adopts a number of assumptions when determining insurance premium rates that may induce adverse selection in the insurance pool. The most basic shortcoming of rate-setting practices is that rates are determined for a large geographic area, the county in which the farm is located. Thus, all individuals with the same average yield in a county pay an identical premium rate for the same crop and practice type.

In the actuarial determination of county-level rates, the FCIC examines several factors. First, the FCIC looks at the twenty-year loss history of a given county and then at the loss-cost ratios (the ratio of indemnities to liability) for the preceding twenty years. The four largest loss-cost ratios are capped at the level of the fifth-largest ratio. The capped data are grouped into a pool (representing a catastrophic loading factor), which is later spread over the entire state. The capped loss-cost ratios plus the sixteen lowest loss-cost ratios are averaged to obtain a county loss-cost ratio, which is then used to construct an actuarially sound rate for each county. The loss-cost ratios are then smoothed across county lines to soften large differences in the cost of insurance for neighboring farms. The catastrophic loading factor is next spread across the entire state, and rates are adjusted accordingly. The resulting rates are set for a given crop practice (for example, irrigated versus dry-land production) at the county level. The smoothing and loss-spreading practices may induce adverse selection into rates, since they tend to lower rates in high loss-risk counties and raise rates in low loss-risk counties.

Rates are next adjusted according to county average yields, as defined by yield data calculated by the National Agricultural Statistics Service. Rates are adjusted inversely with county average yields. Thus, counties with high average yields realize premium rate discounts relative to counties with low average yields, regardless of actual losses or yield variation.

County rates are spread over a range of average yields by a proportional spanning procedure. Nine discrete risk categories are defined, and rates in each category are inversely adjusted according to the farm's average yield. In this way, farms with higher average yields have lower premium rates. In addition, because of the proportional nature of the discounting, as average yields increase the premium falls at an increasing rate. A final constraint faced by the FCIC is a limit on the amount that a rate can increase from year to year. In most cases, premium rates may not increase by more than 20 percent from one year to the next.

An important assumption implicit in the FCIC's actuarial practices involves the relationship between average yields and the likelihood of loss. Botts and Boles (1957) noted that the FCIC's use of average yields in rating assumed a constant relationship between mean yields and the variance of yields. The use of average yields as an indicator of risk may thus introduce adverse selection if the relationship between average yields and relative yield variation is not strong. In reality, considerable differences exist in the

127

relationship between average yields and yield variation across different farms. If rates are determined by average yields, farms with high relative variation in yields are likely to be undercharged for their insurance coverage. Conversely, farms with low variations in yield will be overcharged for insurance and will thus be less likely to buy coverage.

Goodwin (1994) examined the relationship between average yields and relative yield variability (measured by the coefficient of variation calculated from historical yields) using historical yield data for a large sample of Kansas farms. His results indicated that the relationship between average yields and yield variability was weak. He also found that relative yield variation was considerably higher for those farms that purchased insurance. The implication of Goodwin's (1994) analysis is that rating practices that base premiums on average yields may represent risks of loss inaccurately and introduce adverse selection into premium rates.

In 1993 the FCIC introduced an areawide, group risk insurance program (GRP) for soybeans. This program was expanded in 1994 to offer area-yield contracts in more than 1,200 counties (one-third of all counties in the United States) for barley, corn, cotton, peanuts, grain sorghum, soybeans, and wheat. While participation has been limited, the FCIC has a mandate under the 1994 reform act to continue to consider offering GRP contracts for some crops in some counties. The program offers insurance on a county's average yield on the premise that, when the county average yield is low, most farmers in the county will suffer losses (Baquet and Skees 1994). Under the current program, the FCIC forecasts an expected yield for the county using historical data. Farmers may elect coverage of 70, 75, 80, 85, or 90 percent of the expected average yield. If the actual county yield falls below the elected coverage (that is, the trigger yield), the farm receives indemnities. The indemnity payment is based on the percentage decline below the trigger yield, and the indemnity amount (measured in quantity of crop) is converted into a dollar amount by multiplying the quantity indemnity by a protection level (measured in dollars per unit of output) chosen by the farmer. The protection level chosen by the farmer can range from 60 to 150 percent of the expected price.

Disaster payment programs have been an important part of U.S. agricultural policy throughout the 1970s, 1980s, and early 1990s. Between 1985 and 1993, over $25 billion had been spent on direct disaster relief programs, in addition to outlays brought about by excessive losses in the Federal Crop Insurance Program. Recent U.S. disaster relief programs have had three main dimensions: direct payments, emergency loans, and federally subsidized crop insurance. Direct payments are administered through a number of individual programs. In particular, of the $6.9 billion administered by ASCS between fiscal years 1980 and 1989, 81 percent was disbursed through crop disaster assistance payments, 14.2 percent was administered through the Emergency Feed Program, 1.5 percent was administered through the Emergency Conservation Program, and small amounts (less than 0.5 percent) were administered through the Forage Assistance and Tree Assistance Programs.

Under the Emergency Loan Program, loans are provided by the Farmers Home Administration at subsidized interest rates to producers who have suffered crop and livestock losses as a result of natural disasters. The Emergency Feed Program, established in 1977, reimburses producers who lose at least 40 percent of their feed production through natural disasters for up to 50 percent of their commercial feed costs. The Emergency Conservation Program, established in 1978, is a cost-share program that provides emergency funds to restore to productive use farmland damaged by natural disasters such as floods. The Emergency Conservation Program also makes funds available for emergency water conservation measures during severe drought. The Forage Assistance Program, established in 1988, provides funds on a cost-sharing basis to livestock producers for the reseeding of pastures damaged by the 1988 drought. The program also provided funds for facilitating grazing and haying in the late fall of 1988 and early spring of 1989. The Tree Assistance Program, established in 1988, offers funds on a cost-sharing basis to tree producers who suffered seedling losses from the 1988 drought.

Corn producers have been the largest recipient of disaster relief in most years. Wheat and cotton producers are the second and third largest recipients of disaster payments. Disaster relief benefits are also concentrated in particular geographic areas. A recent report by Hoffman, Campbell, and Cook (1994) showed that the top ten congressional districts for disaster assistance received roughly one-third of the U.S. total for disaster assistance from 1985 to 1993. Their report also showed that 60 percent of total disaster aid from 1985 to 1993 went to the top ten states: Texas, North Dakota, Minnesota, Kansas, Iowa, Illinois, Wisconsin, South Dakota, Michigan, and Georgia. Finally, their report demonstrated that many farmers receive disaster relief payments nearly every year. In particular, they found that over 107,000 participants in the ASCS disaster payment program received assistance four or more years out of the seven-year period from 1987 to 1993.

The 1994 Crop Insurance Reform Act

On October 3, 1994, the U.S. Congress passed the 1994 Crop Insurance Reform Act. The provisions of the CIRA will result in several major changes in federal disaster relief programs. The clear intent of the legislation is to reduce federal budgetary outlays on agricultural disaster programs while guaranteeing farmers consistent and reliable access to government support payments when they experience poor crops.

The CIRA contains several important innovations. First, it introduced a catastrophic crop insurance contract mandatory for all insurable crops on farms that participate directly in government programs. If a farm receives deficiency payments for one or more crops, receives a loan from the Farmers Home Administration, or participates in tobacco or peanut programs, the farm must purchase a catastrophic insurance contract for each planted crop for which insurance is available. These cross-compliance requirements of the CIRA will ensure that almost all farmers will participate in the catastrophic component of the crop insurance program.

The catastrophic contract will insure 50 percent of the farm's individual crop at 60 percent of its expected market price at a very low cost. The farmer will be charged a processing fee of $50 per crop, but total farm payments for such contracts will be capped at $200 per farm per county and at $600 per farm. Thus, for farms that operate within a single county, catastrophic coverage for additional crops is free when the farm grows more than four crops. In addition, if a farm is designated as a limited resource operation (that is, it is small), then the catastrophic coverage processing fee will be waived. The processing fee is not intended to operate as a premium but to cover costs incurred by agents and companies that sell such contracts. Thus, in the context of the insurance it provides, the catastrophic insurance will be either nearly or completely free.

Second, because some crops in some counties are not covered by an FCIC insurance program, CIRA established a noninsured crop disaster assistance program. For producers of these noninsured crops, this coverage is equivalent to the catastrophic risk protection available for insured crops.

Third, farmers will be able to buy insurance that provides them with yield and price elections similar to those available under the MPCI contracts offered in 1994. If such insurance is purchased, catastrophic coverage is not required. Two important changes have been introduced, however. First, beginning in 1996, farmers may be able to obtain MPCI contracts with higher, 80 percent, yield elections; that is, a farm may be able to choose a contract that pays an indemnity when the farm's actual yield falls below 80 percent of its average yield.[1] This increase may encourage more participation in the MPCI program in regions where, for

---

1. Under the provision of the 1994 CIRA, FCIC may choose to offer 80 percent yield election contracts but is not required to develop them for all—or, indeed, any—crops in any counties.

some crops, yields exhibit relatively little variation. For major program crops like corn, these areas include parts of Corn Belt states such as Iowa, Indiana, and Illinois. The change may also encourage participation among some producers of irrigated crops in such states as California and stimulate the demand for new MPCI contracts in states that produce fruits and vegetables such as Florida and Massachusetts.

The incentives for participation in MPCI stemming from the increase in the maximum yield election are likely to be enhanced by a subtle but important change in the way in which premiums are subsidized. Under the program as it operated between 1981 and 1994, producers received a 30 percent subsidy on the premiums they paid for contracts with yield elections of 65 percent or less. Farms buying contracts with the higher 75 percent yield election were supposed to pay the full actuarial cost of the additional coverage. Under the CIRA, farms will receive a lump-sum subsidy equal to that provided under the catastrophic contract for buy-up contracts under which the farm chooses up to a 65 percent yield election and a 100 percent price election, or an equivalent contract. If the farm chooses a yield election above 65 percent at 100 percent price election or equivalent contract, however, it receives a larger subsidy equal to the premium established for a 50 percent yield election, 75 percent price election contract. Thus, farms will be able to purchase MPCI contracts with yield elections above 65 percent that offer more heavily subsidized premiums. The combination of higher-yield elections and subsidized premiums for some contracts based on those yield elections may well expand participation in the program but will probably also increase losses (total indemnities less total premiums) because most of the increase in participation will come from new contracts with intentionally subsidized premiums.

Fourth, under the reform bill expenditures under such ad hoc disaster bills would be counted as budget items requiring corresponding cuts in other programs unless majorities above 60 percent prevail in both houses. Currently, expenditures made under ad hoc disaster relief bills do not count as part of the federal budget approved by Congress and are not subject to the same fiscal disciplines as most other government expenditures. The intent of these innovations is to force Congress to exercise self-discipline in relation to agricultural disaster payments. Given that, as a result of the crop insurance reform bill's cross-compliance provisions, almost all farms will have nearly free catastrophic insurance coverage, they should not need additional help in times of hardship. Therefore, the crop insurance reform bill has a rider intended to make it costly for Congress to give farms that additional help. That rider probably has some effective teeth.

The History of U.S. Crop Insurance and Disaster Relief Programs

The current mixture of U.S. agricultural disaster relief programs did not develop in a vacuum, and the programs have had a long and varied history. The first of these programs, initiated in 1938 when Congress established the Federal Crop Insurance Corporation to provide all-risk or multiple-peril crop insurance to farmers, was to afford individual farmers some protection against the financial hardship of substantial crop losses. The private sector offered insurance against risk of crop loss from hail or fire but not general coverage for losses from drought, pests, insect infestations, and the like. Thus, in response to an initiative from President Franklin Roosevelt, Congress developed legislation that shifted the risk of growing crops away from at least some farmers to the taxpayer (Kramer 1983, 181).

In 1944, after large subsidies were required to cover net losses, the program was discontinued for the 1944 crop year but, in response to political pressure, was reintroduced in 1945. Between 1945 and 1973, the program expanded to cover additional crops, although in 1947 sufficiently severe restrictions were placed on the scope of FCIC operations to lead commenters to describe the entire program, as it existed between 1947 and 1980, as experimental (Kramer 1983,

192). In 1973, the Agricultural and Consumer Protection Act established a mandatory federal disaster relief program. From 1973 to 1981 this new program operated in tandem, and in many counties overlapped, with the federal insurance program. The mandatory federal disaster program was discontinued at the beginning of 1981 after passage of the 1980 Federal Crop Insurance Act. As a result of this act, after 1981 federal crop insurance became the only before-the-fact permanent "disaster relief" program for farmers. To function in this new role, the program expanded to cover many more commodities in many more regions of the country. Farmers in many states, however, did receive after-the-fact protection against crop loss through ad hoc emergency disaster relief legislation.

Throughout the fifty-six-year history of the Federal Crop Insurance Program, congressional concerns have focused on three major program-related issues: (1) net losses (or loss ratios) of the crop insurance program and the joint budgetary costs of the crop insurance and disaster relief programs; (2) the extent to which farms participate in the crop insurance program (that is, participation rates); and (3) in the 1980s and 1990s, arrangements for marketing and servicing farmers' crop insurance contracts. Data on annual averages for total premiums, total indemnities, and loss ratios over the periods 1939–1943, 1945–1956, 1947–1955, 1956–1973, 1976–1980, 1981–1983, 1984–1990, and 1991–1993 are presented in table 5–2. The periods are selected carefully to illustrate the effects and causes of important shifts in policy regimes. In all but one of these periods (1956–1973), loss ratios were greater than 1, and over the entire fifty-four-year period the average loss ratio has been 1.33. From the perspective of successive administrations and Congress, an ideal crop insurance program would enjoy high participation rates and provide most farmers with protection against yield losses but, on average, would involve no subsidies and, at the same time, be available to all farms in all states and counties. The evidence suggests that, for individual farm yield insurance based on voluntary participation, these are mutually exclusive goals.

TABLE 5-2
ANNUAL AVERAGE TOTAL PREMIUMS, INDEMNITIES, AND LOSS RATIOS
FOR THE MULTIPLE-PERIL CROP INSURANCE PROGRAM, 1939–1993

Period	Annual Average Premiums (millions of $)	Annual Average Indemnities (millions of $)	Annual Average Loss Ratios[a] (LR)	Number of Years in Which LR > 1
1939–43	58	97	1.65	5
1945–46	44	86	1.16	2
1947–55	195	226	1.16	9
1956–73	593	512	0.86	18
1976–80	674	888	1.32	5
1981–83	1,245	1,504	1.21	3
1984–90	4,395	5,766	1.32	7
1991–93	2,251	3,520	1.56	3

NOTE: After 1980 a 30 percent subsidy was built into the rate-setting procedures.
a. The loss ratio is calculated as total indemnities divided by total premiums (including premium subsidies) and does not account for additional subsidies that covered FCIC administrative expenses.
SOURCE: Federal Crop Insurance Program.

Implications of Economic Theory for the Supply and Demand for Insurance

The theory of insurance has its underpinnings in the neoclassical theory of behavior under uncertainty. Laffont (1989) states that this theory describes the implications of rational choice under conditions of uncertainty. In this context, agents are usually assumed to maximize their expected utility. The neoclassical theory almost universally assumes that agents are globally averse to risk. This risk aversion, in turn, implies that rational agents will always be willing to pay some positive amount to lower risk, holding expected returns constant.

The theory of the demand for insurance implies that risk-averse agents in a competitive insurance market with actuarially fair premium rates will fully insure. Neoclassical theory also suggests that the presence of the pooling equilibrium characteristic of adverse selection will bring about overpurchases of insurance by high-risk agents and under-purchases of insurance by low-risk agents.[2] The theory also has important implications for the elasticity of insurance demand. In particular, it suggests that low-risk agents will be more responsive to premium rate changes and thus will have a more elastic demand than high-risk agents. If premiums are raised across the board in an effort to reduce losses, low-risk agents will drop insurance coverage at a faster rate than high-risk agents. It is conceivable that this effect may be large enough to *worsen* the actuarial performance of the insurance program. Finally, neoclassical theory has important implications for moral-hazard behavior. If an insurance provider cannot monitor the self-protection provided by insured agents, the optimal level of self-protection for an insured agent (which is provided at a cost to the insured agent) will be zero. Thus, if monitoring of self-protection is limited, neoclassical theory predicts the presence of moral hazard.

If one group of agents wants and is able to purchase a certain type of insurance, then another group of agents must be willing to sell it. All that is required for the insurance to be sold is that the insured be willing to purchase the insurance at that premium. Only if the premium is too high will the insurance not be sold. The facts that private insurance companies have never successfully offered multiple-peril crop insurance contracts and that the U.S. government has to provide substantial premium subsidies to get farmers to participate in its MPCI program indicate that the required actuarially sound premium is too high. Borch (1989, 13–14) noted that an insurance premium offered by a private insurer, P_p, has three components: E, the expected claim payment (or expected indemnity); A, the administrative expense of the insurance company; and R, the required return on invested capital. The terms A and R represent the

---

2. The pooling equilibrium is one where individual risks are un-observable. Thus, contracts are based on some average risk, which leads to overcharging low-risk agents and undercharging high-risk agents.

insurer's costs of doing business and are often jointly referred to as the loading factor, $L = A + R$.

The loading factor, L, plays a crucial role in determining whether a market for a particular type of insurance will exist. Risk-averse individuals will buy insurance contracts when the premium, $E + L$, is greater than the expected indemnity, E, but not when the difference, L, is too great. They are willing to pay for the income-smoothing service provided by the insurer, but their willingness to pay for any given level of risk reduction is finite. If the loading factor becomes too large, private markets for a given type of insurance will not exist.

The insurer may be risk neutral, risk averse, or even risk loving. A risk-averse insurer would require a higher value for R than a risk-neutral insurer. Risk neutrality on the part of an insurer can reasonably be assumed when the insurer can either *pool* or *spread* most or all of the risks of an insurance contract. *Risk pooling* (the law of large numbers) is possible when the insurer offers contracts of about the same size to a large number of insured individuals whose individual risks of loss are statistically independent of each other. By pooling such risks, an insurer can reduce the variance of the claims from the insurance pool to almost zero and set premiums without regard to risk of poolwide losses that exceed poolwide premium payments.

Risk pooling is probably not feasible in the case of multiple-peril crop insurance contracts, because crop losses are often driven by weather-related events such as drought and floods or pest infestations and disease that are geographically extensive. Such events cause widespread losses among many insured farmers in the insurance pool and are *systemic risks* that cannot be avoided by the insurer through pooling. Losses among farmers are not independent but positively correlated, and in these circumstances in any given year the insurance company faces a considerable risk that poolwide losses will exceed poolwide premiums by a substantial amount. *Risk spreading*, however, is possible in these circumstances. While in any given year the farm sector as a whole may experience a substantial loss because of crop failure, in an economy such as that of the United States where crop production represents a small fraction (less than 1 percent) of total economic activity, the risk of loss can be spread over the rest of the economy.

Rather than diversifying their book of business, insurance companies often specialize in specific lines of business because each type of business requires specialized knowledge. This failure to diversify leads to managerial diseconomies of scale. In this case, however, insurance companies can still practice risk spreading through reinsurance markets. In reinsurance markets, which are often international in scope, individuals or firms accept some or all the risks of large losses that an individual company takes on in specializing in a specific type of coverage, in return for premiums that cover expected losses and loading factors. By accepting such risks from many different types of specific insurers, the reinsurers are able both to spread and to pool the risks of losses in a particular sector of the economy across many individuals, reducing the cost of risk to close to zero for both the specific insurance company and the individuals it insures. Reinsurance is quite feasible for actuarially fair crop insurance contracts. A priori, there is no reason to presume that insurance companies require a high loading factor for multiple-peril crop insurance because the crop sector experiences exceptionally large systemic risks.

Another factor that affects the administration of the loading factors for crop insurance contracts—moral hazard—is probably more important in deterring private markets for multiple-peril crop insurance. Borch (1982) has shown that when moral hazard is a problem, in most circumstances insurers will have to increase their premiums by at least the amount it costs to monitor the insured individual to prevent behavior that increases the risk of loss. He also showed that premiums will rise by more than these monitoring costs when insured agents refuse to accept large penalties for behavior that violates moral-hazard clauses or for some reason it is infeasible to institute such penalties. Borch's result has powerful implications for multiple-peril crop insurance contracts since it is extremely expensive to monitor a farm's behavior during the entire growing season for moral-hazard violations.

A Review of Empirical Research

The empirical literature on crop insurance has expanded almost exponentially since the mid-1980s but has had a surprisingly long history, especially with respect to analyses of the demand for crop insurance by farmers initiated in the 1940s. This section provides a brief review of recent studies of demand-and-supply issues important to crop insurance. An extensive review of this literature is provided by Goodwin and Smith (1995).

In light of the recent problems of low participation (20.77 percent in the 1980s) and poor actuarial performance (a loss ratio above 2.0 for the period covering 1985–1993), demand issues are of central importance to understanding the actuarial performance of the current program and possible alternatives. In particular, comprehension of the effects of proposed changes requires knowledge of how producers respond to various characteristics of the program, including premium rates. Further, comprehending the interaction between the crop insurance program and the ASCS ad hoc disaster relief programs requires an understanding of how disaster relief influences farmers' demand for insurance.

Recent empirical demand research has given attention to premium effects on participation. In particular, several recent studies have empirically estimated demand price elasticities. Nieuwoudt et al. (1985) estimated the demand for crop insurance using pooled state-level aggregated data for 1965 to 1981. They found that the expected rate of return to insurance was an important factor in explaining participation. They also found that expected yield risk, diversification, crop dominance, tenure, size, and dummy variables for years with disaster relief were significant in explaining participation.

Gardner and Kramer (1986) used fifty-seven county-level observations for 1979 to model the demand for crop insurance. Their results implied an elasticity of $-.92$. Barnett, Skees, and Hourigan (1990) evaluated the demand for insurance in 346 individual wheat-producing counties in thirteen wheat-producing states in 1987. Their study, the first to calculate an explicit demand elasticity, obtained a price elasticity of about $-.2$. They also found that delivery costs, off-farm income, livestock production, and interest payments were significant factors influencing the demand for crop insurance. Calvin (1990) used participation data for individual producers to model the demand for insurance in a discrete dependent variable framework. Her results suggested that expected returns to insurance, age, livestock production, government program participation, and leverage were significant factors in the decision to purchase insurance.

Goodwin (1993) evaluated the demand for insurance using pooled county-level data for Iowa corn production between 1985 and 1990. He found that producers' responsiveness to premium changes was significantly influenced by their risk of loss, which he measured using historical average loss ratios for each county. His results implied that, because of adverse selection, high-risk producers were less responsive to premium changes. Goodwin obtained elasticity estimates of -0.32 for insured acres and -0.73 for liability. His results showed that these elasticities varied from relatively elastic responses for low-risk producers to inelastic responses for risky producers.

Smith and Baquet (1993) used individual producer-level data for insurance purchases by Montana wheat producers. Their results indicate a demand elasticity of about -0.60. Their results also suggest that, because of adverse selection, this elasticity differs with risk of loss and that the nature of this difference depends on whether the farm has a positive or a negative expected return from insurance. Goodwin (1994) investigated the demand for insurance using data from a survey of individual wheat producers in Kansas. His results suggested that farmers who perceived themselves to be protected by disaster relief programs were much less likely (16 percent) to purchase crop insurance.

Coble, Knight, Pope, and Williams (1993) modeled the demand for multiple-peril crop insurance by Kansas wheat producers and obtained a demand elasticity of −0.26 (with demand measured by participation). Their results also suggested that producers may be more responsive to subsidy changes than to premium changes.

Limited evidence exists regarding the effects of moral hazard on insurance purchases and production practices. Horowitz and Lichtenberg (1993) found that farmers who purchased insurance used more agricultural chemicals than uninsured producers. Recent research by Smith and Goodwin (1994), however, suggests that this seemingly paradoxical result may be due to Horowitz and Lichtenberg's modeling approach, which neglected to consider the timing of insurance purchases and simultaneity issues. Smith and Goodwin find that insurance purchasers use significantly less agricultural chemicals than do uninsured farmers.

The feasibility of private insurance markets for multiple-peril or rainfall crop insurance has been addressed by a series of papers (Bardsley et al. 1984; Quiggin 1986; Patrick 1988; and Fraser 1988) largely in the context of Australian wheat production. Bardsley et al. show that private insurance contracts are infeasible even when administrative costs are very low. Patrick investigated Australian wheat producers' willingness to pay for private insurance contracts. He concluded that, in an area in which production risk for wheat is as great as anywhere in the United States, less than 20 percent of the producers would be willing to pay the estimated full costs of insurance. Fraser found that if loading factors for multiple-peril crop insurance are similar to those assumed by Patrick (which are representative of loading factors common across all commercial insurance lines), then private multiple-peril crop insurance would be purchased by very few farmers.

The fact that under the current program guidelines private insurers have to bear some risk raises several empirical issues. Will private insurers, for example, seek to avoid selling MPCI contracts in regions in which losses have been high relative to premiums? Smith and Kehoe (1994) showed that, under the existing reinsurance contract, private insurers will avoid high-loss regions if the actuarial link between premiums and expected losses is weak but that they will be willing to serve such areas if the actuarial link is strong. One way of mitigating the effects of any increase in the private insurer's risk of loss is to develop low-cost ways for the insurer to reinsure its crop insurance book of business in the private market. Using information on the 1993 books of business of ten large private crop insurers, Miranda and Glauber (1994) showed that state-based area-yield insurance options contracts may be able to reduce the riskiness of a private crop insurer's entire book of business to levels comparable with those for automobile insurance or homeowner's insurance (areas in which risk pooling removes almost all the risk). If, then, a subsidized federal MPCI program continues to exist and private reinsurers are to be the only suppliers of the product, one relatively low-cost alternative for ensuring that those companies continue to offer MPCI in all areas might be to subsidize their costs of obtaining reinsurance through such options contracts.

A Summary of Suggested Alternatives to the Current Program

Many alternatives to the current Federal Crop Insurance Program have been proposed, including various forms of revenue insurance and cost-of-production insurance. Several of these proposals, such as notions of revenue insurance, are modeled after existing programs in other countries (for example, Canada's GRIP revenue insurance program). As is the case with the current federal program, each of the various alternatives faces its own limitations and difficulties with respect to implementation.

Revenue Insurance and Revenue Assurance. A number of proposals for some form of revenue "insurance" or "assurance" have recently surfaced in the debate over farm policies. One such proposal is the plan put forward by Harrington and Doering (1993) to provide gross revenue insurance by insuring price and yield separately. Yield coverage would be offered through a conventional form of crop insurance, while price shortfalls would be paid out of a separate insurance fund. The Revenue Assurance Plan advocated by the Iowa 1995 Farm Bill Study Team (1994) is another alternative that would provide joint price and yield protection. Still other alternatives that make use of existing options markets have been recently proposed by Barnaby (1994). Distinctions between revenue insurance and revenue assurance are often drawn. In general, the most important distinction is that when revenue protection is provided under insurance plans, premiums are collected from farmers, while, under assurance plans, protection is provided by the government without charge.

The 1995 Farm Bill Study Team, sponsored by the Iowa Farm Bureau and other Iowa farm groups, has proposed that current price- and income-support programs, insurance programs, and disaster relief programs be largely replaced by a single revenue assurance program. This program would guarantee farmers 70 percent of "normal" revenues and would replace all other government price- and income-support programs, leaving producers free to plant whatever crops they wished. Premiums and administrative costs of the program would be paid by the government. The most significant limitation of the revenue assurance proposal is identifying "normal" levels of revenue. The plan assumes that every participating producer has readily available data to establish individual proven yields for all crops. The FCIC's experience with the Federal Crop Insurance Program since 1980, however, is a testimony to the difficulties of setting program benefits on the basis of individual farm records. The limitations of record keeping and maintaining a proven yield for a revenue insurance or assurance program are probably even more of an obstacle than those that confront the current multiple-peril crop insurance program. Given the implied flexibility of the program, measurement of normal revenues would be further complicated by farmers' shifting production among

143

various crops. Finally, moral-hazard problems would likely be relevant to the revenue assurance plan.

Harrington and Doering (1993) proposed a form of revenue insurance that would restructure U.S. agricultural programs along the lines of current Canadian revenue insurance programs. Their proposal contained two basic provisions: federal crop insurance of the form currently in place and commodity price insurance, which would pay farmers when prices fell below a predetermined target. Price shortfalls would be determined by a comparison of market prices against a ten- or fifteen-year moving average price. Prices that fell below the target (average) would be supported by deficiency payments from a revolving fund financed by farmers or by the government. Harrington and Doering's proposal also suffers from the same maladies that afflict the Iowa plan with respect to the feasibility of developing relevant proven yield histories at the farm level. In addition, because their proposed program is voluntary, farmers could select against adverse price movements as prices moved beneath the fifteen-year moving average guaranteed price.

Barnaby (1994) has pointed out that many of the instruments necessary for revenue insurance already exist in private markets. He proposed a form of revenue insurance that relies on existing options markets to insure price at a target level and a revised form of crop insurance that replaces yield shortfalls at market value (that is, a replacement endorsement). Under this combination, growers are able to insure their revenue at the target price. Barnaby noted that current crop insurance does not guarantee bushels but instead guarantees a fixed dollar amount of indemnities. Replacement coverage, an endorsement already available in some crop insurance markets, pays indemnities on the basis of market prices at harvest.

Under Barnaby's plan, standard multiple-peril crop insurance would include an endorsement that paid indemnities on the basis of actual market prices at harvest. In addition, the government would purchase a put option for each producer at the target price. The government would pay the full premium cost of the target price put plus basis. Investors would then assume the downside price risk. Producers who received the target price put option with replacement value crop insurance would be guaranteed a minimum level of revenue.

A pilot test program of the target put form of revenue insurance was mandated in 1993–1994 for wheat in two Kansas counties and two North Dakota counties, and for corn in nine counties in the Corn Belt. The target put option proposal also faces the same limitations of accurately determining insurable yields as those faced by the current crop insurance program as well as other proposed alternatives for revenue insurance. Accurate individual farm records are necessary to define expected yields. Such a program would presumably use current FCIC procedures for determining insurable yields. In this light, the program would confront the same adverse-selection problems on the yield side as those faced by the current federal crop insurance program. Another limitation of the target put proposal is that its coverage is restricted to crops traded in futures markets or that can be effectively cross-hedged with other crops.

Cost-of-Production Insurance. Recent initiatives for changes in the current Federal Crop Insurance Program have also included a proposal to insure farmers' costs of production. Under such a plan, producers would be guaranteed a certain proportion of their crop production expenses. This proposal is quite similar to the revenue insurance concept except that target revenues are based on farm-level costs of production rather than on expected farm-level total revenues.

The obvious shortcoming of this insurance is the difficulty of measuring a farm's production costs. Although detailed budgets for representative farms are often available from extension sources, the degree to which such budgets could be used to measure individual farms' production costs is likely to be limited. Production costs vary significantly across regions and even across individual farms within a common geographic region. These types of measurement problems are likely to induce adverse selection in such an insurance program. Further, such a program may have an additional incentive for moral hazard since less intensive use of inputs would have the combined effect of lowering production costs and increasing the likelihood of collecting indemnities. In short, the difficulties of accurately defining production costs make such cost-of-production programs highly suspect. It is unlikely that a workable definition of costs of production that would be representative of a range of farms could be constructed. Measurement of individual farms' costs of production requires very detailed farm records, which simply do not exist.

Whole-Farm and Rainfall Insurance. Insurance contracts that consider yield shortfalls among several crops are possible alternatives to the current program that treats contracts for individual crops separately. Revenue insurance is an extreme example of such insurance, in that revenues from all crop enterprises are considered when determining losses and indemnities. A form of insurance that lies between individual crop coverage and revenue insurance could be constructed. Such insurance could cover yields for a combination of crops or, alternatively, for all crops grown on a farm. This approach to insurance recognizes that yield outcomes among different crops on a farm may not be independent of one another (Atwood and Watts 1994).

Many types of whole-farm or partial-farm insurance contracts are imaginable. In general, these contracts face the same limitations of defining expected yields and estimating risks as do existing insurance contracts. The increased complexity of whole-farm contract design may also limit the feasibility of such alternatives. In light of the difficulties of defining risks and appropriate premiums under the current program, workable whole-farm contracts are unlikely to be introduced in the near future.

Another form of insurance, patterned after contracts considered but not implemented in Australia, is rainfall insurance. Proposals have included the formation of a rainfall futures contract and an area-yield insurance contract in which indemnities would be triggered when annual rainfall dropped below a predetermined level. Rainfall insurance proposals are simply area-yield insurance contracts in disguise and, as such, possess all the shortcomings of area-yield contracts. Rainfall contracts suffer even more severely from such problems because areas may experience losses even when annual rainfall appears to be adequate, partly because the timing of rainfall is often critical and partly because rainfall is never the only potential source of crop failure. Given these considerations, rainfall insurance proposals are unlikely to garner much support among policy makers.

Summary and Conclusions

We have raised two fundamentally important questions about disaster relief and crop insurance programs. First, is there any meaningful economic rationale for such programs? Second, if for political economy or other reasons such programs have to be a part of U.S. farm policy, what characteristics should be incorporated to make them as efficient as possible? As far as we can tell, no substantial technical economic efficiency or market failure arguments justify government subsidies for either agricultural insurance or disaster relief programs. One potential argument for such intervention is that private insurance companies are unable to diversify systemic risks like those endemic to crop production. As we have pointed out, however, a substantial international reinsurance market offers risk pooling and spreading opportunities for almost any risk. Thus, the argument that systemic risk is prima facie evidence of the market failure of crop insurance does not appear to be particularly credible. The only justification for government intervention in this case would be that government can diversify such risks more efficiently than private reinsurance. No one has seriously tried to make that case, however.

A second argument for government intervention is that moral hazard and adverse selection are sources of market failure in the market for crop insurance and that the govern-

147

ment should therefore step in to operate welfare-enhancing crop insurance programs. Certainly, there is considerable evidence of both adverse selection and moral hazard in the current federal MPCI program. Adverse selection, however, is a direct consequence of inappropriate procedures for setting premium rates. No evidence suggests that governments, either in the United States or elsewhere, are better at setting premium rates than private reinsurance companies, and, in fact, there may be reasons to suspect the opposite.

A third "quasi-technical" argument for some kind of federal disaster or crop insurance program is that farmers want and are willing to pay for protection against price and production risk but that the private market refuses to supply much-needed all-risk insurance contracts (for whatever reason). The proponents presumably mean that some kind of market failure exists that prohibits the development of an otherwise welfare-enhancing product. Our interpretation of this situation is quite counter to a market failure argument. On the contrary, farmers have a very limited demand for insurance at the prices necessary to make the program actuarially fair. Conceptually, supply and demand do not intersect at a nonzero quantity of insurance. A number of studies of willingness to pay verify this point (see, for example, Bardsley et al. 1984; Fraser 1988; Patrick 1988).

If market failure arguments are not particularly plausible rationales for government intervention in crop insurance markets, what about equity considerations? Although crop insurance and disaster relief programs began at a time when farm households had lower and more variable incomes than nonfarm households, it is no longer clear that this inequity exists. Thus, in general, equity concerns should not be dominant in debates over farm subsidy disaster relief and crop insurance programs.

If crop insurance programs serve no obvious purpose in improving economic efficiency and have little to recommend them with respect to reasonable concerns about equity and social justice, then why do they exist? The answer may be that they are politically palatable ways of transferring income to an effective interest group. Farmers, after all, provide essential commodities and face considerably more unpredictable production risks than do most other industries. In years when disasters hit, they also receive below-average incomes. Thus, in low-income years voters and taxpayers may be more willing to tolerate income transfers to farmers through programs that increase their incomes. Both all-risk crop insurance and disaster aid programs accomplish that purpose.

If crop insurance and disaster relief programs are to continue, they should be designed to minimize the costs of providing the benefits they supply to farmers. We have pointed out a number of shortcomings inherent in current plans. The most serious problem is adverse selection, which has brought about substantial program losses. Improvements in actuarial practices, including greater attention to the risk to yields, should be a priority for policy makers. In addition, the provision of ad hoc disaster relief has been a major factor limiting participation in the MPCI program, especially by lower-risk producers. The fundamental changes brought about by the 1994 Crop Insurance Reform Act should help to alleviate these problems. Only time, however, will prove whether Congress will exercise the discipline necessary to hold to convictions to eliminate ad hoc disaster relief.

Finally, we have reviewed a number of alternative insurance and disaster assistance programs. In general, we find that these programs suffer from the same shortcomings as the current MPCI program. Actuarial problems, adverse selection, low participation, and moral hazard would likely be important issues to be contended with in any alternative programs.

References

Atwood, J. A., and M. J. Watts. "Creating a Crop Portfolio Insurance Policy." Unpublished manuscript. Montana State University, 1994.

Baquet, A. E., and J. R. Skees. "Group Risk Plan Insurance: An Alternative Risk Management Tool for Farmers." *Choices*, 1st qtr., 1994, pp. 25–28.

Bardsley, P., A. Abbey, and S. Davenport. "The Economics of Insuring Crops against Drought." *Australian Journal of Agricultural Economics* 28 (1984): 1–14.

Barnaby, G. A. "Using Private Markets to Achieve Revenue Insurance." Paper presented at the AAEA Risk Management Preconference, San Diego, August 6, 1994.

Barnett, B. J., J. R. Skees, and J. D. Hourigan. "Examining Participation in Federal Crop Insurance." Staff paper 275, Department of Agricultural Economics, University of Kentucky, August 1990.

Becker, G. S. "A Theory of Competition among Pressure Groups for Political Influence." *Quarterly Journal of Economics* 68 (1983): 371–400.

Borch, K. H. "Insuring and Auditing the Auditor." In *Games Economics Dynamics and Time Series Analysis,* edited by M. Deistler, E. Fürst, and G. Schwödiauer. Physica: Verlag, 1982.

———. *Economics of Insurance.* Amsterdam: North Holland, 1989.

Botts, R. R., and J. N. Boles. "Use of Normal-Curve Theory in Crop Insurance Rate Making." *Journal of Farm Economics* 39 (1957): 733–40.

Calvin, L. "Participation in Federal Crop Insurance." Paper presented at the Southern Agricultural Economics Association, Little Rock, 1990.

Coble, K. H., T. O. Knight, R. D. Pope, and J. R. Williams. "An Empirical Test for Moral Hazard and Adverse Selection in Multiple Peril Crop Insurance." Paper presented at the annual meeting of the American Agricultural Economics Association, Orlando, Florida, August 1993.

Fraser, R. W. "A Method for Evaluating Supply Response to Price Uncertainty." *Australian Journal of Agricultural Economics* 32 (1988): 22–36.

Gardner, B. L. "Causes of Farm Commodity Programs." *Journal of Political Economy* 95 (1987): 290–310.

———, and R. A. Kramer. "Experience with Crop Insurance Programs in the United States." In *Crop Insurance for Agricultural Development: Issues and Experience,* edited by P. Hazell, C. Pomerada, and A. Valdez, 195–222. Baltimore: Johns Hopkins University Press, 1986.

Goodwin, B. K. "An Empirical Analysis of the Demand for Multiple Peril Crop Insurance." *American Journal of Agricultural Economics* 75 (1993): 425–34.

———. "Semiparametric (Distribution-free) Evaluation of Discrete Choice under Uncertainty: Adverse Selection, Disaster Relief, and the Demand for Insurance." Unpublished manuscript, Department of Agricultural and Resource Economics, North Carolina State University, 1994.

———, and V. H. Smith. *Economics of Crop Insurance and Disaster Relief Policy.* Washington, D.C.: American Enterprise Institute, 1995.

Harrington, D. H., and O. C. Doering III. "Agricultural Policy Reform: A Proposal." *Choices,* 1st qtr., 1993.

Hoffman, W. L., C. Campbell, and K. A. Cook. *Sowing Disaster: The Implications of Farm Disaster Programs for Taxpayers and the Environment.* Washington, D.C.: Environmental Working Group, 1994.

Horowitz, J. K., and E. Lichtenberg. "Insurance, Moral Hazard, and Chemical Use in Agriculture." *American Journal of Agricultural Economics* 75 (1993): 926–35.

Iowa Farm Bill Study Team. "The Findings of the 1995 Farm Bill Study Team." Unpublished manuscript, Iowa Farm Bureau, 1994.

Kramer, R. A. "Federal Crop Insurance: 1938–1982." *Agricultural History* 57 (1983): 181–200.

Laffont, J. J. *The Economics of Uncertainty and Information.* Cambridge: MIT Press, 1989.

Miranda, M. J. "Area-Yield Crop Insurance Reconsidered." *American Journal of Agricultural Economics* 73 (1991): 233–42.

———, and J. Glauber. "Uninsurable Systemic Risk and the Future of Crop Insurance Markets: A Cure for Area Yield Options." Working paper, Ohio State University, Department of Agricultural Economics, 1994.

Nieuwoudt, W. L., S. R. Johnson, A. W. Womack, and J. B. Bullock. "The Demand for Crop Insurance." Agricultural Economics Report 1985-16, University of Missouri, Department of Agricultural Economics, 1985.

Patrick, G. F. "Mallee Wheat Farmers' Demand for Crop

151

and Rainfall Insurance." *Australian Journal of Agricultural Economics* 32 (1988): 37–49.

Quiggin, J. "A Note on the Variability of Rainfall Insurance." *Australian Journal of Agricultural Economics* 30 (1986): 63–69.

Skees, J. R., and M. R. Reed. "Rate-making and Farm-Level Crop Insurance: Implications for Adverse Selection." *American Journal of Agricultural Economics* 68 (1986): 653–59.

Smith, V. H., and A. E. Baquet. "The Demand for Multiple Peril Crop Insurance: Evidence from the Great Plains." *Montana Ag Research* (Spring 1993).

Smith, V. H., and B. K. Goodwin. "Crop Insurance, Moral Hazard, and Agricultural Chemical Use." Unpublished manuscript, Department of Economics, Montana State University, 1994.

Smith, V. H., and M. R. Kehoe. "The Economics of Marketing Multiple Peril Crop Insurance." Paper presented at the Annual Meeting of the American Agricultural Economics Association, San Diego, 1994.

6

Farm Programs and the Environment

Walter N. Thurman

Agriculture increasingly is found near the center of environmental concern. Public discussion preparatory to the 1995 farm bill makes it clear that environmental interests view the sixty-year-old farm programs as central to their agenda, both because it is believed that farm programs have systematic and bad environmental results and because the farm bill provides a legislative opportunity for new regulation. At a time when creative energy is being applied to redirecting farm programs toward environmental objectives, it seems useful to assess the environmental bias of the current programs. To begin, it is helpful to delimit the proper scope of public policy toward agriculture and the environment.

Where Are the Externalities?

The environmental effects of agriculture are real, and they are significant. They also are site specific, difficult to measure in any particular instance, and even more difficult to summarize in the aggregate.[1] Further, public policy should

---

1. Smith (1992) heroically makes the only published attempt to calculate the total external environmental cost of U.S. crop production. Drawing from a variety of sources, he concludes that "[i]ncluding the instream effects of soil erosion, wetlands conversion, and groundwater contamination, agriculture's crop-related activities yield environmental cost estimates that range from less than one percent to over 40% of the value of crops produced per acre on the land deemed responsible for these impacts" (p. 1077).

concern itself with some environmental effects but not others. Some environmental effects of agricultural production are not externalities.

When a landowner decides to farm in a way that erodes his soil but the erosion has no downstream external effects, for example, then costs and benefits both are focused on the decision maker. There is no externality. Individuals may wish to try to convince the farmer that he is foolish to give the future productivity of his soil so little weight. But apart from, perhaps, educating the farmer as to the value of his soil and the proper way to discount benefits and costs, there is no obvious role for the government.[2]

In another example, some farmers operate tractors without sun protection and thereby increase their risk of skin cancer. No externality is involved, and this environment-related health consequence of agriculture is not an appropriate target of government regulation. A reasonable case could be made for the government to distribute public health information on grounds that such action would be relatively inexpensive and would not be coercive and there may be efficiencies to central coordination of health information distribution. But if farmers are well informed on the subject, an appropriately constrained government should not try to direct the farmer's decision about sun protection.

Similar issues arise in considering the exposure of farm workers to agricultural pesticides. Here too there may be information problems.[3] In the United States this seems most likely where migrant farm workers do not speak English and information costs thus are especially high. (There also

---

2. As an empirical proposition, it is not at all clear that landowners neglect the value of their soil in making farming decisions. Miranowski and Hammes (1984) provide evidence that land markets reflect both the value of topsoil and the erosivity of particular fields.

3. Antle and Pingali (1994) provide evidence from the Philippines that the costs of acquiring and assimilating information regarding pesticide use can be high and can lead to important health problems and productivity impairment. They argue that farmers with low stocks of human capital are likely to behave inefficiently in a changing environment and in particular with regard to their use of hazardous farm chemicals. Also see Antle (1994).

may be the problem of coercion of illegal aliens through exploiting their illegal status.) But the case here is no different in principle from that of the unprotected tractor driver. If the farm workers can be informed of the risks associated with exposure to farm pesticides, then there is no externality. Farm workers will weigh the monetary and nonmonetary benefits of farm employment with the monetary and nonmonetary costs; there are no third-party effects of pesticide application.

What then are the external effects of agricultural production? Have they recently become worse? The land base of U.S. agriculture has remained roughly the same size over the past forty years. Production of crops and animal products has increased dramatically over the period while farm labor has fallen by a factor of three (see Miranowski, Hrubovcak, and Sutton [1991]). The increase in production has resulted from a substitution away from labor and land and toward other inputs, primarily fertilizers and pesticides, and in the case of livestock toward intensification of production on smaller acreage. Input substitution has taken place against a backdrop of constantly improving technical possibilities.

Any increases in the external effects of U.S. agriculture in the aggregate, then, are not due to agricultural production being carried out on a larger geographic scale: they are the result of input substitution. The increased use of fertilizers leads to runoff from fields that overenriches waterways and encourages the growth of algae and other plants and leads to eutrophication. The increased use of pesticides also leads to runoff, where the external effects can be the contamination of drinking water supplies or the poisoning of wildlife. The intensification of production on smaller acreage can increase soil erosion, which can itself impair water quality off site and also carry fertilizer and pesticide residue with it. With animal production the concentration of cattle and poultry operations can raise effluent above the assimilative capacity of the nearby environment.

But the externalities just listed result from the interaction among parties and do not exist in isolation. If there are

155

no downstream water users, then the silting of waterways creates no externality. The reciprocal nature of externality has been stressed by writers following Coase (1960). In the present instance the Coase tradition would argue that those negatively affected by agricultural operations are as responsible for the externality as the on-farm generators of the harm.

The issues of the environmental effects of agriculture and appropriate public policy for dealing with them form a broad set. The focus of the present study is narrower: to analyze critically the often heard claim that traditional farm programs exacerbate externality problems. I attempt to trace out the systematic environmental results from farm programs and their recent modifications and to focus on the results that likely generate externalities.

Varieties of Commodity Programs and Their Environmental Effects

The Generic Effects of Increasing Price. One way to assess the broad environmental impact of commodity programs is to assess their impact on production. The scale effect of program subsidies on production is tempered, however, by the fact that the major commodity programs employ acreage set-asides. Participants in the programs must agree to withhold some of their acres from production. Without commodity programs, set-aside land might be farmed. Miranowski, Hrubovcak, and Sutton (1991) estimated the aggregate production effects of eliminating commodity programs and concluded that program crop production would decline by 7 percent in the long run if production subsidies were removed. Livestock production, they estimated, would decline by 2 percent.

The ultimate effects of production subsidies depend on their effects on the demands for inputs. Miranowski, Hrubovcak, and Sutton considered such effects by analyzing how removal of subsidies would translate into factor demands. They concluded, for example, that the predicted 7 percent decline in program crop production would result in an 8 percent decline in chemical use.

Commodity programs typically increase equilibrium prices. The price increases are achieved through different mechanisms in different programs, and environmental effects are tied to the particular mechanism. Does the government, by raising the price above its unsupported level, encourage the production of environmental externalities? An affirmative answer to this question lies behind much environmental concern over commodity programs.

A link between price and environmental externalities presupposes an output-linked externality. Assume that such an externality exists and that the external effect is related to chemical use. Then an increase in the commodity's price can be seen to influence chemical use on both the intensive and the extensive margins of production.

Consider the supply of the commodity to come from acres of land where the fertility of the soil varies. Assume that chemicals are substitutes for soil quality, at least at the margin: an acre with slightly better soil will rationally apply less chemical than an acre with slightly worse soil. In a competitive equilibrium there is an equilibrium soil quality that earns zero rents in the production of the commodity. All acres inferior to the zero-rent acre will not produce the commodity, and all superior acres will. The zero-rent soil quality defines the extensive margin of production.

Now consider the effects of a program-induced increase in output price. Assuming that the prices of inputs, including chemicals, do not change, there will be two effects. First, the higher output price will lead to a lower zero-rent soil quality. There will be acres that earned negative rents under the lower-price equilibrium and so did not produce the commodity. The new higher price allows positive-rent production on some of those acres, and so they produce. The aggregate amount of chemicals used in the production of the crop increases because of this expansion along the extensive margin, and specific externalities may result.

Chemical use also increases for those acres of high enough quality to be producing both before and after the price increase. Because the increase in output price increases the value of the marginal product of chemicals on the inframarginal acres, there is an increase in chemical use along each producing acre's intensive margin. Preexisting externalities are worsened by expansion along the intensive margin.

As Antle and Just (1991) elegantly demonstrate and emphasize, the environmental consequences of agricultural policy depend on the geographic joint distribution of (here) chemical input use and the environmental attributes of the land, such as erodibility.[4] In our example, knowing the amount of the increase in aggregate chemical use is not the same as knowing the external effects of the price increase. Land heterogeneity is important, and external effects of the price increase are site specific. To evaluate fully the environmental effects, one must know, among other things, where the newly cultivated acres came from. If, for example, the price-supported commodity were corn and the extensive expansion came at the expense of land allocated to soybeans, then the generally acknowledged higher erosivity of corn could lead to external effects. In other cases the extensive increase in planting of program crops could reduce externalities.

Price and Income Support Programs. *Deficiency payments and nonrecourse loans.* The bulk of government payments to farmers is made under a system of nonrecourse loans and deficiency payments. Recipients of these payments are growers of the so-called major program crops: corn, other feedgrains (sorghum, barley, and oats), wheat, cotton, and rice. Of the total $8.2 billion paid to producers by the Agricultural Stabilization and Conservation Service (ASCS) in 1991, fully 70.4 percent went to producers of these crops. (The $8.2 billion total includes payments to farmers under the Conservation Reserve Program, which accounted for 20.2 percent of the total.) Recent changes in the programs, in particular the freezing of program yields and flex acre

---

4. See also Antle and Capalbo (1991) on the evaluation of the external costs of agricultural chemicals.

provisions, have arguably lessened their environmental impacts.

A generic model of a nonrecourse loan program with deficiency payments follows. The government sets a support price, P_s, which is a price floor guaranteed to growers of the crop. If the market price should fall below P_s, then the government agrees to buy the production from program participants at P_s. In modern versions of such programs, P_s is guaranteed on all production by program participants through the mechanism of nonrecourse loans.

The deficiency payment is a transaction separate from the nonrecourse loan. It can be represented as

$$\text{deficiency payment} = [P_T - \max(P_M', P_s)] \cdot A_E \cdot y_P', \quad (6\text{--}1)$$

where P_T is a target price, P_M is the market price, A_E is the (eligible) acreage to which the deficiency payment is applied, and y_P is the (program) yield. The production and acreage effects of deficiency payment schemes vary with the rules that determine A_E and y_P.

If the acreage eligible for payments is somehow fixed, as it currently is, and if yield in the equation above is measured as the current year's actual yield on the farm in question, then the payment scheme creates yield-increasing incentives. On fixed acreage this implies increasing the use of nonland inputs per acre, primarily fertilizers and pesticides. If chemicals leave the farm site through direct runoff, percolation through the soil, or transport on eroded soil particles, then the yield increase can have external effects.

The size of the incentive to increase yield can be measured by the difference between the target price and what would be the market price absent the program. The marginal output price that determines the value marginal product of inputs is the target price, usually substantially above the market price. The wheat target price, for example, has been $4 per bushel for several years, while season average wheat prices have ranged between $3 and $4. For corn, the target price is now—and for several years has been—$2.75 per bushel. The marketing year average price for corn in these years has been as high as $2.50. The 1994 corn price is

159

forecast below $2 and in certain areas below the loan rate of $1.89.

The yield-increasing incentive comes from the direct link between production and the payments described in equation 6–1. If, however, current yield does not affect payments, then no incentive is provided by the deficiency payments to increase yield. This has been the case since an important administrative change in 1986. Program yield at that time was frozen either at 90 percent of the 1985 yield for the specific farm or was tied to a county average. The rule change that no variation in the current yield was to affect program payments effectively eliminated incentives to increase yield.

Prior to 1986, deficiency payment schemes periodically updated a farm's program yield to reflect changes in technology and farming practice. At that time restricting acres through base restrictions induced farmers to increase current yields so as to increase future program payments. Again, because the environmental externalities of production can be linked to chemical use, the updating of base yields exacerbated the environmental effects of program crop production.

The other key policy variable in equation 6–1 is eligible acreage. The variable A_E could refer to actual planted acreage and in fact did in direct payment programs of earlier decades. Currently the acreage used in determining deficiency payments is affected by several program provisions. Continuing the generic deficiency payments example, decompose acreage in the previous equation as

$$A_E = A_b \cdot (1 - arp) \qquad (6-2)$$

where A_b is base acreage and arp (for Acreage Reduction Program) is the proportion of base acreage that is required to be diverted from crop production to participate in the program.

Base acreage for each of the major program crops is determined as a moving average of acreage planted to the crop. For example, a five-year average is used for corn, and a three-year average for cotton. Current deficiency payments are not linked to current acreage choice.

The term $(1 - arp)$ refers to the Acreage Reduction Program (ARP), arp being the proportion of base acreage that the farmer must idle and plant in a cover crop to receive program payments. The ARP percentage is linked by formula to current stocks of the commodity. For 1995 crops, arp likely will be zero for wheat, rice, and feedgrains other than corn. The arp for corn and cotton will likely be 7.5 percent of base acreage. For the participating farmer, the term $A_b(1 - arp)$ imposes a maximum acreage to be planted to the program crop. The farmer may plant less but, with an exception to be discussed, does not receive deficiency payments on acreage he does not plant.

Flex acres and the determination of base. The discussion to this point describes the deficiency payment schemes in the late 1980s. In the 1990 Omnibus Budget Reconciliation Act, the calculation of eligible acreage was further complicated by the introduction of flex acres. The change was made primarily to lower the budget costs of deficiency payment programs. Secondarily, and of most interest here, it addressed the perverse environmental incentives from base acreage calculations.

While the much earlier unlinking of eligible acreage from actual planted acreage was useful in controlling program costs, that unlinking had the unintended effect of encouraging farmers to build base. Because deficiency payments are proportional to acreage base, base is a desirable commodity (Duffy, Taylor, Cain, and Young [1994] calculated its value). One strategy for expanding base is to *not* participate in the program for a year or more and, while not participating, to plant the program crop on a wide scale. During the base-building year the farmer does not receive deficiency payments but does influence future base calculations.

Base building has obvious government budget implications, but it also has environmental implications to the extent that it represents an increase in production generating environmental externalities. Further, and beyond scale effects, the incentive to build base discourages crop rotation. Once classified as base acreage, the moving average base calculation provides continued incentives to plant the program crop without rotation. In most instances rotating crops reduces the desired application of pesticides and, with nitrogen-fixing crops, reduces the desired application of fertilizers as well.

The perverse and budget-straining incentives just discussed were addressed by the 1990 flex acre provisions. Basically the provisions required farmers to divert planting of base acreage away from the program crop. The diverted acreage was to be planted (instead of to a cover crop) to either an alternate marketable crop or to the program crop but without receiving deficiency payments. Broadly the provisions did two things. They reduced the incentive to participate in the program, and they reduced the program penalty for rotating crops for those who did participate.[5] The potency of the incentives and additional flexibility in

---

5. There are two specific flex acre provisions: normal flex acres and optional flex acres. Normal flex acres are better thought of as mandatory flex acres. The 1990 farm act required that 15 percent of base acreage be put in the category of normal flex acres.

A participating farmer is free to plant either the program crop or an alternate crop on normal flex acres, but he will receive no deficiency payments for the acreage. Normal flex acres are an unambiguous bad for farmers who plant their normal flex acres in the program crop: they reduce the farmers' deficiency payments. Conversely, optional flex acres are good from the farmer's view. The 1990 farm act allows up to 10 percent of base acreage to be designated optional flex acres on which the farmer may plant either the program crop or an alternate crop. Unlike normal (mandatory) flex acres, optional flex acres that are planted in the program crop do receive deficiency payments.

The effect of both types of flex acres on deficiency payments can be seen by revising equation (6–2) to reflect the current calculation of eligible acreage:

$$A_E = A_b \cdot (1 - arp - nfa - ofa_o), \qquad (6\text{–}3)$$

where nfa is the proportion of normal (mandatory) flex acres, currently .15, and ofa_o is the part of the optional flex acre proportion (a maximum of .10) that is planted to a crop other than the program crop.

altering crop choice can be known only on a case-by-case basis. Results from Duffy and Taylor (1994) illustrate some important cases.

Remaining incentives to intensify production. The freezing of base yields has almost eliminated any field-level bias in input use from deficiency payment programs. Because deficiency payments are largely decoupled from production decisions, they have no effect on the production of externalities.

One could take several exceptions to this claim. The first concerns the support price (or loan rate). In recent years the support price usually has turned out not to be binding and so ex post should not have had an effect on production. Ex ante, however, by truncating the bottom part of the price distribution, the price support may have increased plantings and the application of inputs with external costs. The nonrecourse loans are not decoupled as deficiency payments are. They apply to all the production of program participants.

Another possible effect of the programs is through the increase in the equilibrium price brought about through acreage restrictions. If acreage restrictions raised the equilibrium price above what it would otherwise be (this is not obviously true), then nonparticipants would increase their acreage; this change could spread production externalities to areas that would not otherwise produce.

Finally, an increase in the equilibrium price would increase the value marginal product of fertilizer and pesticides on each acre and would increase their quantities employed. This would be true both for participants and nonparticipants. Because deficiency payments are no longer linked to actual yields, to know the degree that the programs distort the incentives at the field level, one needs to know by how much the programs increase equilibrium price and not how much higher the target price is than the equilibrium price without the program.

The discussion here has ignored one recent innovation in the deficiency payments programs: the marketing loan provision. Marketing loan programs were created in the 1985 Food Security Act and are an anomalous step away from the decoupling trends represented by base acreage and frozen program yields. But implementation has made the programs relevant only for rice and for cotton. The marketing loan provision encourages farmers not to forfeit their nonrecourse loans and does so by decreasing the price at which farmers may repay their loans. Throughout the marketing year, repayment rates are established slightly below the prevailing market price. Therefore, even when market prices are below the support price, farmers will repay their loans. The purpose of the marketing loan rate option is to minimize the stocks held by the government. The option does not entirely decouple the deficiency and loan payment scheme. In net, farmers are guaranteed not just the support price for their production but also the difference between the market price and the repayment rate.

This last effect suggests a possible reform of the deficiency payment programs for rice and cotton that would be environmentally sound and would reduce government spending as well: freeze yields on loan payments as well as on deficiency payments. A farmer would no longer be guaranteed the support price on all that he produces but rather would be guaranteed the support price on a quantity determined by the product of his allowed acreage and a historically determined yield. This proposal would affect payments only when the market price fell below its support level.

Supply Control Programs. Tobacco and peanuts are the only U.S. crops that are directly supply controlled. Direct control here means mandatory restrictions on the total quantity marketed (tobacco) or domestically marketed (peanuts). The tobacco program limits by transferable quota the total amount that an individual farmer may produce and sell. The peanut program limits by transferable quota a farmer's sales to the domestic market. Anyone, quota owner or not, can grow peanuts in an unlimited amount and sell them for export or for nonedible uses in the United States.

Consider, first, the tobacco industry and tobacco program. Burley and flue-cured tobacco are the two main tobacco types grown in the United States. Together they account for about 80 percent of the crop. The principal burley state is Kentucky, and the principal flue-cured state is North Carolina. There are separate but similar programs for the two types of tobacco. Each employs individual quotas to restrict production directly.

One unit of quota is the right to produce one pound of tobacco per year. While tobacco quota is almost universally discussed in terms of pounds, ownership of quota actually entitles the holder to a share of an aggregate quota, which is adjusted annually. There have been various restrictions on the lease and sale of quota. (See Rucker, Thurman, and Sumner [1995] for an analysis of transferability restrictions.)

The aggregate effect of the tobacco program is to restrict the quantity grown and sold in the United States and to increase its price. A secondary effect comes through the program's fixing of the geographic distribution of production. Because tobacco quota cannot trade across county borders, tobacco is grown now in approximately the same counties as in the 1930s and in approximately the same proportions.

Any environmental effect of the tobacco program must come through the effect on crop choice in the tobacco-growing region. To the extent that alternate crops are more or less erosive, or more or less chemical intensive, tobacco supply controls may have external environmental effects. In general, however, a direct supply control program such as the tobacco program should prima facie be viewed as environmentally benign. Previous versions of both the tobacco and peanut programs, however, controlled supply indirectly—through acreage allotments. Supply control of this sort would not be viewed as environmentally benign because of the effects of acreage restrictions on the use of nonland inputs, particularly pesticides and fertilizers. (See Foster and Babcock [1990 and 1993].)

The important difference between the tobacco and peanut programs is that peanut quota only restricts sales onto the domestic edible market. (See Rucker and Thurman [1990] for a fuller discussion of the peanut program.) If one owns (or rents) quota and sells to the domestic edible market, one is guaranteed the domestic edible support price, currently about $675 per ton. If one produces for the export market, which one can do without quota, the price in recent years has been near $350.

For most of the peanut-producing region, the environmental effects of the current peanut program are more likely to be benign than those of the tobacco program. While the tobacco quota restricts the quantity of tobacco supplied and so affects the distribution of crops grown in quota-owning areas, the peanut program probably does little to restrict the quantity of peanuts supplied. If peanut producers grow their quota amount as well as additional peanuts for the export market, then the marginal price they face is the $350 world price. Without the quota restriction producers would still face the same marginal price and would produce the same amounts. The effect of a quota and support price for domestic sales is entirely inframarginal and results only in a transfer of economic rents from domestic consumers to quota owners. If the peanut program influences the world price, which is at least questionable (Rucker and Thurman 1990), then elimination of the program could have price and production effects.

Borges and Thurman (1994) argue that the peanut program is indeed inframarginal in its effects for North Carolina. Their results likely hold more strongly for the largest peanut-producing state, Georgia. In some regions of the country, however, the quota support price is not inframarginal. In Texas and Oklahoma there are counties where only the quota amount is grown and sometimes not even that. In those areas crop choice is affected by the peanut program and in the same way that crop choice is affected everywhere by the tobacco program. Still, there is no obvious environmental externality generated by the production of peanuts instead of a substitute crop.

Import Control Programs. The sugar program limits the quantity of sugar imported into the United States and thereby raises the domestic price. Congress sets the sugar support price in farm legislation. The executive branch creates import quotas so that the expected domestic equilibrium price reaches the support price. Import quotas are allocated annually to specific producing countries.[6] In recent years the domestic price of sugar has been about twice the world price.

The broad effects of the quotas have been to increase the U.S. domestic price of sugar, to reduce its consumption, and, important to the current discussion, to increase its domestic production. Sugar is produced domestically from two sources, sugar beets and sugar cane. In recent years about 60 percent of domestic production has come from sugar cane (USDA 1993, table 111).

The most publicized environmental effects of sugar production are associated with cane farming, especially near the Florida Everglades. In the United States one-half of cane acreage is found in Florida. The remainder is split largely between Louisiana and Hawaii, with a small acreage in Texas. The environmental problems of cane production are primarily the large quantities of water used, often diverted from wetlands, and the nutrient loads added to water as it leaves sugar cane fields. Hahn (1992) argues that water management is the more critical issue of the two affecting the Everglades. The environmental problems of nearby Lake Okeechobee, also connected with sugar cane farming, are most connected with levels of phosphorous, which harms native plants by encouraging the growth of exotic species.

The domestic environmental effects of the sugar program are due to more sugar cane and beets being grown with the sugar price supports than would be grown without. This is purely a national accounting. Globally the effect

---

6. The allocation of quotas to importing countries has attracted the attention of economists over the years. See, among others, Johnson (1974), Lopez (1989), and Leu, Schmitz, and Knutson (1987).

of raising the U.S. sugar price is to reduce consumption by U.S. consumers and so to reduce equilibrium global production. Without the sugar program less sugar cane would be grown in the United States and more would be grown in, say, Mexico and the Caribbean. There are well-documented environmental problems with sugar cane production in those areas. See, for example, Arteaga (1993) and Little (1993).

Some policy options for dealing with environmental externalities from cane farming have nothing to do with the sugar program. The usual command-and-control approach to environmental problems was typified by a plan drawn up for the Everglades in 1992 by the South Florida Water Management District. The plan called for specific regulations on farming practices as well as the conversion of large areas of farmland (about 56 square miles) to artificial wetlands that could emulate natural wetlands in their regulation of rainwater surges. This plan has since been modified in a 1993 agreement, brokered by the Department of Interior, among sugar growers, the management district, and the National Parks system (see *Sugar y Azucar* [1993]). Hahn (1992) suggests that tradable emission permits are an attractive alternative way to deal with phosphorous problems. Some elements of Hahn's plan have been incorporated into the most recent agreement.

Another instance of the inevitable but unforeseeable interaction of policy is the effect of extensive canal building on the environmental consequences of sugar cane farming. Much of the harm done to the Everglades resulted from drainage and transportation canals dug over several decades by the U.S. Army Corps of Engineers and funded by the federal government. It seems evident that sugar cane production would have a more benign environmental effect and the sugar program could wreak less environmental damage if the canals had not been built.

Dairy Policy. Dairy policy is complicated. It combines three approaches to farm income support: import restrictions, price supports through government purchases, and government-coordinated price discrimination between different end-use markets for milk. Dairying itself is one of the more environmentally costly agricultural activities. Federal and state dairy policy combine to increase the scale of dairying operations over what they would be absent government intervention and to relocate dairy production.

The main environmental externality from dairy production is the same as that from other livestock operations: animal waste discharge into waterways or onto land. Runoff from dairy operations flows from pastures and, in more concentrated form, from barns. One problem resulting from such discharge is the overloading of natural waterways with nitrogen and phosphorous compounds, collectively termed *nutrients*. Excess nutrient loads encourage algae growth, reduce dissolved oxygen, and impair the habitat for fish and other species. A problem from dairying in some areas is the percolation of dissolved minerals into groundwater, contributing to the salinity of water supplies. Moffitt, Zilberman, and Just (1978) discuss this latter problem in the Santa Ana River basin near Los Angeles.

The specific problems caused by runoff vary by the concentration of dairying in the area, the assimilative capacity of the waterway, and the uses made of the waterway. One particularly well-documented instance of environmental problems due to dairying is that surrounding Lake Okeechobee in south Florida. In the river basins draining into Okeechobee, production subsidies from both the sugar program and the dairy program combine to create external costs.[7]

---

7. Boggess, Flaig, and Fonyo (1993) discuss the history of environmental problems and policy of Lake Okeechobee. They cite studies from the 1970s concluding that eutrophication of the lake was an important threat, that the primary enrichment problem in the lake was phosphorous, and that the primary sources of phosphorous were high-density dairy pastures and faulty dairy waste-control systems. More recent studies cited by Boggess, Flaig, and Fonyo report that phosphorous loading of the lake has increased over the past two decades and that agriculture is now the primary source of phosphorous entering the Lake Okeechobee watershed. Broken down by production activity, the major specific phosphorous sources are improved

Two separate policies, plus section 22 import limits, compose the heart of "the dairy program."[8] The first is a price floor on milk manufactured products: primarily butter, cheese, and nonfat dry milk. The price of manufactured products is supported by government purchases at announced support prices; this system implies that the federal government accumulates, and must dispose of, stocks. Section 22 import restrictions protect the U.S. market for manufactured products from lower-price imports. The price support program alone can be expected to lead to milk production levels higher than would exist without the supports.

The second major piece of dairy regulation is the system of federal marketing orders pertaining to sales of fluid milk. Virtually all fluid milk is covered by one of the approximately fifty federal marketing orders or dozen state orders. The orders affect price discrimination between the two sources of demand for fluid milk: milk for consumption in fluid form and milk for use in manufactured products. In particular, marketing orders raise the price of milk for fluid use.

Milk marketing orders also employ blend pricing. The marketing order sells its fluid milk at a high price and its milk for manufactured uses at a low price. But the price per pound of milk that it pays its producing members is the marketing order's average revenue: a quantity-weighted blend of the two prices. This situation implies that the marginal incentive price that an order pays its members is higher than the marginal price at which the marketing order itself sells—and implies an inefficiency in the level of production by the order. Therefore, the marketing orders promote dairy production beyond what would be expected from the price support of manufactured products alone and increase aggregate dairy runoff and its associated problems.

---

dairy and beef cattle pastures (45.8 percent), sugar mills (15.2 percent), dairy barns (14.2 percent), and sugar cane fields (13.5 percent).

8. A fuller discussion of U.S. dairy policy can be found in Helmberger (1991).

LaFrance and de Gorter (1985) measured the effects of the dairy program with an aggregate econometric model. They did not address the issue of environmental externalities from dairy production but, usefully for our purposes, simulated the levels of dairy production that would have obtained without government intervention in the dairy market. They concluded that during the late 1970s eliminating the dairy program would have reduced herd sizes by 7–10 percent.

Several authors (see West and Brandow [1964] and Ruane and Hallberg [1986]) have argued that the dairy program has significant spatial effects. Without the program, they argue, milk production would shift away from certain regions, particularly the South and Northeast, and toward others, especially the upper Midwest and California.

Commodity Program Provisions and Other Agricultural Policies Promoting Environmentally Friendly Production

The Conservation Reserve Program. The Conservation Reserve Program, a product of the 1985 Food Security Act, is the most significant recent attempt to integrate environmental concerns into agricultural policy. Annual CRP payments to farmers to withhold cropland from production approximate $1.8 billion (fiscal year 1994), almost one-quarter of total farm program payments from the Agricultural Stabilization and Conservation Service. Two related, but decidedly more minor, programs are the Wetland Reserve Program and the Water Bank.[9]

The U.S. Department of Agriculture was given substantial discretion in administering the CRP but was subject to the target levels of acreage enrollment specified in the 1985

---

9. Under the Wetland Reserve Program, long-term easements that preclude agricultural production are purchased from owners of wetland areas. In exchange for annual payments, participants agree to restore and protect wetlands that they own. Payments under the Wetland Reserve in 1994 were $67 million. The Water Bank, similar to the CRP, contracts with farmers for ten years at a time to preserve wetland wildlife habitat. Payments under the program were $8 million in 1994.

act. CRP administrators devised a scheme to solicit bids from farmers to voluntarily retire their land from production for ten years. Enrolled land cannot be used for haying, grazing, or commercial crop production and must be planted in grass or tree cover. In return, landowners receive annual rental payments and are reimbursed for one-half of their conservation expenses.

As discussed by Reichelderfer and Boggess (1988), the USDA bidding scheme had three key components. First was an eligibility criterion. To be eligible for CRP contracts, land had to be eroding at rates more than three times a "tolerance" level at which rate the future productivity of the soil is not impaired. Farmers of eligible land submitted bids: offers of willingness to accept their stated amounts in return for idling acreage. The second component of the implementation scheme was the size of the bidding pool. All bids less than a certain threshold were to be accepted for enrollment within a pool. The third component was the setting of the maximum acceptable bid within each pool; the level was not to exceed prevailing rental rates in each region. Once the eligibility criterion and bidding pools were determined, this last component could be manipulated to determine aggregate enrollment in the program.

The program differentiated only between the highly erodible land that was eligible to participate and land that was not. Once declaring certain acreage eligible, the program allowed the quasi-market process of bidding to enroll that acreage with the lowest opportunity cost, at least within a regional pool. Such a scheme minimizes the total costs of enrolling a given acreage but does not distinguish among tracts of land according to erodibility or, more importantly, to the off-site external effects of the tracts' erosion.

Most acreage now in the CRP was enrolled between the enactments of the 1985 and 1990 farm acts. Between 1986 and 1989, 34 million acres were enrolled. Since 1990, only 2.5 million acres have been enrolled. Osborn and Heimlich (1994) characterize the acres enrolled after 1990 as generating greater off-site (read *external*) benefits. This

switch resulted from a change in the way bids for enrollment were accepted.

While CRP bids under the 1985 act were ranked only
according to the dollar value of the farmer's bid, the ranking under the 1990 act was based on the ratio of an estimated environmental benefit per dollar spent by the
government. The environmental benefit was estimated by
an environmental benefits index that gives weight to the
surface and ground water effects of crop production. This
revision in bidding procedures led to a geographic shift in
(the new and smaller) enrollment away from the Great
Plains. Further, the 1990 act designated conservation priority areas, which accounted for higher proportions of post-
1990 enrollment acres. Among these are watersheds draining into the Chesapeake Bay, Long Island Sound, and the
Great Lakes. The retirement of the newly enrolled acres primarily reduced water-caused soil erosion. The 1985–1990
enrollment primarily reduced wind-caused erosion.[10]

The current (before the 1995 farm bill) CRP issue is the
expiration of the ten-year contracts that were first signed in
1985. In 1995, contracts covering 2 million of the 36.4 million
acres will expire. More than 22 million acres will come out
of the CRP over the following two years. The forces behind
a reauthorization of CRP are a coalition of environmental
organizations and farmer groups. The National Farmers'
Union, for example, has strongly supported an extension of
CRP. A meeting of the governors of western states in the

---

10. Miranowski, Hrubovcak, and Sutton characterized the CRP en-
rollments during 1985–1990 as geographically unrelated to the problems of ground water contamination by agricultural chemicals. For
example, most of the Atlantic Coastal Plain, from Florida through
Virginia, lies in an area of "potential groundwater contamination
from agricultural chemicals" (see Nielsen and Lee [1987]), while scant
CRP enrollment during the 1985–1990 period came from the area.
CRP enrollment was then, and remains, primarily from the Great
Plains—from Texas up to Montana and the Dakotas. This area does
overlap substantially the broad central belt of the United States,
where "concentrations of suspended sediment, nitrogen, and phosphorous can impair water uses" (Nielsen and Lee; see their figures 2
and 4).

summer of 1994 produced a statement that also strongly supported extending CRP. In partial response to this pressure, in early September 1994, Secretary of Agriculture Michael Espy announced that CRP funding would be extended for one year beyond the ten-year limit.

A cogent criticism of CRP, at least its 1985–1990 version, is that retiring land is a rather blunt instrument to use to reduce erosion. If there are ways of farming highly erodible land that are not in fact highly erosive, then directly rewarding and subsidizing such practices could reduce erosion at a lower cost. Sinner (1990) makes this argument and claims that a targeted $200 million subsidy could have approximately the same effect on soil erosion as $2 billion spent through the CRP for land retirement. In principle, targeted subsidies could better address particular externality problems in particular locales. In practice, setting nationwide guidelines for distributing subsidies in such a program would be difficult.

A practical problem of a different sort is stressed by Delworth Gardner (1994). He is highly critical of the CRP and characterizes it as meeting only one of its stated goals well: providing income support for farmers. He argues (as do Reichelderfer and Boggess 1988) that CRP payments are distributed broadly across congressional districts although soil erosion problems are geographically concentrated. If implementable versions of CRP require broad geographic sharing of government payments, then narrow targeting of, say, eligibility criteria is not feasible.

Finally, is the goal of the CRP, reducing soil erosion, per se a good thing? The problem of externality in soil erosion occurs when downwind or downstream deposition of soil particles has harmful effects. If so, and if the upwind and downwind parties are prevented by transactions costs from contracting over erosion's effects, then a prima facie case can be made for public action. Osborn and Heimlich suggest that the external effects of soil erosion are associated primarily with water erosion and not with wind erosion. This makes particularly important their claim that the post-1990 CRP enrollment was successful in targeting acres subject to water erosion and, hence, external effects.

Conservation Compliance. The conservation compliance provision of the 1985 Food Security Act encourages farmers to draw up and carry out approved conservation plans by withholding farm program benefits if such a plan is not in place and carried out. The act required the establishment of a plan by 1990. It called for denial of benefits if the plan was not implemented by year-end 1994.

Conservation compliance specifically targeted lands that were identified as highly erodible, measured by an erodibility index. The erodibility index measures the erodibility of a soil in its uncultivated state relative to the amount of erosion consistent with undiminished production. An erodibility index value of one implies that without conservation effort the soil erodes at exactly the rate that would leave crop production unchanged. Higher values of the index imply a deterioration in the fertility of the soil. The definition of highly erodible under the 1985 act came to be soil with an erodibility index of eight or greater. A 1982 inventory of cropland identified 118 million acres that were highly erodible in this sense.

Enforcement of the conservation compliance provision is carried out by field offices of the Soil Conservation Service.[11] They approve conservation compliance plans by criteria that can include the financial burdens imposed by carrying out conservation activities on particular farms.

Conservation compliance and the Conservation Reserve Program aim for the same broad objective, reducing soil erosion, and the provisions of each influence the behavior of farmers regarding the other. In fact the conservation compliance provisions initially were suggested to reduce

---

11. The Soil Conservation Service, since a USDA reorganization, now goes by the name of the National Resource Conservation Service. Throughout the discussion here, I use the older term, Soil Conservation Service or SCS, to refer to the service both before and after the name change.

the Treasury cost of the CRP: owners of highly erodible land would face lower opportunity costs of enrolling their land in the CRP if their alternatives were to farm and receive commodity program payments subject to costly conservation compliance. The lower opportunity costs for highly erodible land should then reduce the CRP bids of owners of such land and make highly erodible land available to the CRP at a lower annual rental rate.[12]

Now that CRP funding may lapse, and lands enrolled in the CRP may return to production, another interaction between CRP and conservation compliance arises. If CRP fades away over the next ten years, owners of CRP-enrolled land will face the decision of whether to return their land to production. Not all land in the CRP is highly erodible (approximately 27 million acres out of a total CRP enrollment of 36.5 million acres), but land that is will face the costs of conservation compliance if it comes back into production. The disincentive from conservation compliance may keep acres out of production even after CRP payments cease.

Has conservation compliance succeeded in reducing erosion from farmlands? That question is hard to answer for two reasons. First, the deadline for implementing conservation was December 31, 1994. Second, there was no attempt to compile farm-level data on actual erosion before and after conservation plans were implemented. Nonetheless, administrators of the program in the Soil Conservation Service (SCS) have claimed great success.

Not everyone is convinced that conservation compliance has resulted in large environmental benefits. A sharp attack on the enforcement of conservation compliance by the SCS comes from Kenneth Cook and Andrew Art (1993)

---

12. The effect of conservation compliance on CRP bids from highly erodible lands has not been verified, and indeed it is hard to imagine how it could be. Both CRP and conservation compliance were created in the 1985 act, and only their joint effects could be measured. Further, it seems unlikely that the conservation compliance provision affected CRP payments because of the administration of CRP as an offer, instead of an auction, system. See Rodney Smith (forthcoming).

at the Center for Resource Economics. They view the success reported by SCS administrators as measuring only lax enforcement.

Can Green Support Programs Deliver What They Promise?

Those who advocate the marrying of current commodity programs to environmental objectives see the possibility of simultaneous progress on at least two social projects: supporting the income of particularly small farm operators and improving environmental quality. The Campaign for Sustainable Agriculture, an umbrella group of more than 200 organizations supporting agricultural policy change, lists a number of objectives that the campaign seeks to meet simultaneously. They include environmental quality, social justice, promotion of family farming, food safety, and humane treatment of animals.

The literature of the campaign taken at face value suggests that its goals are mutually consistent and that agricultural policy, if carefully done, will promote small, wise, and profitable farms at the same time that it prevents environmental abuse. The realities of the environmental externalities generated by agriculture suggest otherwise.

Lynch and Smith (1994) compare the geographic distribution of the environmental effects of agriculture with the geographic distribution of farm program payments using county-level ASCS data. They use an Environmental Benefits Index developed by USDA's Economic Research Service to measure the environmental impact of agriculture and weight the index by affected population. Assuming that marginal damage from agricultural externalities is correlated with total damage (as measured by the Environmental Benefits Index), they conclude that a green support program that maximized environmental quality would be concentrated in the heavily populated Northeast and Chicago lake plain, the southern Piedmont, the Mississippi Delta, and parts of southern California and south-central Arizona. Conspicuously absent from this list are the major program payment-receiving regions in the Great Plains.

177

To proponents of green support programs, the low spatial correlation between current program payments and agricultural externalities presents a formidable problem. If one views current commodity programs as effectively addressing the farm income support goals of the nation, then the current distribution of payments is geographically appropriate. If one also agrees that subsidies for environmentally friendly farming are needed mostly elsewhere, then it is hard to imagine green support programs that can meet both income and environmental objectives without breaking the federal budget.

If one views current commodity programs more cynically as simply a political equilibrium (for elaboration see Bruce Gardner [1987]), then no less a problem arises. One may wish to redistribute farm subsidies to areas where the value of externalities is large and to subsidize certain production techniques in those areas, but this action implies redistributing income away from current members of a politically powerful coalition. At the outset, then, one must doubt the efficacy and the political feasibility of a green support program that attempts to address both income support and externality problems.

Lessons learned from the decoupling debate are useful here. Many have advocated decoupling farm subsidies from production outcomes on economic efficiency grounds: that lump sum subsidies transfer income more efficiently than subsidies that distort market signals. Recent and proposed agricultural policy reform moves in this direction. There is a parallel, and powerful, argument for decoupling farmer income support programs from programs addressing agricultural externalities. The goal of an environmental policy should be to alter the incentives that farmers face and substitute for a missing market incentive. Stated this way, this is fine-tuning of the highest and most demanding order, and one should be skeptical of the ability of any program to provide such a finely tuned signal. (Skepticism is particularly appropriate when one considers the information and transaction costs that led to the problem of externality in the first place.) But regardless of one's optimism toward the ability of government to implement Pigovian solutions to externality problems, the policy design problem will be complicated by coupling environmental goals with the goal of supporting certain farmers' incomes in certain regions.

Conclusions

There are good reasons to believe that major crop farm programs, through their effects on yield-increasing chemical inputs and through their discouragement of crop rotation, increased the external costs of agriculture. Most yield-increasing incentives, however, are gone from current versions of the programs. The supply control programs no longer rely on acreage allotments and already employ what proponents of green payments have dubbed bushel-based supply management. More important (because of the size of the feedgrain and foodgrain sector), the deficiency payment programs are no longer direct payment programs. They no longer base payments on realized yield and no longer provide incentive to apply yield-increasing chemicals. Further, through the recent flex provisions, they now allow some rotation of crops within a farmer's acreage base.[13]

But not all is environmentally well with current farm programs. A program that encourages domestic production of a commodity generating negative environmental externalities can properly be blamed for making environmental problems worse. This is the case with the dairy program. It also is the case with the U.S. sugar program, which protects the domestic sugar industry but fails to protect the environmentally fragile lands on which sugar cane is grown.

---

13. A successful environmental reform, but not of a commodity program, appears to be the post-1990 version of the Conservation Reserve Program. The CRP established in 1985 has been widely and justifiably criticized for buying little environmental bang for the buck. The expenditures on land enrolled after the 1990 farm act apparently bought more. Admittedly, the post-1990 version was much more modest than the 1985 version. (Only 2.5 million acres were enrolled after 1990 compared with 34 million acres before). But the acres enrolled have, by design, been those responsible more for water erosion than wind erosion and more responsible for off-farm externalities; they have been located where agricultural runoff causes greater harm.

FARM PROGRAMS AND THE ENVIRONMENT

The examples cited of frozen yields, conversion of acre-age controls to output controls, and flex acre provisions demonstrate that environmental reform of commodity programs is possible. Although agricultural commodity programs can be and have been made more environmentally friendly, there is further room for improvement. But this conclusion does not imply an answer to the broad question, should farm programs be used as tools to fix environmental externalities?

There are several reasons for thinking that farm programs should not be so used. One important and obvious problem with using farm programs to improve environmental quality is that there are no programs for the beef, pork, and poultry industries. All three are growing, pork and poultry rapidly, and all three produce concentrated animal waste that causes locally important surface water, ground water, and odor problems. Externalities generated by these industries cannot be addressed by farm programs unless we are willing to widen the ring of government subsidy to include them.

Another problem with building environmental incentives into farm programs is that the inherent time variation in farm program payments limits their value in correcting environmental externalities. The traditional rationale for farm programs has been the correction of distributional problems created by markets. To the extent that this rationale continues to justify these programs, the specific subsidies they offer will be tied to market conditions: the rewards to farming in environmentally benign ways will be tied to market conditions. The amount of environmental benefit will then be tied to conditions that may have something to do with the costs of environmental controls but little to do with their benefits.

Finally and perhaps most important from the view of someone truly seeking environmental improvement is an issue of truth in labeling. If farm programs are sold to the public on the grounds that they are buying environmental quality, they are bound to be disappointed. Making payments to the traditional coalitions supporting farm programs is a different task from making payments to promote environmentally friendly production. The attempt to make farm programs green can only disappoint citizens interested in improving environmental quality.

Sumner (1990), in a discussion of the distribution of program benefits across farm sizes and wealth, concludes that other means may achieve distributional objectives better than commodity programs. The same can be said of environmental objectives. In a phrase that arises frequently in discussion of commodity programs and the environment, commodity programs are blunt instruments with which to deal surgically with externalities.

References

Antle, John M. "Choice, Efficiency, and Food Safety Policy." Paper presented at the American Enterprise Institute conference, "Future Directions in Agricultural Policy," November 3 and 4, 1994, Washington, D.C.

Antle, John M., and Susan M. Capalbo. "Physical and Economic Model Integration for Measurement of the Environmental Impacts of Agricultural Chemical Use." *Northeast Journal of Agricultural and Resource Economics* 20 (1992): 68–81.

Antle, John M., and Richard E. Just. "Effects of Commodity Program Structure on Resource Use and the Environment." In *Commodity and Resource Policies in Agricultural Systems,* edited by Richard E. Just and Nancy Bockstael. Berlin: Springer-Verlag, 1991.

Antle, John M., and Prabhu L. Pingali. "Pesticides, Productivity, and Farmer Health: A Philippine Case Study." *American Journal of Agricultural Economics* 76 (1994): 418–30.

Arteaga, V. "Environmental Impact of Sugar Cane Production in the Central Region of Venezuela." Paper presented at the technical program of the 1993 Inter-American Sugar Cane Seminar.

Boggess, W. G., E. G. Flaig, and C. M. Fonyo. "Florida's Experience with Managing Nonpoint-Source Phosphorous Runoff into Lake Okeechobee." In *Theory, Modeling and Experience in the Management of Nonpoint-Source Pollu-*

tion, edited by Clifford S. Russell and Jason F. Shogren. Boston: Kluwer Academic Publishers, 1993.

Borges, Robert B., and Walter N. Thurman. "Marketing Quotas and Random Yields: The Marginal Effects of Inframarginal Subsidies on Peanut Supply." *American Journal of Agricultural Economics* 76 (1994): 809–17.

Coase, Ronald H. "The Problem of Social Cost." *Journal of Law and Economics* 3 (1960): 1–44.

Cook, Kenneth A., and Andrew B. Art. "Countdown to Compliance: Implementation of the Resource Conservation Requirements of Federal Farm Law." Washington, D.C.: Center for Resource Economics, 1993.

Duffy, Patricia A., and C. Robert Taylor. "The Effects of Increasing Flex Acres on Farm Planning and Profitability." *Agricultural and Resource Economics Review* 23 (1994): 47–57.

Duffy, Patricia A., C. Robert Taylor, Danny L. Cain, and George J. Young. "The Economic Value of Farm Program Base." *Land Economics* 70 (August 1994).

Foster, William E., and Bruce A. Babcock. "Commodity Policy, Price Incentives, and the Growth in Per-Acre Yields." *Journal of Agricultural and Applied Economics* 25 (1993): 253–65.

Foster, William E., and Bruce A. Babcock. "The Effects of Government Policy on Flue-Cured Tobacco Yields." *Tobacco Science* 34 (1990): 4–8.

Gardner, B. Delworth. *Plowing Ground in Washington.* San Francisco: Pacific Research Institute, 1995.

Gardner, Bruce. "Causes of U.S. Farm Commodity Programs." *Journal of Political Economy* 95 (1987): 290–310.

Hahn, Robert W. "Saving the Environment and Jobs: A Market-based Approach for Preserving the Everglades." Unpublished manuscript, Economists Incorporated, April 21, 1992.

Helmberger, Peter G. *Economic Analysis of Farm Programs.* New York: McGraw-Hill, 1991.

Johnson, D. Gale. *The Sugar Program: Large Costs and Small Benefits.* Washington, D.C.: American Enterprise Institute, 1974.

LaFrance, Jeffrey T., and Harry de Gorter. "Regulation in

a Dynamic Market: The U.S. Dairy Industry." *American Journal of Agricultural Economics* 4 (1985): 821–32.

Leu, Gwo-Jiun, Andrew Schmitz, and Ronald D. Knutson. "Gains and Losses of Sugar Program Policy Options." *American Journal of Agricultural Economics* 69 (1987): 591–602.

Little, D. W. "Sugar Cane Agriculture and the Jamaican Environment." Paper presented at the technical program of the 1993 Inter-American Sugar Cane Seminar.

Lopez, Rigoberto A. "Political Economy of the United States Sugar Policies." *American Journal of Agricultural Economics* 71 (1989): 20–31.

Lynch, Sarah, and Katherine Reichelderfer Smith. "Lean, Mean and Green: Designing Farm Support Programs in a New Era." Unpublished manuscript, Henry A. Wallace Institute for Alternative Agriculture, Greenbelt, Md., November 1994.

Miranowski, John A., and Brian D. Hammes. "Implicit Prices of Soil Characteristics for Farmland in Iowa." *American Journal of Agricultural Economics* 66 (1984): 745–49.

Miranowski, John A., James Hrubovcak, and John Sutton. "The Effects of Commodity Programs on Resource Use." In *Commodity and Resource Policy in Agricultural Systems*, edited by Richard E. Just and Nancy Bockstael. Berlin: Springer-Verlag, 1991.

Moffit, L. Joe, David Zilberman, and Richard E. Just. "A 'Putty-Clay' Approach to Aggregation of Production/ Pollution Possibilities: An Application in Dairy Waste Control." *American Journal of Agricultural Economics* 60 (1978): 452–59.

Nielsen, E. G., and L. K. Lee. "The Magnitude and Costs of Groundwater Contamination from Agricultural Chemicals: A National Perspective." USDA-ERS, Staff Report AGES870318, Washington, D.C., 1987.

Osborn, Tim, and Ralph Heimlich. "Changes Ahead for Conservation Reserve Program." *Agricultural Outlook*, July 1994, pp. 26–30.

Reichelderfer, Katherine, and William G. Boggess. "Government Decision Making and Program Performance:

The Case of the Conservation Program." *American Journal of Agricultural Economics* 70 (1988): 1–11.

Ruane, J. J., and M. C. Hallberg. "Spatial Equilibrium Analysis for Fluid and Manufacturing Milk in the United States." Pennsylvania Agricultural Experiment Station Bulletin 783, June 1986.

Rucker, Randal R., Walter N. Thurman, and Daniel A. Sumner. "Restricting the Market for Quota: An Analysis of Tobacco Production Rights with Corroboration from Congressional Testimony." *Journal of Political Economy* 103 (1995): 142–75.

Rucker, Randal R., and Walter N. Thurman. "The Economic Effects of Supply Controls: The Simple Analytics of the U.S. Peanut Program." *Journal of Law and Economics* 33 (1990): 483–515.

Sinner, Jim. "Soil Conservation: We Can Get More for Our Tax Dollars." *Choices*, 2d qtr., 1990, pp. 10–13.

Smith, Rodney B. "The Conservation Reserve Program as a Least-Cost Land Retirement Mechanism." *American Journal of Agricultural Economics*, forthcoming.

Smith, V. Kerry. "Environmental Costing for Agriculture: Will It Be Standard Fare in the Farm Bill of 2000?" *American Journal of Agricultural Economics* 74 (1992): 1076–88.

Sugar y Azucar, August 1993.

Sumner, Daniel A. "Targeting and the Distribution of Program Benefits." In *Agricultural Policies in a New Decade*, Kristen Allen, editor. Washington, D.C.: Resources for the Future and National Planning Association, 1990.

U.S. Department of Agriculture. *Agricultural Statistics 1993.* Washington: U.S. Government Printing Office, 1993.

———. "Ending the Everglades Gridlock." In *Agricultural Statistics*. Washington, D.C.: 1993.

West, D. A., and G. E. Brandow. "Space-Product Equilibrium in the Dairy Industry of the Northeastern and North Central Regions." *Journal of Farm Economics* 46 (1964): 719–36.

7
Choice, Efficiency, and Food Safety Policy

John M. Antle

Food safety is a goal everyone shares. But a food supply that is 100 percent safe is an unattainable goal, and improving the safety of food is costly. Choices must be made between different dimensions of food safety—for example, between the regulation of pesticide use and the prevention of food-borne illness—and also between a safer food supply and other uses of public and private resources. The more efficiently society's demand for food safety is met, the more resources are available for other uses.

The concepts of choice and efficiency, however, have not played a central role in the design of most legislation dealing with human health risk and food safety. Most legislation is written, and most regulatory decisions are taken, without explicit recognition of the choices that have to be made within the domain of food safety regulation or between food safety and other goals. These choices are therefore made implicitly, and the outcomes often yield surprising, costly, and in some cases deadly consequences.

Today heart disease and cancer are the leading causes of death in the United States; 25 percent of Americans die from some form of cancer. Experts increasingly recognize that certain types of behavior—diet, smoking, and lifestyle—are strongly associated with the risk of various types of cancer. This knowledge provides individuals with many opportunities to reduce the risk of death from cancer at relatively low cost. Put in terms of a lifetime risk of death, all forms of cancer represent a risk of 250,000 in 1 million. The

185

Centers for Disease Control estimates that 9,000 deaths per year are associated with food-borne disease, at a risk of about 2,400 in 1 million over a seventy-year lifetime. At the same time, the Environmental Protection Agency's regulation of agricultural pesticides has attempted to achieve a lifetime cancer mortality risk of 1 in 1 million or less. Estimates based on actual pesticide residues in food indicate that fewer than 10 excess cancers per year may be caused by pesticide residues.

Clearly, unless the cost of reducing an additional death from heart disease, cancer, or food-borne disease were thousands of times higher than the cost of reducing the risk of a cancer death from pesticide residues, the current emphasis in food safety regulation on prevention of cancer from chemical residues represents a wildly inefficient allocation of public funds. This inefficiency exists within the food safety domain, as well as between that area and other areas of health and safety policy. Such misregulation is more than an academic or even an economic issue—it is undoubtedly costing American lives every year. Ironically, pesticide regulations themselves raise the cost of one method of averting heart disease and cancer—consuming a diet rich in fruits and vegetables—and thus discourage behavior that lowers the risk of these diseases.

How can this seemingly absurd situation result from well-meaning food safety legislation? One answer is that federal legislation does not require an efficient allocation of resources among the various aspects of food safety and health policy. Only coincidentally are health and safety regulations efficient in the sense that the last dollar spent on each program yields the same risk reduction. In addition, most food safety regulation is based on a paternalistic view of government—the view that government can make food safety choices better for people than they can make for themselves. This paternalism then becomes an excuse for inefficiency—people cannot choose for themselves, so it is better to have inefficient government regulations protecting people than to leave them at the mercy of the marketplace.

An equally important but more subtle source of inefficiency is the type of regulations that are typically imposed by agencies such as the Food and Drug Administration. One of the FDA's principal regulatory tools is the imposition of good manufacturing practices, that is, prescriptions for how the production process should be designed and managed. One major lesson of the past two decades of environmental regulation is that design standards are a notoriously *inefficient* way to achieve regulatory goals. Every firm's plant, equipment, and management are different, and it is impossible for bureaucrats to tailor design standards that would be efficient for every firm. Inflexible design standards discourage innovation, the key source of long-term productivity growth. To the extent that conforming to design standards is a fixed cost independent of plant size, such standards also tend to put small firms at a competitive disadvantage relative to larger firms.

The importance of these factors is underscored by the intention of the FDA and the U.S. Department of Agriculture (USDA) to mandate the Hazard Analysis Critical Control Points system of quality control for the entire food industry (Food and Drug Administration 1994; USDA 1995). Advocates of HACCP argue that it has been successfully used in the food industry for several decades. But HACCP advocates seem to ignore the difference between a technology voluntarily adopted by a firm and tailored to its needs and one designed and enforced by government bureaucrats and inspectors. Moreover, because compliance with HACCP regulations involves a significant start-up cost that is independent of size of operation, the economic survival of small firms may be at stake.

There is widespread sentiment that it is time to reconsider the design of food and agricultural policy in the United States. Partly this view is brought about by the recognition that the commodity emphasis of U.S. agricultural policy is an anachronism of Great Depression–era policies; partly it is brought about by the recognition that government regulation is often costly and ineffective. But the desire for the reform of food policy is also brought about by the changing priorities of the public. As real incomes grow

187

both domestically and internationally, people place a greater emphasis on the quality of food consumed and less on the quantity.

The purpose of this study is to take a fresh look at issues of food safety policy from an economic perspective. We consider the following questions:

- What are the key issues of food safety, and how do federal policies address them?
- Under what conditions—what aspects of safety, consumer behavior and knowledge, and market conditions—is regulation of food safety needed?
- What economic principles should guide the design of food safety regulation when it is needed?
- What kinds of changes in existing legislation would move the current system toward the goal of a safer food supply at lower cost?
- What role should farm bill legislation play in achieving food safety policy goals?

Summary of Findings

Efficient regulation of food safety is a desirable social goal because more safety is thus obtained—there are fewer illnesses and deaths from food risks—at every level of regulatory effort. A truly efficient system of food safety regulation would also select the level of regulatory effort that gives people the opportunity to obtain the degree of safety that they are willing and able to pay for.

Because of inefficient regulation, consumers are not obtaining the degree of safety that they are willing to pay for, and what safety they are obtaining is costing them more than necessary. This study finds that the current food safety system in the United States is inefficient for a variety of reasons. The principal reasons follow:

- a misallocation of effort: too much effort devoted to the avoidance of cancer risk from chemical residues, too little effort devoted to risks associated with food-borne diseases and diseases associated with diet

• an overreliance on statutory regulation in general and on outmoded and inefficient process design standards in particular

• an underreliance on incentives for firms and informed individual choice for consumers (education and product labeling)

Yet the elements of a more efficient system are in place, a system that could produce the degree of safety that consumers are willing and able to pay for at minimum cost to both consumers and producers. Based on the background and analyses presented in this study, recommendations for the reform of food safety policy conclude this essay:

• Conduct an independent assessment of priorities to achieve an efficient use of resources across major areas of concern—dietary causes of disease, biological hazards and food-borne disease, and chemical contamination—and amend existing legislation to allow regulatory agencies to allocate effort accordingly.

• Make the first priority of food safety policy to expand research and education to enhance the capacity of producers and consumers to make informed safety choices.

• Replace outdated and inefficient design standards with a combination of safety labeling and efficient performance standards that pass an objective benefit-cost test. In particular, subject proposed HACCP regulations to independent benefit-cost analysis tests.

Food safety policy has not traditionally been a major part of farm legislation. Clearly, this study's recommendation that research, consumer education, and labeling substitute for statutory regulation is consistent with the research and education titles of past farm bills. Many who argue for the consolidation of responsibility of food safety regulation in one agency, however, do not necessarily advocate that these responsibilities be assigned to USDA. But unless this single-agency model becomes a reality, the farm bill could be a vehicle for reform of at least those parts of the food safety regulatory system—notably, meat and poultry inspection—for which USDA currently has responsibility.

In conclusion, the simple message of this study is that we can have safer food at lower cost simply by putting basic economic considerations into the priority setting, design, and implementation of food safety policy.

Background on Food Safety Legislation

The modern era of food safety regulation in the United States began with the passage of the Pure Food and Drug Act of 1906 and the Meat Inspection Act of 1906. Periodic amendments to these acts occurred in 1938, in the 1950s, and subsequently. Other major laws include the Federal Insecticide, Fungicide, and Rodenticide Act (FIFRA) of 1947 and its amendments and the Wholesome Meat Act of 1967. For a history of the Meat Inspection Act, see Libecap (1992). Middlekauff (1989) provides a view of these laws and their amendments, summarized in table 7–1.

The Pure Food and Drug Act and its amendments give the major responsibility for food safety in general, as well as safety and inspection of seafood, to the Food and Drug Administration. The Commerce Department's National Marine Fisheries Service conducts inspection and grading of fish products. Meat, poultry, and egg inspection and related research and education activities are the responsibility of the Department of Agriculture's Food Safety Inspection Service (FSIS). The USDA's Animal and Plant Health Inspection Service has responsibility for programs related to plant health, plant pests and diseases, pest management, and animal disease control, including testing and quarantine of imports. The Environmental Protection Agency is responsible for pesticide regulation in the areas of human health and the environment under FIFRA and section 408 of the Federal Food, Drug, and Cosmetic Act of 1938 (FFDCA). The U.S. Department of Treasury's Bureau of Alcohol, Tobacco, and Firearms is responsible for ingredients in alcoholic beverages and tobacco products.

The FDA and the USDA are also responsible for food labeling. The FSIS is responsible for the regulation of labels for meat and poultry products pursuant to the Federal Meat

TABLE 7–1
SIGNIFICANT EVENTS IN THE REGULATION OF FOOD SAFETY,
1906–1992

Year	Event	Year	Event
1906	Pure Food and Drug Act of 1906 and Meat Inspection Act of 1906 enacted.	1968	Wholesome Poultry Products Act enacted.
1927	Food, Drug, and Insecticide Administration (renamed Food and Drug Administration in 1931) became a separate unit of the U.S. Department of Agriculture.	1969	Good Manufacturing Practices regulations first adopted.
		1970	Egg Products Inspection Act enacted.
1938	Federal Food, Drug, and Cosmetic Act of 1938 enacted.	1975	Corporate officer criminally convicted for sanitation problem in food-containing facility.
1946	Agricultural Marketing Act enacted.	1985	FDA proposed *de minimis* exception to Delaney clause for a food additive in its entirety to allow continued use of methylene chloride to decaffeinate coffee.
1947	Federal Insecticide, Fungicide, and Rodenticide Act enacted.		
1953	Congress gave FDA authority to inspect a plant, after written notice to the owner, without a warrant and without permission of the owner.	1986	FDA stated that food produced by new biotechnology could result in a level of substance that "may be injurious to health."
1957	Poultry Products Inspection Act enacted.	1990	Nutrition Labeling and Education Act enacted.
1958	Food Additives Amendment of 1958 enacted.	1992	U.S. Ninth Circuit Court of Appeals overturned EPA's use of *de minimis* standard for pesticide cancer risk.
1967	Wholesome Meat Act enacted.		

SOURCE: Middlekauff (1989) and the author.

Inspection Act and the Poultry Products Inspection Act. Under FFDCA, the FDA has the responsibility for most other food labeling. The Nutrition Labeling and Education Act of 1990 directed the FDA to improve nutrition labels, a task completed in May 1994. In September 1994 the Clinton administration proposed the Pathogen Reduction Act to modernize regulations for meat inspection. In January 1995 the USDA announced its new plan to modernize meat and poultry inspections systems and to require the use of HACCP by processing plants.

As detailed in the companion to this chapter (Antle 1995), a complex array of laws and public agencies deals with food safety regulation in the United States. These laws and institutions evolved from concerns in the early part of the century with ensuring that only healthy animals enter the food system and that processed food not be adulterated. Today, the breadth and complexity of issues have expanded. Laws and regulations deal with microbial contamination of fresh and processed foods and transmission of food-borne diseases, chemical contamination of fresh and processed foods, the health implications of genetically engineered foods and drugs, the use of irradiation, the health implications of nutrition and food labeling, and international trade issues associated with food safety regulation. Estimates of the costs of food-borne illness run into billions of dollars per year. But estimates of cancer deaths associated with pesticide residues range widely, depending on whether EPA's "conservative" estimates are used or estimates are based on actual food residues.

The Market for Food Safety

Food products have differing safety attributes. Raw seafood is much more likely to contain food-borne disease than a well-done piece of ground beef. In this sense markets exist for food safety, or, more precisely, markets exist for foods with varying safety attributes. In safety as in many other aspects of life, people have differing needs and wants; business firms discern these demands in the marketplace and profit by meeting these demands.

Many choices in safety, however, are not available. Consumers will not buy a product that they consider unsafe. No one willingly buys contaminated meat that will cause illness or death, and firms that sell such products quickly find themselves out of business. Some choices are not available because the government has established universal safety standards. Food safety legislation has provided federal agencies with broad authority to establish standards for fresh and processed foods. But are these regulations necessary? Can't the unregulated market provide the level of food safety consumers are willing and able to pay for?

To answer this question, we need to understand how product markets, with the particular characteristics of food products, work according to economic theory. In this way we can gain an insight into the situations in which the market can provide the level of food safety demanded by consumers. This understanding then provides the basis for considering whether government intervention in these markets can improve on the efficiency of the unregulated market.

Market Information and Market Equilibriums. The textbook theory of competitive markets assumes that consumers and firms possess perfect information about prices and products in the market. But clearly information is costly and imperfect in many markets. By imperfect information we mean that all the attributes relevant to the value of the product are not known. Stiglitz (1989) reviews the literature on product markets with imperfect information, which shows that the properties of market equilibrium depend on the characteristics of the product, on the cost of communicating information among consumers, and on the ability of consumers to use that information.

One way to look at product quality is to ask under what conditions the market will provide the degree of quality that consumers want to purchase. When prepurchase information about product quality is imperfect, then consumers are uncertain about the quality of the product being purchased. Firms could offer a product with a higher price to reflect its higher quality, but this process raises a theoretical problem. If price is used by firms to communicate quality to consumers, then how will the process of competition work, as consumers seek out the lowest price?

In their seminal contribution, Klein and Leffler (1981) resolve this paradox. They ask the question, under what conditions will the unregulated market ensure contractual performance in the sense that firms provide the product quality that consumers believe they are buying? They argue that as long as a substantial number of knowledgeable consumers in the market demand a high-quality product and are willing to pay for it, the higher price is sufficient to ensure that nonperformance (supplying an inferior product) results in a loss greater than the gain from nonperformance. Price in such a market equals minimum average cost, where that cost includes conventional average production costs plus the costs to the firm of establishing its reputation for supplying high quality.

For this discussion of information about attributes of food quality, it is useful to distinguish several types of information.

• *Perfect information.* Both seller and buyer have perfect information about the product. This is the assumption used in the textbook model of a competitive market. In food safety this would occur when a seller credibly reveals product quality to consumers or when consumers can ascertain quality from examination of the product before purchase.

• *Asymmetric imperfect information.* Information is perfect for the firm but imperfect for the consumer. This would be the case if a firm knowingly applied a pesticide to a crop but the consumer could not perceive the residues.

• *Symmetric imperfect information.* Information is imperfect for consumer and producer before and after purchase. This is typically the case of a food-borne disease transmitted through meat, as neither the firm supplying the product nor the consumer is aware that the meat is contaminated.

The literature has identified three categories of goods according to the way consumers obtain information about them (Caswell and Padberg 1992; von Witzke and Hanf 1992). Search goods are those for which consumers have perfect information before purchase; experience goods can be judged only after purchase; and credence goods are those whose quality cannot be judged even after purchase. Thus, both experience goods and credence goods correspond to cases of imperfect information, either asymmetric or symmetric, because their definition does not consider the type of information available to the firm. The distinction between asymmetric and symmetric imperfect information plays a key role in the analysis of efficient regulation.

Properties of Market Equilibriums. Some qualities of food safety are detectable by sight, smell, or touch, that is, by organoleptic inspection. Firms may declare a food's qualities, as in branded, genetically altered foods with desirable nutritional or safety qualities. In these cases the consumer may have nearly perfect safety information.

Even though food products may be differentiated by safety and nutritional characteristics, a competitive market can exist for the product as long as the standard conditions supporting competition exist. In the ideal case of perfect information, identical informed consumers, and free entry for identical, competitive producers, the perfectly competitive market functions efficiently. It provides consumers with the product they demand at the minimum average cost of production.

When competitive firms can produce products with different levels of safety, then the marginal cost of safety is equated with the marginal benefit of safety in competitive equilibrium: the competitive market achieves the "right" level of safety. The market then provides just as much safety as consumers are willing and able to buy.

If safety were costless, everyone would want perfect safety. But because safety is costly, perfectly informed, rational consumers generally choose less than 100 percent safety. One important policy implication is that regulations striving to achieve zero risk are misguided on two counts. Zero risk is rarely achievable at any cost, and even if achievable, it is rarely desired by those who know the true benefits and have to pay the costs of achieving it.

Few product markets meet the conditions of the perfectly competitive market, but many approximate them well enough for an efficient allocation of resources. Important violations of the perfectly competitive conditions may, however, result in an inefficient level of safety. We now consider those violations of the perfectly competitive market model and discuss their effects on market equilibrium.

Imperfect information means that consumers lack perfect information about quality before they purchase a product. But when consumers realize the quality of the product after purchase, reputation can play an important role in determining the property of market equilibrium. This is typical of acute illness from toxic residues or of food-borne disease contracted immediately after consumption. If consumers repeatedly buy a product, firms that provide a higher quality (more safe) product can charge a higher price for it, and the market with imperfect prepurchase information can achieve the same outcome as the market with perfect information. When consumers purchase a product only once, an efficient equilibrium can be attained as long as consumers can exchange product information or otherwise obtain product information at low cost. Here again firms can establish a reputation for a high-quality product and charge a commensurately high price to cover the cost of producing the product and of establishing its quality reputation.

Many food markets satisfy the conditions that allow firms to establish reputations for quality. Repeat purchases are typical of virtually all households' demand for food consumed at home. Moreover, low-cost information about product quality is available by word-of-mouth, newspapers, consumer information publications, and so forth. In addition, the rise of fast-food chains has made repeat purchases typical for food consumed outside the home.

Consumers usually cannot know about product quality either before or after purchase when that quality involves the chemical composition of the food, contamination with toxic chemicals, or the presence of microorganisms. Whereas acute effects of chemical contamination may be associated with the food source, the chronic effects of low-level exposure to toxins, such as cancer-causing substances, are difficult to know because the effects are delayed for many years. Moreover, because the causes of cancer and many other diseases are not well understood, it is difficult for consumers to associate exposure to any particular substance with a disease. Some acute effects of toxins or food-borne illness are delayed enough to prevent associating the disease with the consumption of a contaminated food. Consumers typically cannot discern quality that is related to the production process, as when food is irradiated or milk is produced with animals treated with genetically altered growth hormones.

Because under these conditions it is difficult for firms to establish reputations for quality, the distinction between asymmetric imperfect information and symmetric imperfect information becomes important. With the latter, the firm itself does not know all the quality attributes and so cannot reveal them even if it wants to or is required to do so by law. As the discussion of policy options in the next section reveals, this difference plays a role in designing appropriate policies when the market fails to achieve the efficient degree of safety.

Clearly, when consumers cannot distinguish low-quality from high-quality products, the reputation mechanism cannot work effectively to achieve an efficient level of safety. Consequently, a Gresham's law of product quality applies, with bad (low-quality, low-cost) products chasing good (high-quality, high-cost) products out of the market. Thus, under these conditions the market fails to provide consumers who want a high-quality, safer product with the opportunity to buy it.

Consumer Knowledge of Safety. A knowledgeable consumer can assess the quality attributes of a product if the information is available; a consumer lacking such knowledge cannot assess product quality even with perfect quality information. Clearly, if none of the consumers were knowledgeable about food safety, there would not be a de-

TABLE 7–2
Efficiency of Equilibriums in the Market for Food Safety

Product and Consumer Types	Perfect	Imperfect with quality realized after purchase	Imperfect with quality not realized after purchase
		Type of Information	
Repeat purchases or low-cost information	Efficient	Efficient	Inefficient
Single purchases and high-cost information	Efficient	Inefficient	Inefficient
Unknowledgeable consumers	Inefficient	Inefficient	Inefficient

Source: Author.

mand for safety. For most long-standing safety issues, it can be assumed that there are many knowledgeable consumers, whereas most consumers may be unknowledgeable about new issues such as the use of bovine growth hormone to raise dairy cow production.

Under these conditions, competitive markets with symmetric perfect information or with imperfect information and reputable firms will provide an efficient level of safety for the knowledgeable consumers for the reasons described above. But what about the consumers who lack the knowledge to use product safety information? Generally, the market provides whatever safety characteristics are economically feasible. The uninformed consumer is provided these options but does not know how to evaluate them in terms of safety and would have to select among them according to criteria other than safety, such as price. Assuming that unknowledgeable consumers select the product with the lowest price, and therefore the lowest quality, some will obtain less safety than they would if they were knowledgeable. But because the market does not fail to provide consumers with choices, we cannot conclude that the market is inefficient.

When Is the Market Efficient? Based on the preceding discussion, we can conclude that efficient outcomes in the market for food safety can be obtained not only in the textbook case of a competitive market with perfect information but also in other important cases:

• when products are repeatedly purchased or low-cost product information is available and when consumers can ascertain product quality either before or after purchase so that firms can establish reputations for product quality and charge a higher price for high-quality products
• when a sufficient number of knowledgeable consumers exist to generate a demand for safety representative of the preferences of the larger population

Second, inefficient outcomes in the market for food safety can be obtained under several circumstances:

• when information is imperfect, consumers purchase a product only once, and information costs are high
• when information is imperfect for consumers both before and after purchase
• when a majority of consumers are unknowledgeable about product safety attributes

The principal results of this discussion are summarized in table 7–2. In three of these nine stylized cases, the unregulated market achieves efficient equilibriums. Assuming that a relatively large proportion of the population is knowledgeable about food safety reduces the number of inefficient cases to three. Additionally, many food purchases are characterized by repeat purchases or relatively low-cost information. Thus in all these cases economic theory predicts that the unregulated market is likely to meet the food safety demands of the public efficiently. Only when consumers' information is imperfect, both before and after purchase, is the market likely to fail to provide the desired degree of food product safety efficiently.

TABLE 7–3
EFFICIENT POLICY TOOLS IN THE MARKET FOR FOOD SAFETY

Product and Consumer Types	Perfect	Imperfect with realization after purchase	Asymmetric imperfect without realization after purchase	Symmetric imperfect without realization after purchase
		Type of Information		
Repeat purchases or low-cost information exchange	Market	Market	Labeling	Performance standards
SIngle purchases and high-cost information exchange	Market	Liability	Labeling	Performance standards
Consumers lacking safety knowledge	Education	Education and liability	Education and labeling	Education and performance standards

SOURCE: Author.

Principles and Tools for Efficient Food Safety Regulation

The previous section described several key conditions that may give rise to inefficient outcomes in the market for food safety. Imperfect information, incomplete markets, and uninformed consumers were identified as possible causes of market inefficiency. Thus government regulation may have a role in the market for food safety.

But saying that there *may* be a role for regulation does not mean that there *should* be regulation, nor does that possibility tell us what form regulation should take when warranted. Four economic principles should guide the design of food safety regulations and the policy options that are available and used in the food safety area. We refer the reader to the companion monograph (Antle 1995) for a detailed discussion of these principles.

Principle 1. Food safety regulations designed to correct market failures are justified if, and only if, they pass a benefit-cost analysis test.

Principle 2. Regulatory benefit-cost analysis should be conducted independently of regulatory agencies and should provide comparable treatment of the uncertainties in benefit estimation and in cost estimation.

Principle 3. Informed individual choice of safety is preferred to statutory safety standards when risk preferences are heterogeneous.

Principle 4. Performance standards and incentive-based regulation are more efficient than design standards.

Efficient Food Safety Regulation. We now consider how these principles lead to a choice of policy tools that would be best suited to the cases where the market may not be efficient, as identified in table 7–3. Although the table is not an exhaustive delineation of situations in food safety, it is representative of important cases. For this discussion, we consider the following policy tools:

• *Product safety research and consumer education.* This category includes research on food safety knowledge and technology that are public goods and educational programs designed to convey food safety knowledge to consumers.

• *Product labeling requirements.* Firms are required to label products regarding their ingredients or any other characteristics that are deemed relevant to safety.

• *Safety performance standards that pass a benefit-cost analysis test.* Products marketed by firms are required to conform to standards of safety defined by law or by a regulatory agency.

• *Liability.* The design of rules regarding negligence or strict liability that allow private individuals or groups of individuals to seek compensation from harm caused by a firm's product through the courts.

As table 7–3 shows, markets for products that consumers repeatedly purchase are efficient when information is perfect and also when information is imperfect and firms can establish a reputation for product quality. These markets are inefficient when consumers cannot discern product quality either before or after purchase, as with low levels of pesticide residues in foods. Consequently, reputation or low-cost exchange of information among consumers does not provide an incentive for firms to provide more than the minimal degree of safety that consumers can ascertain.

As long as consumers are knowledgeable about the use of food safety information, the obvious solution to the information problem is to require firms to label products with information relevant to safety. Firms know what pesticides they have used in food production; some form of labeling could be devised, as with nutrition labeling, to provide consumers with usable safety information. Viscusi (1993) discusses some issues that arise in product safety labeling. Consumers could choose among products with different price and safety attributes.

As Shavell (1987) notes, one situation in which safety standards are likely to be more efficient than liability is when consumers have difficulty knowing or proving harm *ex post*. Consumers do not know, for example, if the foods they eat contain pesticide residues and would have difficulty proving that chronic exposure to toxic chemicals in food caused cancer. Even when consumers have heterogeneous safety preferences, consensus for a minimal degree of safety is likely. Therefore a statutory minimum safety standard that passes a benefit-cost analysis test could be efficient. With a system of required safety labeling, those consumers who preferred a higher degree of safety than the minimum could obtain it if such a market were economically feasible.

With symmetric imperfect information neither the firm nor the consumer knows all of a product's safety attributes. The seller of produce, for example, may know that certain pesticides are used in the production process but may not know whether sufficient residues are likely to be present in the product to pose a health risk. Clearly such information about pesticides is a public good, and there is an inadequate incentive for individual firms to produce it. Thus there is also a role for public funding of research to generate health and safety information.

The tourist-trap restaurant is an example of a single-purchase product with high-cost product quality information. These markets are efficient with perfect information but inefficient with imperfect information. With a high cost of information, firms are unable to establish reputations for quality, and so the market equilibrium provides only low product quality. Because health risks often involve acute effects, as with food-borne illnesses, firms typically exercise some degree of precaution. In these situations nonperformance is usually idiosyncratic and can be handled effectively through liability. A well-functioning liability law would induce an efficient level of precaution in these cases except for firms with few assets; those cases may require firms to have liability insurance. It might be argued, for example, that with fresh meat, poultry, and fish products, liability would not be sufficient to ensure that small processing firms would take adequate safety precautions, whereas larger firms would. If insurance markets for small firms are not functioning well, then the appropriate policy would be to correct the failure in the insurance market.

The most glaring fact in table 7–3 is that, regardless of information regime, the outcome is not efficient when most consumers lack knowledge of the safety attributes of a product. Even a well-functioning competitive market cannot make choices for people. Clearly such knowledge is a public good, and therefore public consumer education is warranted. Publicly funded research can develop the knowledge that consumers need.

Despite educational efforts, some consumers may remain unable to make decisions for themselves or their families. Indeed, this is an issue much studied in the nutrition field (National Research Council 1990). Consumer ignorance is not an indication of an inefficiently functioning market, but it apparently is an important motivation for the paternalistic view that government is responsible for those who seemingly cannot take care of themselves. It can be argued that because education, labeling, and liability rules are ineffective to protect these individuals, statutory regulations should be invoked.

According to principles 1 and 2 cited earlier, a performance standard designed to protect unknowledgeable consumers should pass a benefit-cost analysis test. The setting of an acceptable standard will depend on the number of consumers who benefit from the standard and the costs associated with the standard. One cost of a uniform standard is lack of choice for those informed consumers who would prefer a lower level of safety than is imposed by the standard. Without a standard the market provides the minimal degree of safety that knowledgeable consumers demand. A benefit-cost analysis can determine if more people would fare better with a statutory standard.

The results of this analysis are summarized in table 7–3. For most cases, education, labeling, and liability are efficient solutions. Notably, even when consumers have imperfect quality information before and after purchase of a product, product labeling requirements can solve the consumers' information problem as long as producers and sellers have quality information. The one class of problems where statutory regulation is indicated as a possibly efficient solution is when *both* consumers and producers have imperfect information about product quality.

Toward Regulatory Reform

The preceding sections of this chapter analyzed the efficiency of the unregulated market for food safety and outlined principles for efficient regulation in those cases where market outcomes are not efficient. This discussion applies those analyses to assess the current regulatory system. This assessment in turn provides the basis for recommendations for regulatory reforms.

The earlier analysis identified characteristics of food product markets that are likely to cause those markets to function efficiently in terms of food safety quality. Two broad sets of conditions appear to be necessary for market efficiency:

• Firms must be able to establish reputations for quality and to charge a price that reflects this quality.
• Enough consumers in the market must have the knowledge needed to evaluate safety attributes of foods.

Remarkably, then, economic analysis suggests that the majority of product markets can provide the efficient measure of food product safety with, at most, labeling requirements. When some consumers lack adequate knowledge of food safety, public education programs are warranted.

Existing nutrition labeling and education policy is broadly consistent with this analysis. Rather than attempt to legislate what kinds of foods people eat, nutrition education efforts such as those in the Nutrition Labeling and Education Act are designed to complement labeling. Recent efforts by the USDA's Food Safety Inspection Service to use safety labeling and education have emphasized the importance of consumer information and education in reducing the incidence of food-borne illness. The analysis in this study supports an expanded role for consumer research and education to develop safety labeling and education as a substitute for unnecessary and inefficient standards and design regulations implemented under FFDCA.

Most statutory regulation of food safety under FFDCA is broadly *inconsistent* with the conclusions of the preceding analysis. The food adulteration concepts of the act have led to a heavy reliance on design standards rather than performance standards. Moreover, the provisions of sections 408 and 409 of FFDCA regarding food additives and the regulation of pesticides involve the imposition of zero-risk standards that are inconsistent with the economic analysis of efficient regulatory procedures.

The preceding analysis indicates one general set of conditions under which statutory safety standards may be required, namely, when both firms and consumers have imperfect information about product safety before and after purchase. These conditions correspond to the contamination of food with microorganisms, chemicals, and other hazards that are not readily tested for in the manufacturing process and affected consumers cannot readily associate with a food source.

Recommendations for Regulatory Reform. The full-length monograph (Antle 1995) details existing legislation and the degree to which it is consistent with the regulatory principles outlined above. Based on the preceding discussion of economic theory and regulatory principles and on this assessment of existing regulation, we propose the following recommendations for regulatory reform.

Recommendation 1. Undertake an independent, across-the-board assessment of priorities to determine whether research, education, and the various forms of regulation are being efficiently utilized and how food safety regulatory activity of the federal government would be most efficiently organized.

Numerous consumer groups, industry representatives, and scientists argue that regulation of food safety would be conducted more efficiently if all responsibilities were assigned to one agency. The single-agency model could facilitate the assessment of priorities and resource allocation across the various areas of such regulation. It does seem reasonable to ask whether it is time to consider consolidating the diverse laws and agencies that are involved in food safety regulation.

There are several problems, however, with the single-agency model. First, where does food safety responsibility end and health, environment, and other areas of responsibility begin? Many areas of health and safety overlap. Would the assignment of all responsibilities to a single agency provide the correct incentives within the bureaucracy? It could be argued that a multiagency system of checks and balances would be better. Independent rather than in-house benefit-cost analyses are needed to assure objectivity. This problem suggests a different, decentralized model for the redesign of food safety regulation, wherein legislation assigns responsibility for benefit-cost analyses to an independent agency or even an extragovernmental organization and also requires implementing agencies to allocate effort and resources accordingly.

Recommendation 2. A principal goal of food safety policies for research, education, and design of statutory standards should be to enhance the capacity of producers and consumers to make informed safety choices.

• Research and education to support safe storage, handling, and cooking by consumers and food service workers.

• Research and education to improve knowledge about the linkages between diet, nutrition, and health.

• Research to develop criteria for safety labeling. Various questions must be addressed to implement safety labeling. How should safety be integrated with nutritional considerations in design of labels? How can a system of variable safety standards and labeling replace the system of uniform standards? What types of safety concerns can be supported with this type of system?

• Develop safety labeling for products produced with new technologies when risk data indicate they are appropriate. Allow new technologies with higher risks to be used subject to labeling requirements that indicate scientifically established risks. Revise technology approval rules to streamline the approval process for technologies that are considered to be low risk.

• Allow products to be labeled as certifiably produced by a process, with the costs of such certification borne by producers and consumers of those products (for example, brandname labeling of foods genetically engineered for longer shelf life, improved nutritional content, or greater safety; labeling of products as organically grown without pesticides; labeling of dairy products as not produced with cows treated with rBST).

Recommendation 3. Where industrywide food safety performance standards are indicated as the most efficient regulatory approach and where firms and consumers have imperfect safety information both before and after production and consumption of a food product, the standards should pass an objective benefit-cost analysis test.

- Replacement of the Delaney clause with a *de minimis* risk standard to be applied to all products, whether raw or processed. Pesticide registration should be allowed for those products that exceed *de minimis* risk if they pass a benefit-cost analysis test. Foods that are expected to contain higher than *de minimis* residue levels should be labeled accordingly.
- Research to support development of efficient performance standards and testing procedures.
- Development of integrated economic, medical, and biological data for risk assessments needed to set efficient standards.
- Research to compare the efficiency of HACCP systems with final product performance standards.
- Benefit-cost analysis tests for hazards to be controlled and for critical control points in HACCP systems.

Recommendation 4. Process design standards should be replaced by a system of performance standards and incentives.

- Development of safety standards and labeling to support product markets for safety-differentiated products.
- Research funding to support development of efficient standards and testing procedures for biological, chemical, and physical hazards. Specifically, the integration of economic, disease incidence, and health data to support the identification of hazards for control.
- Definition of HACCP systems as performance standards, not as design standards, at each stage of production.

Implications for the 1995 Farm Bill. Food safety was not a principal objective of the 1990 farm bill or its predecessors. Whether the 1995 farm bill should have such a goal is questionable. Advocates of an overhaul of food safety legislation, such as the Safe Food Coalition, would have all food safety regulatory authority assigned to one agency, such as the FDA. These consumer groups argue that food safety reform should assign responsibility for meat inspection to the FDA. According to this view, clearly food safety legislation should not be incorporated into the 1995 farm bill. But unless such comprehensive food safety reform is undertaken and food safety responsibility is assigned to an agency other than USDA, it seems appropriate to consider the degree to which the food safety policy reforms outlined above could fit into new farm legislation, perhaps in the form of a food safety title. Several important aspects of needed reforms could be addressed in the 1995 farm bill.

• *Research.* Publicly funded research is needed in important areas to improve the science base for food safety education and to devise more efficient regulations such as those for safety labeling. The USDA has a substantial capacity to conduct this research in land-grant universities, private universities, and the private sector. To ensure that this research is performed on a competitive basis, a component of a national research initiative could be targeted to address the research questions in the food safety area.

• *Education.* Consumer education is a critical aspect of an efficient approach to food safety policy. The farm bill could specifically direct cooperative extensions to address needed food safety education to complement the Nutrition Labeling and Education Act of 1990.

• *Efficient regulation.* The recent USDA reorganization established an office to conduct benefit-cost analyses of USDA regulations. The above recommendations are consistent with the goal of subjecting USDA's regulations to benefit-cost tests, but the proposal to conduct these analyses within USDA has several problems. First, USDA's Economic Research Service has the capacity to conduct benefit-cost analyses and has done a number of such studies (for example, on ethanol policy, the Conservation Reserve Program). Second, as noted, regulatory benefit-cost analyses need to be done independently of implementing agencies to ensure objectivity.

References

Antle, J. M. *Choice, Efficiency, and Food Safety Policy.* Washington, D.C.: AEI Press, 1995.

Caswell, J. A., and D. I. Padberg. "Toward a More Comprehensive Theory of Food Labels." *American Journal of Agricultural Economics* 74 (May 1992): 460–68.

Food and Drug Administration. "Food Safety Assurance Program; Development of Hazard Analysis Critical Control Points; Proposed Rule." *Federal Register*, August 4, 1994: 39888–39896.

Klein, B., and K. B. Leffler. "The Role of Market Forces in Assuring Contractual Performance." *Journal of Political Economy* 89 (August 1981): 615–41.

Libecap, G. D. "The Rise of the Chicago Packers and the Origins of Meat Inspection and Antitrust." *Economic Inquiry* 30 (April 1992): 242–62.

Middlekauff, R. D. "Regulating the Safety of Food." *Food Technology* 43 (September 1989): 296–307.

National Research Council, Committee on the Nutrition Components of Food Labeling. *Nutrition Labeling: Issues and Directions for the 1990s.* Washington, D.C.: National Academy Press, 1990.

Shavell, S. *Economic Analysis of Accident Law.* Cambridge: Harvard University Press, 1987.

Stiglitz, J. E. "Imperfect Information in the Product Market." In *Handbook of Industrial Organization,* edited by R. Schmalensee and R. D. Willig. Vol. 1. Amsterdam: North-Holland Publishing Co., 1989.

U.S. Department of Agriculture, "Statement by Richard Rominger on New Food Safety Proposals." Office of the Secretary, January 31, 1995.

Viscusi, W. K. *Product Safety Labeling: A Federal Responsibility.* Washington, D.C.: AEI Press, 1993.

von Witzke, H., and C.-H. Hanf. "BST and International Agricultural Trade and Policy." In *Bovine Somatotropin and Emerging Issues: An Assessment,* edited by M. C. Hallberg. Boulder: Westview Press, 1992.

8
Farm Credit Policy

Peter J. Barry

Public credit programs and financial policies have long played a significant role in agricultural finance. The channels of influence come through government loan programs, government-sponsored enterprises, and regulations of depository institutions. The general rationale for public intervention is usually based on two issues (Bosworth, Carron, and Rhyne 1987). First, private credit markets cannot meet the social objectives and priorities affecting the allocation of resources and distribution of income. Second, perceived imperfections in private credit markets result in credit rationing, market failure, or other types of credit gaps. Programs that focus on correcting market imperfections need not require subsidization; they are considered to be the more successful government programs in credit markets. In contrast, efforts to achieve public purposes generally involve subsidization, with significant questions raised about the form, magnitude, length, measurability, and recipients of the subsidies.

This chapter discusses farm financial policy with an emphasis on public credit programs and their effects on the farm sector. First, the chapter reviews the major characteristics of U.S. agriculture and sources of agricultural credit. Then, public credit programs—in particular, the programs of the Farmers Home Administration, the Farm Credit System, and the Federal Agricultural Mortgage Corporation—are evaluated.[1] A concluding section considers the general

---

1. The restructuring of the U.S. Department of Agriculture in 1994 resulted in the termination of the Farmers Home Administration and

implications for the role of public credit in financing a diverse agricultural sector.

U.S. Agriculture and Agricultural Lenders

Over the years, U.S. farmers have relied heavily on credit to finance their capital base, to mechanize and modernize their farming operations, to conduct marketing and production plans, and to serve as a valuable source of liquidity in responding to risks. Readily available credit has facilitated many of the significant, long-term changes in the farm sector—larger farm sizes, fewer numbers, greater specialization, greater capital intensity, adoption of new technology, stronger market coordination, and others. Thus, equitable access to credit is important to the economic contributions and financial performance of the agricultural sector.

Despite these structural changes and the related role of credit, public credit programs have played important historical roles in maintaining a pluralistic, smaller scale, and largely (but by no means complete) noncorporate organization of agricultural production units, arrangements seemingly consistent with the public interest. Credit has been viewed as a facilitating tool for aggregate structural change but not as a driving force (Gustafson and Barry 1993). The increasing "industrialization of agriculture," however, especially in livestock and poultry production, is challenging this historic perspective.

In the mid-1990s, agriculture can be characterized as a capital-intensive industry, in which the dominance of farm real estate has brought liquidity and debt-carrying problems, with significant reliance on leasing of farmland by farm operators. Production units are mostly of smaller scale, although the gap is widening between numerous small, part-time farms and the relatively few but much

---

the transfer of its farm loan programs to the new Consolidated Farm Service Agency. This chapter, however, will continue to refer to the Farmers Home Administration for familiarity and in reference to its programs of the past.

more economically significant commercial-scale operations. Considerable consolidation of production units is continuing to occur, especially in livestock, along with movements toward greater contract, integrated, and financial arrangements with input suppliers and food companies (Barkema and Cook 1993a, 1993b). Reductions in the availability of government contracts through traditional commodity programs will likely bring greater contractual opportunities for crop producers with input suppliers and processors. Business and financial risks in agriculture are high, but numerous risk management options are available, especially for larger operators. In general, a tri-modal distribution of agricultural production units is emerging to include (1) large, independent, commercial-scale farms and ranches operated by one or more farm families; (2) the industrialized component of production agriculture, involving vertical integration, contract production, and other forms of vertical coordination; and (3) a large number of small, part-time, or limited-resource farms, many of which rely heavily on earnings from nonfarm employment and investments. Diminishing in number and importance are the medium-sized family farms, which dominated the agricultural landscape of the past.

The major sources of financial capital (besides equity capital) for agricultural production units include the Farm Credit System (FCS), commercial banks, life insurance companies, the Farmers Home Administration, agribusiness firms, and individuals (see table 8–1 for the levels and market shares of total farm debt held by these credit sources). The FCS institutions began the 1980s with the largest market share of farm debt, especially farm real estate debt. Since the mid-1980s, however, the FCS has experienced a substantial decline in loan volume, massive institutional restructuring, rebuilding of the system's equity capital, and the burden of repaying $1.26 billion of federal assistance acquired during the 1980s.

Commercial banks, which were surpassed by the FCS as the dominant farm lender in the 1970s, reestablished that position in the late 1980s, with especially strong growth in

213

TABLE 8–1

TOTAL U.S. FARM DEBT, EXCLUDING OPERATOR HOUSEHOLDS, 1976–1993
(millions of dollars)

Year	Farm Credit System	Commercial banks	Farmers Home Administration	Life insurance companies	Total	Individuals and Others[a]	Total Debt
			Debt Owed to Reporting Institutions				
1976	29,007	28,077	4,963	6,828	68,874	27,191	96,065
1977	32,992	31,289	6,378	8,150	78,808	32,047	110,855
1978	37,564	34,435	8,833	9,698	90,529	36,871	127,400
1979	45,376	37,125	14,442	11,278	108,222	43,329	151,551
1980	52,974	37,751	17,464	11,998	120,188	46,636	166,824
1981	61,566	38,798	20,802	12,150	133,316	49,065	182,381
1982	64,220	41,890	21,274	11,829	139,214	49,592	188,806
1983	63,710	45,422	21,428	11,668	142,228	48,842	191,070
1984	64,688	47,245	23,262	11,891	147,086	46,701	193,787
1985	56,169	44,470	24,535	11,273	136,447	41,152	177,599
1986	45,909	41,621	24,138	10,377	122,044	34,926	156,970
1987	40,030	41,130	23,553	9,355	114,069	30,342	144,411
1988	37,138	42,706	21,852	9,018	110,714	28,654	139,368
1989	36,218	44,795	18,974	9,045	109,030	28,201	137,231
1990	35,567	47,425	16,950	9,631	109,573	27,794	137,367
1991	35,382	50,169	15,213	9,494	110,259	28,612	138,871
1992	35,616	51,571	13,504	8,718	109,410	29,860	139,270
1993[b]	35,556	53,739	12,211	8,521	110,028	31,327	141,355

Percentage Distribution of Total Debt

Year							
1976	30.2	39.2	5.2	7.1	71.7	28.2	100.0
1977	29.8	28.2	5.8	7.4	71.1	28.9	100.0
1978	29.5	27.0	6.9	7.6	71.1	28.9	100.0
1979	29.9	24.5	9.5	7.4	71.4	28.6	100.0
1980	31.8	22.6	10.5	7.2	72.0	28.0	100.0
1981	33.8	21.3	11.4	6.7	73.1	26.9	100.0
1982	34.0	22.2	11.3	6.3	73.7	26.3	100.0
1983	33.3	23.8	11.2	6.1	74.4	25.6	100.0
1984	33.4	24.4	12.0	6.1	75.9	24.1	100.0
1985	31.6	25.0	13.8	6.3	76.8	23.2	100.0
1986	29.2	26.5	15.4	6.6	77.7	22.3	100.0
1987	27.7	28.5	16.3	6.5	79.0	21.0	100.0
1988	26.6	30.6	15.7	6.5	79.5	20.5	100.0
1989	26.4	32.6	13.8	6.6	79.5	20.5	100.0
1990	25.9	34.5	12.3	7.0	79.8	20.2	100.0
1991	25.5	36.1	11.0	6.8	79.7	20.6	100.0
1992	25.6	37.0	9.7	6.3	78.6	21.4	100.0
1993[b]	25.2	38.0	8.6	6.0	77.8	22.2	100.0

a. Includes individuals and others (land for contract, merchants, and dealers credit, etc.), CCC storage and drying facilities loans, and Farmer Mac loans.
b. Preliminary figures.
SOURCE: U.S. Department of Agriculture (1994).

farm real estate debt. Banks were also hard hit by farm loan problems in the 1980s, but the greater diversity in loan portfolios and shorter average maturities of agricultural loans allowed quicker identification and resolution of loan problems. Much of the commercial bank debt (56.3 percent in 1993) is provided by smaller, agricultural banks that are heavily dependent on their local communities for lending opportunities and sources of deposits. Continued geographic liberalization, including the interstate banking legislation of 1994, however, is moving the banking industry toward greater involvement in agricultural lending by larger banking systems.

Market shares of farm real estate debt held by individuals (mostly sellers of farmland) have declined substantially, from above 30 percent of total farm real estate debt before 1981 to the 21–23 percent range in the 1990s. Market shares of life insurance company loans for farm real estate have declined modestly, although fewer insurance companies have been making larger loans with a shift away from the Midwest toward the South and the West Coast. Financing provided to farmers by input suppliers and other agribusiness firms has long been an important source of non–real estate credit. In recent years, trade firms have become a dominant source of financing for farm machinery, and a number of large agribusinesses have begun to provide line-of-credit financing to their customers.

Farm lending by the U.S. government has come from the Farmers Home Administration and the Commodity Credit Corporation. FmHA lending has fluctuated inversely with the financial performance of the agricultural sector. It increased sharply during the 1980s, reflecting various types of emergency loan programs and the serious economic problems of agriculture during these times. Agricultural lending by state credit programs and the Small Business Administration (mostly in the 1970s and early 1980s) has been relatively small.

Perspectives on Public Credit Programs

The rapid growth in public credit programs and their prominent position in the financial markets have brought increasing attention to the intended goals, mechanisms, subsidies, payoffs, accounting procedures, and general effectiveness of these programs (Bosworth, Carron, and Rhyne 1987; Budget of the United States 1994). Major questions have been raised about the appropriateness of credit programs relative to other mechanisms for providing subsidies. Credit programs have weaknesses in transmitting subsidies because the loan funds may be used for unintended purposes, the borrowers may have access to credit from other sources, the subsidy benefits may accrue to private lenders rather than to borrowers, or favorable terms of credit may be capitalized into the value of assets being financed.

More fundamentally, using credit markets to transmit subsidies undermines the integrity of inherently fragile financial markets. A financial market's primary function is to facilitate financial intermediation by adjusting the liquidity and risk positions of savers and investors. Because credit transactions involve intangible financial assets and promises to repay, high levels of confidence, trust, discipline, and stability are needed for these markets to function effectively. Extensive government regulation contributes to market effectiveness. Adding a subsidy, however, is counterproductive to effectiveness. Thus, the larger the subsidy needed to achieve the public purpose, the less the assistance should be channeled through public credit programs.

Since the early 1980s, the federal government has substantially upgraded its concepts and procedures for managing, controlling, and accounting for federal credit programs. In 1984, the Office of Management and Budget issued guidelines for a more systematic budget and accounting process that clearly shows the magnitude, composition, and form of federal credit and estimates the subsidies conveyed to borrowers. In addition, the Federal Credit Reform Act of 1990 fundamentally changed the budgetary treatment of direct loans and loan guarantees by requiring budgeting for the costs of these programs. Recording the full cost as a requirement when the government

217

enters into a loan obligation or guarantee commitment replaces the previous procedure of accounting for loan disbursement and repayments on a cash basis. The cost approach provides more accurate information for public decision making and for comparing interprogram lending costs. The estimated 1995 subsidy rates for the farm lending programs of FmHA, for example, were 13.03 percent for direct loans and 2.49 percent for guaranteed loans. In general, the lower "costs" of guaranteed loans relative to direct loans make guarantees the preferred method of assistance and explain the dominance of guaranteed-loan programs over direct loan programs.

The Farmers Home Administration

The FmHA was established in 1946 as the result of a lengthy series of legislative enactments and agency developments intended to meet the financing needs of agricultural borrowers who could not obtain credit from commercial sources. The characteristics of these borrowers have changed over time but have generally included impoverished, destitute farm families; young farmers entering the sector; small yet potentially viable farms; limited-resource farms; and larger farms experiencing significant distress due to natural disasters and economic emergencies. In addition to its farm loan programs, the agency has also provided extensive credit programs for the nonfarm activities of rural residents and rural communities. Included over the years have been loans for rural housing, water facilities, waste disposal systems, rural businesses, and other development programs.

Downsizing versus Responding to Financial Stress. At the beginning of the 1980s, there were a clear understanding and widespread agreement that direct public lending through FmHA to agriculture had become excessive and needed curtailment to restore the agency's last-resort role (Lee and Gabriel 1980; Barry 1985). Curtailment at that time seemed feasible because of (1) the high taxpayer cost of public credit and other farm programs; (2) stronger financial performance expected for the farm sector; (3) slower growth in farm debt; (4) expanded use of the revised federal crop insurance program for disaster protection; (5) more effective use of loan guarantees in public credit programs; and (6) more effective risk management by agricultural lenders.

This redefinition of FmHA lending was thwarted, however, by considerable financial stress on farms in the 1980s, political pressures involving farm credit, and ineffectiveness of the crop insurance program. Instead of downsizing, the agency increased its provision of financial assistance to the agricultural sector and even now continues to carry a great deal of adversely classified credit in its loan portfolio. It is not surprising, however, that public credit would increase in stress times and that the lingering effects of the financial stresses of the 1980s would weigh more heavily on the lender of last resort, in contrast to the quicker recoveries of agricultural banks and the Farm Credit System. In addition, the significant amount of federal assistance channeled through FmHA in the 1980s probably reduced the adversity experienced by the FCS and agricultural banks. In the absence of FmHA, the needs for financial assistance by the FCS would probably have been much greater than the $1.26 billion actually used. Loan losses of the agency totaled $16.19 billion over the 1986–1993 period, compared with losses of $3.1 billion for the FCS, $2.18 billion for commercial banks, and $2.49 billion for life insurance companies (U.S. Department of Agriculture 1994).

Current Developments in the Farmers Home Administration. By 1994 the FmHA had achieved two major accomplishments. First, the level of credit channeled through its farm programs was substantially reduced. New loan obligations declined from $6.28 billion in 1980 to $5.92 billion in 1985, $2.17 billion in 1990, and $2.13 billion in 1993. Similarly, farm debt outstanding from direct loans from FmHA declined from $24.54 billion in 1980 to $12.21 billion in 1993, although a major part of this reduction is attributed to loan losses (U.S. Department of Agriculture 1994).

Second, the form of FmHA lending swung significantly toward guaranteed loans rather than direct loans. Considering the farm ownership and operating loans only, new obligations were 97.1 percent direct loans and 2.9 percent guaranteed loans in 1980, 78.4 percent direct and 21.6 percent guaranteed in 1985, and 29.5 percent direct and 70.5 percent guaranteed in 1993. The shift toward guaranteed loans is consistent with the mandate of the Office of Management and Budget in 1984 and legislative enactments in 1985. The shift reflects the lower subsidy cost and other merits of guaranteed loans cited earlier. The agency is sensitive to these subsidy costs and to the concept of cost control along with an operating goal of serving as many farm borrowers as possible, given the size of the annual allocations.

Graduation Attributes of the Loan Programs. A continuing issue in FmHA farm loan programs has been the length of participation by individual borrowers and the prospects for "graduating" these borrowers to commercial credit (Barry 1985). Agency regulations define graduation as "the payment in full of an FmHA loan before maturity by refinancing through other credit sources." Graduation is the ultimate objective of a public credit program in which eligible borrowers are presumed to have potential for future viability and development of creditworthiness sufficient to qualify for commercial financing. Since 1989, the agency has used a credit-scoring model for its direct loan borrowers, taking account of five factors: (1) the agency's security margin in collateral pledged as loan security; (2) the borrower's debt-to-asset ratio; (3) the current ratio; (4) return on assets; and (5) repayment ability. The model places borrowers in one of five credit classes: commercial, standard, substandard, doubtful, and loss.

The commercial class includes borrowers who would appear to be acceptable for financing by commercial lenders. Personnel in county or local FmHA offices have assessed graduation potential by following several steps: they monitor fund availability and credit conditions in their local credit markets; they build familiarity and rapport with local agricultural lenders (primarily commercial banks and FCS lending associations); and they periodically send loan documentation of commercial-classed borrowers to local lenders for possible acceptance as a loan customer. Lack of acceptance by the commercial lenders means the applicant continues as an agency borrower.

The recently adopted credit classification system represents an improvement over the old FmHA guidelines in which a specified percentage (that is, 10 percent) of the local office's borrowers were reviewed for possible submission to local lenders. Nonetheless, under both the old and the new approaches, the graduation decision still rests with the acceptance or rejection decisions of commercial lenders, who are evaluating the potential profitability of the borrower as a new loan applicant. The process is also vulnerable to moral hazards (LaDue 1990) by the farm borrower who may prefer to remain eligible for the more favorable, subsidized credit terms of FmHA. The lender too may exhibit moral-hazard behavior by preferring to reject a borderline borrower, knowing that the borrower may continue as an agency client.

Several other options could be considered to facilitate the graduation process. FmHA could adopt provisions that would, after some period of time, change graduation from a discretionary decision to a mandatory discontinuation of financing, either by graduation or by departure from farming. A maximum length could be placed on an individual borrower's participation in the farmer program, as is the case with the new young farmer program, in which ten- and fifteen-year limits are placed on the participation in the direct and guaranteed-loan programs, respectively. Using the credit-scoring models of local commercial lenders rather than the agency alone could be part of this process.

Greater consideration could also be given to providing rewards and incentives for borrower progress and graduation. One example is to adjust the borrower's financing costs downward as progress occurs, with a partial rebate of interest payments when early graduation occurs or according to other terms agreed upon by the agency and the borrower. Another example is for the agency to compensate the private lender for accepting the borrower by paying part of the borrower's interest payments for a stipulated period of time—similar to the interest buy-down programs of the 1980s. A third incentive could provide rewards to FmHA personnel for the speed, efficiency, permanency, and other attributes with which borrowers graduate into private sector lending. Any personnel incentives associated with program magnitude (number of borrowers served, loan volume, or staff size) could be deemphasized.

The shift to loan guarantees facilitates graduation by providing a bridge between the direct loan status and complete graduation. With a guarantee, the borrower becomes a direct customer of the commercial lender, and the goal is then to provide a bridging of credit risks that eventually qualifies the borrower for an unfettered credit relationship with the commercial lender. Periodic expirations of guarantees or potential refinancing to private status may flow more naturally from the guarantee status than from direct loans.

Finally, eligibility for FmHA credit might be based on a first refusal by any guaranteed-loan programs provided by individual states. Many states have such programs, although their small size and limited personnel would hinder this approach. Perhaps a federal-state partnership program could be developed to shift more of the funding and administration to the states.

USDA Restructuring. The USDA restructuring program proposed by former Secretary of Agriculture Mike Espy and signed into law in 1994 also has important implications for public credit programs for agriculture. Under restructuring, FmHA has been dissolved as a USDA agency, with the farm programs transferred to a new Consolidated Farm Service Agency (along with the Agricultural Stabilization and Conservation Service and the Federal Crop Insurance

Corporation), and the rural housing and business development loans have been transferred to the Rural Development Agency. In principle, the service capacity to farmers would be enhanced by consolidating the programs of these agencies into one local office, and the types of farm loans would remain the same. The restructuring has increased the number of contact points of FmHA programs with rural communities but not in terms of specialized credit personnel.

Considerable uncertainty remains about the credit knowledge of the local Consolidated Farm Service Agency office; the role of county committees composed of farmers, which have now been disbanded; and adjustment costs of the consolidations of dissimilar data, computer, communications, other information, and employment systems across the consolidated agencies. These details can be disruptive in the transition process and can detract from the quality of credit decisions and loan monitoring over the long term.

Management, Control, and Risk Exposure. In recent years, FmHA has come under substantial scrutiny and criticism regarding the management, control, and risk exposure of its loan programs. It faces a nearly chronic dilemma of balancing a lender-of-last-resort and emergency credit role against the need to operate as an efficient, responsive agency that maintains effective programmatic oversight and control and that ensures full compliance of operations by its lending personnel with guidelines and directed procedures.

On the one hand, the agency has borne the brunt of the public credit syndrome in which credit programs are popular responses to all sorts of financial adversity. The financial horror stories of the 1980s are well known, and it simply became unacceptable (illegal for a time because of foreclosure moratoriums) for the agency to put distressed farmers out of business. The agency was asked to take on a massive relief mission without commensurate growth in administrative resources. Perhaps it functioned as best it could under the circumstances, especially in light of the rather weak and ambiguous signals received from Congress about the agency's mission and goals. While FmHA is intended to function as a lender of last resort, providing a temporary source of credit, it has no clear statutory guidelines in defining the conditions under which it can resolve its relationship with many types of borrowers.

On the other hand, FmHA has experienced substantial criticism over the years regarding the management, control, and risk exposure of its lending programs. A series of reports from the Government Accounting Office (GAO) has cited the agency's inability to develop an effective information system (despite substantial resources devoted to the effort) and long-standing planning and oversight problems and thus has raised serious questions about its planning process. The criticisms extend to the management and control of the agency's loan programs. In an April 1992 report, GAO states:

> By almost any measure, FmHA's loan programs have become good examples of how programs should not be implemented and managed. Because legislation has not established clear priorities for FmHA's mission, the agency has tried simultaneously to meet conflicting objectives—to be fiscally prudent and to provide high risk borrowers with temporary credit to keep them in farming until they secure commercial credit. Arguably, FmHA has not achieved either objective. Its shaky loan portfolio does not reflect the operations of a prudent lender. Furthermore, as an assistance agency, FmHA has had little success in graduating borrowers to commercial sources of credit, as was originally anticipated. Ironically, some of FmHA's clients are financially weaker after FmHA's help than before.

Of course, many positive contributions and success stories for FmHA borrowers could be cited as well, but the concerns have become large issues.

Those criticisms represent the classic case of an overloaded credit program forced to carry relief and welfare functions well beyond the proper scope and mission of a credit program. The effective workings of a credit market are being undermined by asking the agency to bear too much of a fuzzy or even undefined responsibility that seems intended to keep marginal farmers in business. Moreover, the agency does not have sufficient resources or types of loan personnel to function consistently as a complement to commercial lenders—that is, as a temporary repository of soon-to-be creditworthy borrowers. Instead, a credit agency is serving a welfare purpose.

The Farm Credit System

The Farm Credit System is a system of federally chartered, privately owned banks, lending associations, and service units organized as cooperatives with the purpose of providing credit and related services to agricultural producers, rural homeowners, and agricultural cooperatives in the United States. The FCS is one of several government-sponsored enterprises established to serve the credit needs for agriculture, housing, and college students—groups viewed as not being well served by the existing credit markets when these institutions were created. The FCS is regulated and examined by the Farm Credit Administration, an independent agency in the executive branch of the U.S. government.

The late 1980s began a period of significant structural change for the FCS because of the financial stress in agriculture, financial problems affecting the FCS institutions that eventually led to $1.26 billion in federal assistance, and greater competition in the financial markets. (The subsequent rapid financial recovery of system institutions portends an early payback of the federal assistance.) Through consolidations and restructuring, the number of lending associations declined from 915 in 1980 to 240 by 1994. The remaining associations are much larger in size and include several multistate associations. The 1987 agricultural credit act also required the old federal land banks and federal intermediate credit banks to merge to form farm credit banks. Some interdistrict mergers of farm credit banks have also occurred, and the original thirteen banks for cooperatives merged into two banks for cooperatives.

The 1980s legislation and experiences brought several other changes to the FCS. The Farm Credit Administration became an arms-length regulator with more stringent powers for regulating and examining the FCS institutions. Virtually all the borrower-owned equity capital of the lending associations is now considered "at risk" and is largely generated by retained earnings with less reliance on stock purchase requirements of borrowers. Minimum capital requirements for FCS institutions were expressed by an equity-to-capital ratio of 7 percent or greater, and the Farm Credit System Insurance Corporation (FCSIC) was established to provide a safety reserve for investors in farm credit securities, thus reducing the likelihood of needs for public assistance for the FCS in the future. Besides the FCSIC, the farm credit banks and the banks for cooperatives also entered into several collective, self-initiated actions to build financial control, discipline, safety, and soundness across the respective banks.

In general, the FCS has placed a high priority on the monitoring and management of various types of risks experienced by the FCS institutions, in recognition of the system's mission to provide specialized credit services to an inherently unstable agricultural industry. The catastrophic nature of risks facing the FCS, however, is difficult to insure against. Severe risks tend to become concentrated in relatively short periods of time. The financial adversities of the 1980s, for example, were the system's first major loss experience since the 1930s, indicating a loss concentration covering a four- to five-year period out of about fifty years. It remains unclear whether the new risk protection mechanisms employed by the FCS can prevent a similar recurrence during the next fifty years.

Agency Status Issues. While the FCS is considered privately owned and operates much like other commercial financial institutions, its major source of funds is from the sale of farm credit securities (bonds, medium-term notes, and discount notes) that are treated as "government agency securities" in the financial markets. Debt issuances by other government-sponsored enterprises receive the same treatment. The rationale is that the statutory mandate to be a reliable, specialized agricultural lender creates the need for a reliable source of funds. Thus, agency status is accorded these securities even though it is explicitly stated in the statute that they are not guaranteed against default by the U.S. government. Agency status results from a set of regulatory exemptions and preferences of these securities as they are traded in the financial markets and the perception of implied government backing if the FCS experiences severe financial difficulty. Agency status is a significant factor in the ability of the farm credit banks to market large volumes of securities at interest rates slightly above the rates paid on U.S. government securities with similar maturities.

Agency status of the Farm Credit System and other government-sponsored enterprises has been closely scrutinized over the past fifteen years, with a view toward eventual and complete privatization of these institutions. That scrutiny reflects questions about the general role of and specific needs for government-sponsored enterprises, the missions of the respective institutions, and the implied contingent liability of the U.S. government in upholding the financial obligations of such enterprises. As indicated earlier, agency status for the FCS may ensure reliable access for funding in return for the highly concentrated, single industry (agriculture) characteristic of the system's loan portfolio. Moreover, continuation of agency status has seemed appropriate during the system's recent financial recovery. Thus, it is likely that agency status will continue to invite policy debate in the future.

Expanded Authorizations. Confining the mission of the FCS primarily to financing agricultural production and agricultural cooperatives in the United States results in a significant concentration of risk in the system's loan portfolio. Consideration is occasionally given to broadening the range of eligible borrowers to increase the system's risk-carrying capacity and more effectively meet the financing needs of rural America. Modest increases in FCS lending authority have occurred over time. The Farm Credit Amendments Act of 1980 allowed system institutions to finance the on-farm marketing and processing of farm-related business activities of eligible borrowers with 1990 legislation allowing additional financing of agribusiness activities based on through-put requirements for previously eligible agricultural borrowers. Other broadening of lending authority has included rural housing loans, international lending by the banks for cooperatives, loans to aquatic and timber producers, and the ability of the banks for cooperatives to provide credit enhancements for some types of rural development lending.

In 1994, two pieces of legislation were introduced to broaden further the lending authorities of the FCS institutions. The provisions of the Rural Credit and Development Act of 1994 (called the Clayton Bill) include (1) broadened authority to lend to rural and agricultural businesses that provide related goods and services to farmers and ranchers; (2) permission for FCS institutions to purchase such loans originated by others; (3) broadened authority to lend to businesses serving cooperatives that are, in turn, eligible for FCS financing; (4) authority for FCS institutions to lend to rural communities for facility projects; (5) authority for FCS lending to rural utilities; and (6) expanded authority to provide rural home mortgage credit by increasing the present community size limitation of 2,500 to 20,000 population and increasing the portfolio limitation from 15 percent to 20 percent.

The second piece of legislation (the CoBank Bill), which was enacted into law, removes or reduces a number of restrictions on the banks for cooperatives with respect to joint-venture financing, import-export financing, and loan participation authority. As a result, banks for cooperatives will have a stronger capacity to engage in financing international trade of agricultural commodities.

The long-run goals of these proposals are to enhance the risk-carrying capacity of system institutions and to provide a competitive source of credit from the national financial markets for rural borrowers, communities, and cooperatives whose financing needs are otherwise unmet or inequitably served. Opponents of these proposals argue that existing credit sources are available to meet these financing needs adequately, especially through commercial banks, and that expanding the lending authorities might detract from the FCS financing of its traditional agricultural clientele. Judging from past experience, new lending authorities for FCS institutions will likely continue to evolve, although incrementally, and perhaps be accompanied by other statutory changes affecting those institutions.

In contrast with that in other countries, the U.S. Farm Credit System is more narrowly defined. Some of the world's largest agricultural lenders (for example, Credit Agricole, Rabbobank) were originally organized as local cooperative banks that now have international deposit-gathering and lending authorities. The home environment of these international banks, however, did not typically include a decentralized commercial banking system that was inclined to finance agriculture and serve rural residents, compared with the community-oriented banks in the United States. Thus, more broadly based rural credit institutions were needed in these countries. The need for such breadth at this time in the United States is much less.

The Future Outlook. The Farm Credit System's major contribution has been the provision of reliable, long-term credit to agricultural borrowers to finance the purchase of improvement of farm real estate. The absence of effective long-term credit programs was a major gap when the federal land bank system was established in 1916. A major gap would likely be the case again today in the absence of the Farm Credit System, especially if the public sector continues to favor a largely pluralistic, smaller-scale structure for agriculture. While farm real estate lending by commercial banks has increased substantially in recent years, it is unlikely that the banking system could completely replace the long-term credit provided by the FCS. A well-developed secondary market for selling farm real estate loans or pooled shares in loans would then be needed (a successful version of the Federal Agricultural Mortgage Corporation, or Farmer Mac), similar to the case in residential housing, but even then the government-sponsored enterprises (the Federal National Mortgage Association, or Fannie Mae, and Freddie Mac) have been needed to make the secondary market work.

The Farm Credit System has also provided an important source of non–real estate credit for farmers that enhances market competition, especially in selected rural financial markets where commercial banks are less involved in agricultural finance. Finally, the targeted availability of credit to agricultural cooperatives has played a major role in the growth and performance of these cooperatives in the United States, including the financing of a modest yet significant amount of international lending. If further privatization of the FCS is needed, through the removal of agency status, then a broadening of lending, service, and funding authorities may be appropriate to consider.

As restructuring and consolidations within the FCS continue, the need for the farm credit bank component of the system may ultimately be called into question. Fewer banks (for example, one, two, or three) and larger lending associations may shift the role of the banks to a provider of services to the associations and reduce the bank's role in the FCS intermediation process. Lending associations may eventually supplant the banks and remove one of the tiers from the FCS systems.

Further restructuring and consolidations may also reduce the importance of the cooperative organization of the FCS. Shifting to outside ownership of stock traded on the public stock exchanges (similar to several other government-sponsored enterprises) would broaden the ownership base, further strengthen risk-bearing capacity, and provide a different perspective and degree of financial discipline among the boards of directors of the FCS institutions. At the same time, however, it would dilute the familiarity with local agricultural conditions that now characterizes the boards of most smaller lending associations.

Federal Agricultural Mortgage Corporation

Creation and Purpose. Farmer Mac was created by the Agricultural Credit Act of 1987 to oversee the development of a secondary market for farm real estate loans. The purposes of the secondary market, indicated in the 1987 act, are (1) to increase the availability of long-term credit to farmers and ranchers at stable interest rates; (2) to provide greater liquidity and lending capacity in extending credit to farmers; (3) to facilitate capital market investments providing long-term agricultural lending, including funds at fixed rates of interest; and (4) to improve the availability of credit for rural housing.

The secondary market is to achieve a separation of loan origination, servicing, funding, and risk bearing so that the farm mortgage market will function more efficiently. The original function of Farmer Mac was to oversee the purchases by poolers of eligible farm mortgages originated and perhaps serviced by a primary lender. The poolers (organized by life insurance companies, commercial banks, FCS institutions, or others) aggregate the loans into portfolios and then sell pooled participation securities to investors based on a pass-through of principal and interest payments by borrowers, or based on sales to investors of securities backed by the loan pools. In turn, Farmer Mac provides guarantees on these securities to ensure their safety for financial market investors.

Several safety mechanisms are contained in the Farmer Mac system to deal with loan delinquencies and losses and thus protect investors in Farmer Mac securities. These mechanisms include (1) a cash reserve or subordinated participation interest held by originators or poolers equal to at least 10 percent of the loan; (2) a Farmer Mac reserve funded through fees charged to participating financial institutions; (3) Farmer Mac's own equity capital; and (4) a line of credit up to $1 billion with the U.S. Treasury.

Growth Problems. While Farmer Mac was created by the 1987 act, the first pooling operation did not begin until 1991. By 1994, only eight poolers had been certified, and little pooling activity had occurred. The total volume of credit under the Farmer Mac program is in the $800 million to $900 million range. The slow development has been attributed to several factors: (1) weak loan demand in recent years; (2) strong liquidity of agricultural banks; (3) stringent capitalization requirements by bank regulators; (4) uncertain loan volume in the secondary market; (5) questionable interest rate competitiveness; and (6) slow acceptance by investors of the unique and complex features of real estate mortgages in agriculture (GAO).

Expanded Authorizations. Beginning in 1990, Farmer Mac received two new authorities intended to stimulate and expand the development of the secondary market. The first new authority allowed Farmer Mac to serve as the pooler for secondary sales of loans guaranteed by the Farmers Home Administration. This activity is called Farmer Mac II, while the original program is Farmer Mac I.

The volume of FmHA-guaranteed loans sold through Farmer Mac II totaled $39.5 million in 1993, up from $24 million in 1992 (USDA). Despite the growth, the 1993 figure is less than 5 percent of the fiscal 1993 guaranteed loan volume of FmHA eligible for Farmer Mac II sale. Either the program has significant growth opportunity, or it is not viewed as an attractive alternative by most lenders using the loan-guarantee program.

The second change in late 1991 authorized Farmer Mac to fund loan pools by issuing its own unsecured debt securities, having agency status similar to that of other government-sponsored enterprises. That program, called the linked portfolio strategy, has attracted renewed pooler interest. Two new poolers began to purchase complete farm loans from originators in 1993, under the terms of the linked portfolio strategy program, with a variety of maturities and pricing methods for borrowers. In addition, most sales of FmHA-guaranteed loans now occur under Farmer Mac's program of linked portfolios.

Farmer Mac activities are also receiving a boost through the formation of a network of mini-poolers. These mini-poolers provide a bridge between loan originators (primarily small banks) and larger poolers. They also play a major role in applying Farmer Mac's underwriting standards to evaluate eligibility of loans for pooling. The degree of success of the mini-pooler concept remains to be seen.

Future Outlook. The slow development of Farmer Mac has raised serious questions about the program's long-term viability, even with the recent development of the Farmer Mac II and the linked portfolio components. The ultimate demand for the program, even with stronger growth in loan demand, remains unclear.

Other questions, issues, and perspectives about the future of Farmer Mac are also important to consider. It is interesting, for example, that commercial banks were able to increase their volume of farm real estate loans substantially—from $7.6 billion in 1982 to $19.3 billion in 1993 (while aggregate farm debt was declining)—without the direct assistance of the Farmer Mac program. Some of the growth came at the time of FCS problems and when fund availability from banks was strong. But the growth in loan volume is still substantial.

Moreover, the creation of Farmer Mac in 1987 occurred in legislation directed primarily toward the financial recovery of the Farm Credit System. To some extent, the major competitors (that is, life insurance companies and commercial banks) of the FCS may have used the circumstances of those times and the political process to gain a financial innovation (Farmer Mac) as a concession from the FCS for the public financial assistance that aided its own recovery. Thus, Farmer Mac may have been created, in part, as a quid pro quo rather than as a response to a strong need-driven demand.

Perhaps the most fundamental question is whether two government-sponsored enterprises, the FCS and Farmer

Mac, are needed to make the farm real estate loan market work effectively. If the agency status of FCS securities were changed to result in a greater privatization of the system, then the secondary market role of Farmer Mac might take on greater significance.

The development of the secondary market for farm mortgage loans was a major financial innovation for agricultural finance. Given the significant transition occurring in agricultural finance markets, it is too early to abandon Farmer Mac as only an interesting, yet failed experiment. We need to see how its potential role may change as the financial markets for agriculture continue to evolve.

Concluding Comments

Both agriculture and its financial markets are experiencing substantial transition. A trimodal structure is emerging in agriculture, characterized by the coexistence of large industrialized units, commercial-scale family operations, and small, part-time, or limited-resource farmers. Commercial lenders, including the Farm Credit System, are meeting the financing needs of the industrialized units. These units neither need nor use subsidized credit programs. Commercial-scale family operations and small farms are financed by a variety of sources, including public credit programs. For these producers, the availability of public credit seems more important. The traditional mid-sized family farms, which have been a major focus of FCS lending, are diminishing in number and relative importance.

Several sources of credit are financing this changing structure of agriculture: the banking system and other commercial lenders, two government-sponsored enterprises, and a government-owned lender of last resort. These public credit programs have responded to each of the major rationales for public credit. The FCS, which filled a major real estate financing gap, provides a reliable specialized, competitive source of operating and capital credit for agricultural borrowers. The specialization has helped to overcome the information problems and relatively high transaction costs of agricultural lending. Without the FCS, farm real estate financing would suffer considerably, and the secondary market operations of Farmer Mac would become more important. Farmer Mac was created to improve the workings of the farm real estate credit market, although the need for two separate government-sponsored enterprises—one for direct lending and another for secondary transactions—is an interesting issue. Finally, the geographic liberalization and increasing size of the commercial banking systems could create a financing gap for some types of agricultural borrowers, who might then seek public credit.

FmHA has served the public purposes of facilitating resource adjustments in agriculture, providing liquidity in times of adversity, and assisting many agricultural borrowers in meeting the creditworthiness requirements of commercial lenders. In the process, the agency has provided substantial subsidies, although the shift to guaranteed loans has reduced subsidization. FmHA, however, is especially vulnerable to the political economy of credit programs that easily lead to institutional overload. The fuzziness and varying nature of its mission, especially in the 1980s, have led to weak loan quality (even for a lender of last resort), slow graduation of borrowers to commercial credit, management and control problems, and a major welfare role. Some observers (for example, Herr [1994]) even question the continuing need for these programs. How the agency's programs will fare in the proposed USDA restructuring is unclear.

Key questions remain about public preferences, if any, toward the structural features of the agricultural sector. The FCS and FmHA play a major role in preserving the traditional pluralistic, small-scale organizational and ownership structure of the sector. But the forces of industrialization are working against this traditional view. If these forces continue to work their course, then the traditional scope, missions, and operations of the FCS and FmHA are subject to change as well. Changes will not likely occur overnight, but the journey may have begun.

References

Barkema, A., and M. Cook. "The Industrialization of the U.S. Food System." *Food and Agricultural Marketing Issues for the 21st Century*. Food and Agricultural Marketing Consortium, FAMC 91-1, Texas A&M University, 1993a.

————. "The Changing U.S. Pork Industry: A Dilemma for Public Policy." *Economic Review, Federal Reserve Bank of Kansas City*, vol. 78, no. 2 (1993b): 49–66.

Barry, P. "The Farmers Home Administration: Current Issues and Policy Directions." *Looking Ahead*. National Planning Association, Washington, D.C. 8 (September 1985): 4–12.

Barry, P. J. "Needed Changes in the Farmers Home Administration Lending Programs." *American Journal of Agricultural Economics* 67 (1985): 341–44.

Bosworth, B., A. Carron, and E. Rhyne. *The Economics of Federal Credit Programs*. Washington, D.C.: Brookings Institution, 1987.

Budget of the United States Government. *Analytical Perspectives FY1995*. U.S. Government Printing Office. Washington, D.C., 1994.

Gustafson, C., and P. Barry. "Structural Implications of Agricultural Finance." In *Size, Structure and the Changing Face of American Agriculture*, edited by A. Hallam. Boulder, Colo.: Westview Press, 1993.

Herr, W. "Are Farmers Home Administration's Farm Loan Programs Redundant?" *Agricultural Finance Review* 54 (1994): 1–14.

LaDue, E. "Moral Hazard in Federal Farm Lending." *American Journal of Agricultural Economics* 72 (1990): 774–79.

Lee, J., and S. Gabriel. "Public Policy toward Agricultural Credit." *Future Sources of Funds for Agricultural Banks*. Federal Reserve Bank of Kansas City, Kansas City, 1980.

U.S. Department of Agriculture. *Agricultural Income and Finance*. Situation and Outlook Report, Economic Research Service, AIS-52, Washington, D.C., February 1994.

U.S. General Accounting Office. *Federal Agricultural Mortgage Corporation: Secondary Market Development Slow and*

Future Uncertain. GAO/RCED-91-181, Washington, D.C., September 1991.

———. *Farmers Home Administration: Billions of Dollars in Farm Loans Are at Risk.* GAO/RCED-92-86, Washington, D.C., April 1992.

9
Revitalizing R&D

Julian M. Alston and Philip G. Pardey

Agricultural productivity has grown rapidly in the United States relative to productivity in the economy more generally. Many people attribute much of this growth to public sector agricultural research and extension, which operates primarily through land-grant colleges and research agencies of the U.S. Department of Agriculture (USDA), in a system introduced over a century ago. In recent years the agricultural sciences have increasingly been asked to do more with less. Questions have arisen about whether the old research and development (R&D) institutions are still needed, or about how they should adapt to accommodate changes in science, in scientific institutions, in society and social attitudes, in government, in agriculture itself, and in the economy more generally.

This chapter analyzes U.S. federal government policies directed toward agricultural research and development and extension. We draw on the relevant economic principles to review and evaluate the past and present policies against the changing market and institutional setting as a basis for considering policy directions for the future. We emphasize public sector agricultural R&D as a mechanism for correcting private sector underinvestment, from a national perspective, in research. We consider the economics of alternative approaches toward financing, organizing, and managing public sector agricultural R&D and propose five principal types of changes to increase the economic efficiency of agricultural R&D:

- an increased emphasis on economic principles, economic efficiency criteria, and an economic way of thinking in research planning and management
  - an increased investment in agricultural R&D
  - a greater use of check-off funding
  - an increased use of regional research organizations instead of national or state-based institutions
  - a greater emphasis on competitive grants rather than special grants and formula funds

Economic Principles for Government Intervention in Research

Rationales for Government Intervention. Market failure in agricultural R&D seems to be widely taken for granted, mainly because of inappropriability. Often those who invest in R&D cannot capture all the benefits—others can "free ride" on an investment in research, using the results and sharing in the benefits without sharing in the costs. Hence, private benefits to an investor (or group of investors) are less than the social benefits of the investment, and, as a result, some socially profitable investment opportunities remain unexploited. Specifically, in the absence of government intervention, the investment in agricultural research is likely to be too little, because

- the nature of research, which is usually long term, large scale, and risky, means that the typical firm in agriculture is not able to carry out effective research (although it can help to fund it) and institutions may need to be set up on a collective basis[1]
- the returns to new technologies or processes are often high, but the firm responsible for developing a technology may not be able to appropriate all the benefits accruing to

---

1. There are exceptions to the *typical* situation, but even when firms are large enough to find it profitable to carry out some research there is still likely to be too little research for the other reasons (appropriability and externalities).

the innovation, often because fully effective patenting or secrecy is not possible[2]

- some research benefits (or costs) accrue to people other than those who use the results

The first reason concerns the economics of the research enterprise as it relates to the size of farm firms. The second and third concern the asymmetry between the incidence of benefits and the costs of research. Both types of problem can be important. These conventional reasons for private sector underinvestment in agricultural R&D can explain the major result from the empirical literature across different commodities and different countries: agricultural R&D has been, on average, a highly profitable investment from society's point of view, which suggests that research has been underfunded and that current government intervention may be inadequate.

Other reasons for government intervention in agricultural R&D relate to more general market failures, including distortions due to externalities.[3] The existence of externalities means that marginal *private* costs (or benefits) from economic activities differ from the corresponding marginal *social* costs (or benefits) and that, as a result, private decisions will not be socially optimal: a market failure. Hence, in the absence of government intervention, commercial decisions will tend to produce too much pollution and preserve too little pristine wilderness. Agricultural R&D can affect the balance by generating technologies that are both privately profitable and, say, environmentally friendly, rel-

---

2. This appropriability problem extends beyond relations among single individuals to relations among collectives such as one producer cooperative or industry group versus another, and among states and even countries.

3. Externalities arise when one individual's production or consumption activities have spillover effects on other individuals that are not compensated through markets. Groundwater pollution with agricultural chemicals is an example of a *negative* externality. Free riding by others on an individual's research results, as discussed above, is a type of externality, too—a *positive* externality, having favorable spillover effects.

ative to the current technology. But the very nature of (negative) externalities is that it does not pay private investors to make an effort to reduce them, either in the choice of production practices with given technology or in the choice of technological evolution through research, development, and adoption decisions.

Similar arguments apply to the development and adoption of technologies that consume stocks of unpriced or underpriced natural resources. Hence, private incentives are likely to lead in the direction of the development and adoption of excessively consumptive technologies unless government acts to modify the incentives and "internalize" the externalities. These arguments mean that, even in the absence of market failures associated with the atomistic nature of agricultural production, distortions in incentives may bias the direction of research against externality-mitigating technologies and in favor of externality-exacerbating technologies. There is too little R&D because of inappropriability; the mixture of R&D is biased because of externality effects.

Forms of Government Intervention. It is one thing to establish a case of market failure but another to determine the best action for the government to take to reduce the social costs of that failure. Indeed, taking *no* action may be the optimal policy. Many interventions occur in agricultural R&D. They include improvements in private property rights (for example, recent changes in intellectual property rights that apply to plant variety protection or "utility patents" for plants), enhanced incentives for private R&D (for example, through the provision of tax breaks, direct subsidies, or other incentives), the provision of public funds for publicly or privately executed R&D through competitive grants, or the creation of new public or private sector R&D institutions (for example, legal arrangements under which an industry funds research cooperatively). Another way to finance public sector agricultural R&D is to sell the scientific results (even public sector organizations such as universities now often patent their research results where possible and sell the product).

The dominant U.S. strategy has been to use government revenues to finance public or private sector R&D. This strategy includes the provision of tax breaks and other financial incentives for private R&D, which creates a loss of government revenues, as well as the direct use of government funds both to finance private R&D, through grants and contracts, and to finance the production of knowledge in a variety of publicly administered R&D organizations.

These alternatives may all differ in their incentive effects, the net social (dead-weight) cost of distortions in the quantity and mixture of research, and the total social cost of financing R&D. An intervention is justified only if it improves the situation by reducing the social costs of market failure—the benefits of the intervention must be greater than the costs. Different interventions will be more or less effective at correcting different types of market failures; they will also have different distributional (or equity) consequences.

Evolution of U.S. Agricultural Research Policy

Agricultural R&D Institutions. Since the USDA and the land-grant colleges were founded over a century ago, U.S. public sector agricultural science has evolved into a major enterprise. An important element has been the long-standing close association and integration of agricultural research with extension and higher education.[4] The 1862 Act of Establishment focused on the discovery and diffusion of knowledge as the primary function of the Department of Agriculture. This led to the establishment of a substantial scientific institution within the federal government, which was ultimately organized as the Agricultural Research Service (ARS). The formalization of intramural research within

---

4. These events have been documented in much greater detail by Moore (1967), Rasmussen and Baker (1972), and Kerr (1987), among others. Huffman and Evenson (1993) provided an economist's perspective.

the USDA was accompanied by the development of the land-grant colleges, following the passage of the 1862 Morrill Land Grant College Act.

In 1887, federal funding of extramural USDA research began with the passage of the Hatch Experiment Station Act, which authorized annual appropriations to state agricultural experiment stations (SAESs) "established under the direction" of the land-grant colleges. The two streams of agricultural research—intramural USDA labs and the SAESs—have since developed in parallel, with some tension in the USDA's dual role as research funder and research performer.

The Smith-Lever Act of 1914 established a federal role in agricultural extension, which had been provided by state governments alone, and introduced formula funding and a requirement that federal funds be matched by state appropriations (innovations that would later be adopted for research as well as extension). The formula established the amount of federal support according to each state's share of the total rural population of the United States.

Formula funding has evolved over time. The core of the Hatch Act funding of the SAESs, both in its original form and following the 1955 amendments, has been the distribution of block funds with little or no programmatic direction by the federal government. In the original Hatch Act of 1887, the Adams Act of 1906, and the Purnell Act of 1925, which expanded federal support of the SAESs, the determination was particularly simple: the appropriated funds were simply divided equally among the various states. The sole control vested by Congress in the USDA was a requirement that the funds be used to support research. The 1935 Bankhead-Jones Act imposed a formula that tied SAES support to each state's share of the nation's rural population; a more complicated formula was used in the Research and Marketing Act of 1946, with some funds divided equally among states, others distributed on the basis of rural population, and a third based on farm population. The 1955 Hatch Act amendment that replaced the original Hatch, Adams, and Purnell Acts included a similar formula; formula funding also found its way into the 1962 McIntire-Stennis Forestry Research Act, the Research Facilities Act of 1963, and the periodic farm bills reauthorizing SAES support.

A generally rising total federal budget for agricultural R&D, a sequence of changes in the institutional arrangements for administering those funds, including attempts to make the experiment stations more accountable to the USDA, and a rising congressional role in the decisions about allocating the funds have characterized the postwar period. In place of pure formula funding, a structure of planning and coordinating committees developed, with an increasing role of oversight and administrative overhead.

The Bankhead-Jones Act's establishment of nine regional research laboratories in 1935 marked the beginning of congressional designation of the programmatic uses for federal agricultural research funds.[5] In addition, the Special Research Fund established as part of the same act, and later called the Special Research Grants program, gave prior authorization for congressional appropriations for designated research tasks, including specific research projects at identified facilities. The increasing complexity and politicization of the funding system were apparent in title 14 of the Food and Agriculture Act of 1977,

> a title whose eleven subtitles and seventy sections included a little of everything for everyone. To the questions of what problems deserved priority attention and who in the scientific community might best address them, Congress seemed to answer that all were important and every scientist could contribute to their solutions. (Kerr 1987, 149)

The trends of strong congressional direction of research funding, combined with a substantial federal management

---

5. Four more regional facilities, concentrating on the discovery of new industrial uses for surplus farm commodities, were established by the Agricultural Adjustment Act of 1938. A preoccupation with the marketing of agricultural surpluses continued in the postwar period with the 1946 passage of the Research and Marketing Act.

superstructure, continued in the early 1980s, with the reauthorizations of the 1981 amendments to title 14. The 1985 reauthorization continued these trends, and the same is broadly true of the 1990 legislation, which extended the preexisting arrangements.

The major innovation of the 1990 farm bill in the area of research funding was the National Research Initiative (NRI), which authorized a substantial increase in competitive grants (first introduced in 1977), an increase that was not to be specifically earmarked but rather was to support the development and application of advanced technologies. As in the past, however, Congress has resisted the attempt to retain flexibility in the research funding process and has funded the NRI at well below its authorized levels.

Public Sector R&D Expenditures. Public sector R&D in the United States is big business by most measures. In 1994, the federal government spent just over $64 billion on R&D compared with only $178 million in 1949 (table 9–1). About $38.8 billion, or 57.1 percent, was spent on defense-related research, down from its 69.7 percent share of total R&D spending in 1987. In 1994, about $29.1 billion went for non-defense research, of which federally funded agricultural research accounted for just $1.142 billion, or 1.7 percent of the total. Table 9–2 gives a more detailed, longer-run perspective on agricultural R&D spending in the United States. In 1889, shortly after the Hatch Act was passed, federal and state spending totaled $859,300. A century later the public sector agricultural R&D enterprise had grown to over $2.6 billion, an annual rate of growth of 8.0 percent in nominal terms. Intramural research by the USDA dominated the national system in 1889. By 1993, the SAESs accounted for 74 percent of total public spending on agricultural R&D, with federal laboratories operated by the USDA making up almost all the remaining 26 percent.

The sources of funds for SAES research have also changed markedly. During their early formative years, the SAESs received a relatively small but growing share of their funds from state sources. The proportion of state funds

TABLE 9-1

FEDERAL OUTLAYS FOR RESEARCH AND DEVELOPMENT, 1949–1994
(millions of dollars)

		Nondefense							
Year	National Defense	General science, space, and technology	Energy	Transportation	Health	Agriculture	Natural resources	Total	Grand Total
1949	762	82	—	—	—	—	—	178	940
1960	5,937	570	159	77	277	107	68	1,385	7,322
1970	8,021	4,203	451	407	1,073	246	301	7,132	15,153
1980	14,643	5,445	3,289	861	3,682	563	951	15,592	30,235
1990	41,078	7,927	2,342	973	8,253	937	1,220	22,732	63,810
1991	37,887	8,741	2,501	1,127	8,528	990	1,323	24,296	62,183
1992	38,170	9,157	2,593	1,348	9,656	1,070	1,593	26,558	64,728
1993	40,396	9,546	2,517	1,504	10,374	1,129	1,762	27,982	68,378
1994	38,883	9,740	2,470	1,816	10,878	1,142	1,825	29,181	68,064

NOTE: Dashes = data not available.
SOURCE: Executive Office of the President (1994), table 10.2.

TABLE 9-2
PUBLIC SECTOR FUNDING FOR AGRICULTURAL RESEARCH AND
DEVELOPMENT, 1889–1993
(millions of dollars)

| Year or Decade Average | State Agricultural Experiment Stations[a] | | | | USDA[b] | U.S. Total |
	State	Federal	Miscellaneous fees and sales	Total		
1889	0.08	0.59	0.06	0.72	0.14	0.86
1890–99	0.22	0.70	0.11	1.04	0.21	1.25
1900–09	0.65	0.87	0.31	1.84	1.04	2.88
1910–19	2.24	1.43	1.09	4.76	4.48	9.24
1920–29	6.01	2.11	2.09	10.21	18.44	28.65
1930–39	8.25	4.88	2.60	15.72	30.68	46.40
1940–49	15.81	7.42	5.44	28.67	40.97	69.64
1950–59	56.17	19.10	14.27	89.55	46.08	135.63
1960–69	132.10	42.87	25.20	200.18	109.32	309.50
1970–79	289.13	131.14	63.41	483.68	258.58	742.26
1980–89	646.44	359.41	207.04	1,212.89	500.37	1,713.25
1990	927.15	500.86	338.07	1,766.07	614.08	2,380.15
1991	961.73	532.15	358.72	1,852.59	650.62	2,503.22
1992	956.29	582.06	376.52	1,914.87	689.97	2,604.84
1993	960.41	632.39	387.54	1,980.33	692.29	2,672.63
Annual growth rates (%)						
1889–93	9.52	6.95	8.93	7.96	8.50	8.04
1980–89	7.87	6.87	9.57	7.86	5.06	7.04
1990–93	1.18	8.08	4.66	3.89	4.08	3.94

a. Data include experiment stations and cooperating institutions for U.S. contiguous states (excluding data for Alaska and Hawaii).
b. Series approximates intramural research by USDA and consists of total appropriations to the Agricultural Research Service, the Economic Research Service, and the Agricultural Cooperative Service less appropriations to contracts, grants, and cooperative agreements with the SAESs made by these USDA agencies.
SOURCE: SAES data compiled by Pardey, Eveleens, and Hallaway (forthcoming) from various USDA sources, including USDA *Inventory of Agricultural Research* for years after 1980. USDA data from Huffman and Evenson (1993, table A4.1) for period 1889–1990, updated with data from *Inventory of Agricultural Research* for more recent years.

peaked at 69 percent in 1970 and has fallen steadily since to average only 48 percent in 1993. Funding from miscellaneous sources, fees, and sales (including funds from grants and industry check-offs) has grown steadily as a share of the total since the early 1970s and now accounts for nearly 20 percent of SAES funds.

Between 1972 and 1993 total support for the SAESs grew by 8.5 percent per year in nominal terms and only 2.8 percent in real terms (table 9–3). About 51 percent of the money from the federal government comes from funds administered by the Cooperative State Research Service (CSRS) including funds dispersed on a formula basis, some earmarked funds, and funds made available to the states as part of the competitive grants program.[6] The remainder (about 49 percent) of the federal funds going to the states comes from other earmarked funds, funds derived from USDA grants, contracts, and cooperative agreements, as well as funding received from agencies such as the National Science Foundation, the National Institutes of Health, the Department of Defense, and so on. These types of funds have accounted for a rising share of the SAES total, well up from their 33 percent share of federal funds just two decades ago.[7] Revenues from the sale of services and products (including royalties from patents) account for only 5.4 percent of total funds. Industry funds from grants, check-offs, and the like still account for only 7.2 percent of the total, although this is one of the faster-growing components of funds received over the past two decades.

The USDA both disperses and consumes federal R&D funds. Table 9–4 details the deployment of federal appro-

---

6. In October 1994 the USDA initiated a major reorganization that, among other changes, merged the CSRS and the Cooperative Extension Service into a newly created Cooperative State Research, Education, and Extension Service (CSREES). Since the text refers for the most part to the previous institutional structure, for convenience we continue to refer to the (now defunct) CSRS.

7. As a share of the total, not just federal, funds going to the SAESs, these sources of funds collectively accounted for 9.7 percent of the total in 1972 and 15.7 percent in 1993.

priations to the USDA. Since 1970, an increasing share of the USDA resources earmarked for research and education has gone to research, with a corresponding contraction in the share going to education and extension services; they now account for a quarter of total funds, whereas in 1970 they took one-third of the available resources. The ARS accounts for about one-third of all USDA expenditures on research and education, a share that has remained fairly constant over recent years. CSRS administers slightly more than one-fifth of the USDA expenditures on research and education, mostly funding earmarked for SAES and other cooperating institutions, although some of the competitive grant funds that CSRS oversees are spent by agencies within the USDA.

Public sector research spending as a share of the gross value of farm marketings (the agricultural research intensity ratio) grew by 3.8 percent per year from 0.0031 in 1950 to 0.014 in 1990 (table 9–5). If private sector R&D expenditures were included, the contemporary research intensity ratio would increase from 0.014 to about 0.03, or 3 percent of the value of output. Given that $1.90 is spent on research for every public dollar spent on extension, extension expenditures now represent around 0.74 percent of the gross value of agricultural output, about half the corresponding public sector research intensity ratio. Some figures suggest that the United States may be falling behind in agricultural R&D. Australia and Canada, for instance, comparable in many ways to the United States, report public sector agricultural research intensity ratios for recent years that would exceed the combined U.S. public and private sector intensity ratio.

Economic Consequences of Agricultural Research

Changing Structure of Agriculture. During the twentieth century, U.S. agriculture has changed dramatically, with big changes in numbers of farms, farm sizes, and technologies; input and output mixtures; the nature of farmers and farming; consumers and markets for farm products; and the role

TABLE 9–3

SOURCE OF FUNDS TO STATE AGRICULTURAL EXPERIMENT STATIONS AND OTHER COOPERATING INSTITUTIONS, 1972–1993

(millions of dollars)

Year	Federal				Nonfederal					Grand Total
	CSRS administered[a]	USDA[b]	Other[c]	Total	State	Sales	Industry[d]	Other	Total	
1972	71.5	7.0	28.2	106.7	205.5	23.2	16.6	11.0	256.3	363.0
1973	78.2	7.7	29.6	115.4	222.1	28.1	17.7	11.7	279.6	395.1
1974	83.2	8.8	32.0	124.0	247.5	32.4	21.0	12.2	313.0	437.0
1975	92.0	11.1	35.3	138.4	284.7	37.3	24.0	15.0	361.1	499.4
1976	104.8	10.5	40.8	156.1	309.7	30.7	28.3	16.4	385.2	541.3
1976[e]	26.2	2.6	10.2	39.0	77.4	7.7	7.1	4.1	96.3	135.3
1977	118.9	12.6	55.6	187.0	321.2	39.1	32.7	21.9	414.8	601.8
1978	134.5	16.5	57.9	208.8	374.9	40.1	34.7	22.4	472.1	680.9
1979	156.3	21.1	64.6	242.1	413.5	46.7	37.1	27.2	524.6	766.6
1980	162.8	27.5	71.6	261.9	456.4	55.9	48.4	30.5	591.3	853.1
1981	174.3	33.3	83.0	290.6	501.2	59.1	53.5	38.2	652.1	942.7
1982	199.2	36.2	107.6	343.0	545.2	62.5	61.3	45.5	714.6	1057.6
1983	204.9	38.9	95.2	339.0	576.5	65.4	66.7	49.1	757.7	1096.7

Year									
1984	210.5	38.5	103.2	352.3	621.8	66.3	71.0	54.4	813.5	1165.7
1985	221.0	35.9	112.4	369.4	678.3	70.5	79.1	61.5	889.3	1258.7
1986	222.7	35.8	140.6	399.1	741.7	69.4	85.1	70.2	966.5	1365.6
1987	230.8	36.8	148.1	415.7	778.9	75.4	93.8	85.1	1033.1	1448.8
1988	247.8	42.2	153.5	443.5	823.4	84.8	99.1	91.1	1098.3	1541.8
1989	261.0	48.9	169.7	479.6	894.4	92.4	111.3	102.1	1200.2	1679.8
1990	272.8	54.1	188.6	515.5	950.1	102.4	126.6	112.4	1291.5	1807.0
1991	290.8	57.8	199.4	548.0	985.9	113.6	134.0	114.9	1348.4	1896.3
1992	316.6	60.7	221.3	598.7	981.5	116.1	143.4	121.0	1362.1	1960.7
1993	331.0	68.6	249.0	648.5	985.4	110.0	146.1	134.8	1376.3	2024.8
Annual growth rates (%)										
1972–93	7.6	11.5	10.9	9.0	7.7	7.7	10.9	12.7	8.3	8.5
1989–93	6.1	8.8	10.1	7.8	2.5	4.5	7.0	7.2	3.5	4.8

NOTE: Includes all state agricultural experiment stations, forestry schools, 1890/Tuskegee institutions, veterinary schools, and other cooperating institutions.

a. Includes formula funds, special grants, and competitive grants.

b. Includes money received from USDA grants, contracts, and cooperative agreements.

c. Includes contract, grant, and other money received from agencies such as the National Science Foundation, Energy Research and Development Administration, Department of Defense, National Institutes of Health, Public Health Service, National Aeronautics and Space Administration, Tennessee Valley Authority, and so on.

d. Includes money received through industry grants and agreements.

e. Includes appropriations for the transition quarter, which covers the period from July 1, 1976, to September 30, 1976.

SOURCE: USDA, *Inventory of Agricultural Research*, various annual issues, table IV-E.

TABLE 9–4
USDA Appropriations for Research and Education,
1970–1995
(millions of dollars)

	CSRS Administered			Agricultural Research Service
Year	Competitive	Others	Total	
1970	—	62.7	62.7	160.1
1971	—	69.6	69.6	178.6
1972	—	83.0	83.0	191.7
1973	—	91.5	91.5	208.1
1974	—	90.1	90.1	205.0
1975	—	101.8	101.8	224.4
1976	—	114.5	114.5	282.8
1976[a]	—	28.6	28.6	64.4
1977	—	129.0	129.0	282.9
1978	15.0	142.9	157.9	313.9
1979	15.0	159.3	174.3	328.0
1980	15.5	170.4	185.9	358.0
1981	16.0	184.7	200.7	404.1
1982	16.3	204.3	220.6	423.2
1983	17.0	215.3	232.3	451.9
1984	17.0	220.7	237.7	471.1
1985	46.0	230.6	276.6	491.0
1986	42.3	227.3	269.6	483.2
1987	40.7	253.0	293.7	511.4
1988	42.4	260.7	303.1	544.1
1989	39.7	270.9	310.6	569.4
1990	38.6	288.0	326.6	593.3
1991	73.0	300.3	373.3	631.0
1992	97.5	316.9	414.4	670.6
1993	97.5	317.5	415.0	671.7
1994	112.1	325.2	437.3	679.2
1995[b]	130.0	272.1	402.1	712.7
Annual growth rates (%)				
1970–80	1.7[c]	10.5	11.5	8.4
1980–90	9.6	5.4	5.8	5.2
1970–94	13.4	7.1	8.4	6.2

(Table continues)

TABLE 9-4 (continued)

Year	Forest Service	Economics and Statistics			Total Research
		Economic research service	Statistical service	Total	
1970	45.6	—	—	17.0	290.3
1971	48.8	—	—	18.4	320.3
1972	54.4	—	—	18.8	358.0
1973	57.8	—	—	20.6	387.9
1974	64.7	—	—	22.0	386.9
1975	77.6	—	—	24.9	433.5
1976	82.3	—	—	28.9	516.0
1976[a]	22.3	—	—	7.4	124.6
1977	89.8	24.5	4.7	29.2	539.7
1978	90.6	26.0	5.0	31.0	609.8
1979	95.0	28.2	5.4	33.6	648.2
1980	95.9	26.1	5.0	31.1	687.5
1981	108.4	39.5	7.5	47.0	778.0
1982	112.1	39.4	7.0	46.4	816.3
1983	107.7	38.8	7.6	46.4	856.6
1984	108.7	44.3	8.2	52.5	886.7
1985	113.8	46.6	8.4	55.0	956.2
1986	113.6	44.1	8.0	52.1	945.1
1987	126.7	44.9	3.4	48.3	1,002.2
1988	132.5	48.3	3.6	51.9	1,054.6
1989	138.3	49.6	2.9	52.5	1,097.9
1990	150.9	51.0	2.8	53.8	1,155.3
1991	167.6	54.4	3.2	57.6	1,265.4
1992	180.5	59.0	3.6	62.6	1,371.4
1993	182.7	58.9	3.9	62.8	1,373.0
1994	193.1	55.2	3.5	58.7	1,413.6
1995[b]	204.0	53.7	3.5	57.2	1,429.4
Annual growth rates (%)					
1970–80	7.7	2.1[d]	2.3[d]	6.2	9.0
1980–90	4.6	6.9	−5.6	5.6	5.3
1970–94	6.2	4.9	−1.7	5.3	6.8

(Table continues)

TABLE 9–4 (continued)

Year	National Agricultural Library	Education Extension service	Education Other	Education Total	Total Research and Education
1970	—	146.2	4.8	151.1	441.4
1971	—	165.6	5.5	171.0	491.3
1972	—	182.2	6.1	188.3	546.3
1973	—	197.9	6.5	204.3	592.3
1974	—	206.7	6.8	213.6	600.4
1975	—	217.2	7.9	225.0	658.6
1976	—	230.2	8.3	238.4	754.4
1976[a]	—	56.0	2.1	58.1	182.8
1977	—	232.7	9.2	241.9	781.6
1978	6.6	257.5	20.8	278.3	888.1
1979	7.0	263.8	21.2	285.0	933.2
1980	7.3	274.0	21.5	295.5	983.0
1981	8.2	292.2	22.4	314.6	1,092.6
1982	8.2	315.7	11.0	326.7	1,143.0
1983	9.1	328.6	11.9	340.5	1,197.1
1984	10.4	334.3	18.2	352.5	1,239.2
1985	11.5	341.2	21.3	362.5	1,318.7
1986	10.8	328.0	18.4	346.4	1,291.5
1987	11.1	339.0	18.7	357.7	1,359.9
1988	12.2	358.0	19.8	377.8	1,432.4
1989	14.3	361.4	21.9	383.3	1,481.2
1990	14.7	369.3	28.6	397.9	1,553.2
1991	16.8	398.5	34.8	433.3	1,698.7
1992	17.8	419.3	35.8	455.1	1,826.5
1993	17.7	428.4	35.7	464.1	1,837.1
1994	18.2	434.6	37.5	472.1	1,885.7
1995[b]	19.6	432.4	38.9	471.3	1,900.7
Annual growth rates (%)					
1970–80	5.2[c]	6.5	16.1	6.9	8.3
1980–90	7.3	3.0	2.9	3.0	4.7
1970–94	6.5	4.6	8.9	4.8	6.2

NOTE: Dashes = data not available.
a. Includes appropriations for the transition quarter, which covers the period from July 1, 1976 to September 30, 1976.
b. Estimate only.
c. Growth rate is for the 1978–90 period.
d. Growth rate is for the 1977–90 period.
SOURCE: USDA, unpublished *Budgetary Tables*, various fiscal years.

TABLE 9–5
AGRICULTURAL RESEARCH AND EXTENSION INTENSITY RATIOS, 1950–1990

	1950	1960	1970	1980	1990	Annual Growth Rate
Percentages						
Relative to agricultural output						
Research	0.3	0.6	0.9	0.9	1.4	3.8
Extension	0.3	0.4	0.6	0.5	0.7	2.7
Constant 1980 Dollars per Farm						
Relative to farm numbers						
Research	75.5	158.9	265.4	497.6	588.0	5.3
Extension	62.1	102.0	168.6	279.8	307.0	4.1
Constant 1980 Dollars per Capita						
Relative to total population						
Research	2.8	3.5	3.8	5.3	5.0	1.5
Extension	2.3	2.2	2.4	3.0	2.6	0.3

SOURCE: Compiled by the authors. Alston and Pardey (1995) give more details.

of agriculture in the economy. Agricultural R&D has played a major role in bringing about those changes.

Agriculture's share of total employment and gross domestic product accounted for almost half the total economic activity in the United States at the turn of the century. Beginning around 1890, the relative importance of agriculture in the economy has steadily and substantially declined. Agriculture's share of U.S. GDP declined from 12.8 percent in 1890 to 1.4 percent in 1990. Although the nominal and real value of agricultural output has increased markedly, the rest of the economy has grown faster.

Labor-saving technological change has been important. Although agricultural output has risen steadily in real terms, total labor use in agriculture has declined. Agriculture has become less labor intensive both relative to the rest of the economy and in absolute terms. Much of the reduction in the agricultural labor force has come from the consolidation of farms into larger units so that fewer but larger farms remain and less owner-operator and family labor is used—hence, the total number of U.S. farms declined from almost 6 million in 1900 to about 2 million in 1995. The process of consolidation is often attributed to the adoption of new technology, particularly embodied in machinery, that directly reduced labor requirements and increased economies of size. Such innovations imply a less labor-intensive and larger minimum efficient scale in farming operations. Rising nonfarm wages, however, played a role in stimulating the development and adoption of these innovations. Whether labor has been "pushed" from agriculture because of technical changes in that sector or "pulled" from agriculture by better employment opportunities in other sectors is yet to be resolved. The full explanation probably involves some of both forces, with the relative importance varying over time (for example, see Kislev and Peterson [1981]).

While farms are bigger than before, they are different in some other ways as well. Farms have become more specialized. As a result of the incorporation of modern machines and methods, farming is more sophisticated and technically demanding, but at the same time it has become less arduous, less taxing, and less dangerous. Today's tractors, with insulated cabins, stereos, and safety features, are safer and more comfortable as well as more powerful and more efficient than their predecessors.

Changes in agribusiness—the industries that supply inputs to farmers and that buy farm products and process and distribute them—have been perhaps more profound than in agriculture itself. These industries are relatively highly concentrated, especially from the view of regional markets, and have evolved to a position where value added beyond the farm gate is much greater than value added by farmers. The declining importance of farm commodities in the food chain can be attributed to (1) changing *relative prices* of various processing inputs and farm commodities; (2) changing *technology* in the industries that transport, store, process, distribute, and merchandise food products; and (3) changing *consumer demand*—associated with generally rising consumer incomes, changing demographics, an increasing proportion of women in the work force, changes in household technology, and changes in information about the nutritional and health consequences of diet. Some changes appear in the form of new consumer food products or in new characteristics of traditional products; others are reflected in the cost of supplying otherwise unchanged products to retail. Most of these changes have been driven by, or at least accompanied by, technical change.

Implications of Structural Change for R&D Policy. The U.S. farming industry continues to be characterized by large numbers of firms that typically have small gross sales, market share, or number of employees and by decentralized production and marketing decisions. As a consequence of this atomistic structure, individual farm firms are small both in the sense that they are price takers in input and output markets and in the sense that they cannot afford individually to undertake broadly applicable agricultural R&D that might be adopted by the industry as a whole. Such claims do not apply equally to every sector of the farming industry. Producers in some industries have developed institutions that empower a group of producers of a commodity to act in their collective interest when they are individually unable to exert market power; such institutions include marketing orders and producer cooperatives, some of which include arrangements to raise funds for collective goods such as promotion and research. In a few other cases, the farming industry does not fit the atomistic archetype (for example, vertically integrated broiler production), and a relatively small number of firms that control most of production have strong incentives to undertake R&D.

The picture is quite different beyond the farm gate either upstream, in the industries that supply inputs to farmers, or downstream, in the industries that process, distribute, and market farm products. Because these industries are typically highly concentrated relative to the farming sector, they are less likely to suffer market failure in their R&D activities, since the benefits from their innovations are more clearly appropriable through secrecy or patents. Moreover, the divergence between social and private benefits and costs is likely to be small in the typical agribusiness firm compared with the typical farm firm. Hence, public sector agricultural R&D should play a smaller role in relation to farm-input development and food-processing technologies since, for the most part, market failure in R&D is less likely beyond the farm gate than in on-farm technology.

Outputs, Inputs, and Productivity. Over time, mixtures of agricultural outputs and inputs have evolved. It is difficult to distinguish between effects of technological change and effects of changes in prices and other incentives, but clearly technology has played a role in much of the change in input and output mixtures, as either a fundamental cause or an intermediate factor.

Outputs. U.S. farmers produced almost twice as much agricultural output in 1985 as they did in 1949 (the output

TABLE 9–6

VALUE SHARES OF U.S. AGRICULTURAL OUTPUT, 1949–1985
(percent)

		Value Shares			
Year	Field crops	Livestock	Fruit	Vegetables	Output Quantity[a]
1949	39.0	51.5	3.3	1.8	100.0
1955	38.5	50.0	4.1	2.2	110.0
1960	36.6	51.5	4.4	2.2	120.4
1965	37.1	50.7	4.4	2.6	130.3
1970	32.4	56.3	4.1	2.3	140.1
1975	45.4	43.5	3.8	2.8	155.1
1980	43.1	45.6	4.6	2.1	172.8
1985	40.3	45.8	4.9	2.7	191.9
Annual growth rates (%)					
1949–60	−0.6	0.0	2.6	1.6	1.70
1960–70	−1.2	0.9	−0.5	0.7	1.53
1970–80	2.9	−2.1	1.1	−0.9	2.12
1980–85	−1.3	0.1	1.1	5.0	2.12
1949–85	0.1	−0.3	1.1	1.1	1.83

a. Index, 1949 = 100.
SOURCE: Pardey, Craig, and Deininger (1994).

quantity index increased from 100 to 192). This number represents an average increase in agricultural output of 1.8 percent per annum. Different categories of output grew at different rates, however. Thus, the composition of agricultural production changed markedly over the postwar period. Higher-valued products such as vegetables and greenhouse and nursery products, as well as fruits and nuts, all accounted for a larger share of the value of agricultural output in the 1980s than they did in the immediate postwar period (table 9–6). Development patterns also display some important regional differences.

Inputs. The national average of a 92 percent increase in agricultural output was achieved with a 7 percent increase in agricultural inputs (table 9–7). The composition of the inputs used in agriculture has also changed over the post-

TABLE 9–7
COST SHARES OF U.S. AGRICULTURAL INPUTS, 1949–1985
(percent)

Year	Land	Labor	Capital	Purchased inputs	Input Quantity[a]
			Cost Shares		
1949	18.3	44.7	11.4	25.7	100.0
1955	18.4	39.6	13.1	28.9	100.4
1960	19.1	36.0	13.9	30.9	99.8
1965	19.0	35.2	13.4	32.4	99.5
1970	18.8	33.7	13.3	34.2	100.9
1975	19.6	28.7	12.8	38.9	99.8
1980	19.7	24.4	14.3	41.6	112.4
1985	18.8	27.2	14.4	39.6	107.0
Annual growth rates (%)					
1949–60	0.42	−1.93	1.83	1.70	−0.02
1960–70	−0.17	−0.66	−0.46	1.01	0.11
1970–80	0.49	−3.20	0.75	1.98	1.09
1980–85	−0.95	2.24	0.14	−1.00	−0.99
1949–85	0.09	−1.37	0.66	1.21	0.19

a. Index, 1949 = 100.
SOURCE: Pardey, Craig, and Deininger (1994).

war period. The cost share of purchased inputs (for example, electricity, feed, fertilizer, fuels and oil, and seed) has increased from 23 percent in 1949 to 36 percent in 1985. The share of capital services—including physical inputs such as automobiles, tractors, trucks, and combines, as well as biological inputs such as dairy cows, ewes, and breeder pigs— has grown modestly, from 11 percent in 1949 to 14 percent in 1985. Land's share has stayed virtually constant at around 19 percent. Meanwhile, labor use in agriculture declined. Thus, between 1949 and 1985, the cost share of labor fell from 45 percent to 27 percent.

Productivity. Multifactor productivity measures express *aggregate* output per unit of *aggregate* input, where the input aggregate includes all *measurable* inputs such as land, labor,

TABLE 9–8

MULTIFACTOR PRODUCTIVITY IN U.S. AGRICULTURE, 1949–1985

Year	Multifactor Productivity[a]	Year	Multifactor Productivity
1949	100.0	1968	136.6
1950	97.8	1969	137.7
1951	100.2	1970	138.9
1952	103.7	1971	148.1
1953	104.8	1972	147.8
1954	107.3	1973	151.6
1955	109.5	1974	146.6
1956	112.3	1975	155.5
1957	111.3	1976	149.6
1958	119.2	1977	154.8
1959	120.1	1978	149.9
1960	120.6	1979	156.9
1961	122.8	1980	153.7
1962	122.4	1981	170.1
1963	127.0	1982	171.8
1964	126.8	1983	149.6
1965	131.0	1984	171.9
1966	130.8	1985	179.3
1967	135.1		

a. Index, 1949 = 100.
SOURCE: Pardey, Craig, and Deininger (1994).

capital, and purchased inputs. If outputs and inputs are carefully measured and aggregated so as to capture changes in their quality and composition, then the growth in aggregate output that cannot be explained by the growth in measured inputs is a measure of the growth in multifactor productivity. Changes in multifactor productivity can then be explained by things that are not reflected in measured inputs or outputs—such things as improvements in rural infrastructure (for example, communication and transport facilities), environmental degradation, build-up of pest populations, and research-induced technical changes. Figures on multifactor productivity for the 1949–1985 period, presented in table 9–8, show that multifactor productivity grew by 1.6 percent per year and that output grew by 1.8 percent while inputs grew by 0.2 percent per year, accounting for part of the growth in output. The measured productivity growth rate has not been constant over the entire period, nor is it uniform across states within the United States.

Rates of Return to Research. There is no general agreement on the determinants of agricultural productivity, although there is a consensus that agricultural research effectively enhances productivity. Alston and Pardey (1995) documented the results of many studies of rates of return to agricultural research. The overwhelming conclusion is that estimated rates of return to agricultural research have been high, typically well above 20 percent per year. Hence, there appears in general to have been a gross underinvestment in agricultural research. Some reservations can be raised about this evidence. Most of those studies have not adjusted for the effects of price-distorting policies on the measures of research benefits, an omission that might lead to over- or understatement of the benefits and the rate of return (Alston, Norton, and Pardey 1995). Most have not adjusted for the effects of the excess burden of taxation on the measures of costs, an omission that will lead to a systematic understatement of the social costs and an overstatement of the social rate of return (see, for example, Fox [1985]).[8] Many have estimated average rather than marginal rates of return, and it is the latter that is most relevant for marginal changes in R&D. In contrast, a number of factors could lead to *underestimated* rates of return to agricultural R&D, including the omission of spillovers from agricultural R&D into nonagricultural applications and the consequences of such things as environmental, food safety, and social science research that are not reflected in conventional productivity or rate-of-return measures. If we allow for all these potential sources of error, on balance it seems likely that the rate of

---

8. The "excess burden" is due to the social costs of market distortions arising from taxation as well as the costs of enforcement, compliance, collection, and administration of taxes (see, for example, Fox [1985] and Fullerton [1991]).

return to agricultural R&D has been high and that there has been underinvestment.

Getting Research Right

The economic justification for government intervention in agricultural R&D is that economic efficiency will improve as a result. In this context, economic efficiency is an inclusive concept that refers to the achievement of the greatest net benefits for the society as a whole, taking a broad view of net benefits. It includes, for instance, benefits such as sustainability (to the extent that there are net benefits from the development and adoption of more sustainable patterns of resource use), environmental objectives (for example, where R&D can lead, economically, to a reduction in pollution), and nutritional objectives (to the extent that net benefits arise from R&D directed toward improving dietary quality and health). Such nonpecuniary benefits are included along with pecuniary benefits, in a broad concept of net national benefits. The idea of economic efficiency is to make those net national benefits as great as possible.

Objectives for Public Sector Agricultural R&D. Applying the same economic principles and arguments also leads to the conclusion that the only reasonable objective of public sector agricultural research is the pursuit of economic efficiency. This is not to say that other objectives are illegitimate, irrelevant, or unimportant. Rather, alternative, less costly ways can be used to achieve these other objectives instead of moving the agricultural R&D portfolio away from programs that will maximize total national net income. Agricultural R&D is a blunt and ineffective instrument for objectives other than economic efficiency. Hence, distorting the agricultural R&D portfolio away from economic efficiency in the pursuit of nonefficiency objectives is likely to impose a high social opportunity cost.

While the research program may be designed primarily to increase the size of the national economic pie, the shape of the pie and the way it is sliced among groups will inevitably be affected by the choice of research priorities. Unless other policies are in place that can correct fully for any unintended effects of agricultural research on other objectives, it may be necessary to trade off efficiency gains from research for other objectives such as equity or security. In our view, such trade-offs should be limited, and it is appropriate to focus largely, if not exclusively, on economic efficiency considerations when choosing how to finance, organize, and manage public sector agricultural R&D.[9]

Whether the potential improvements in economic efficiency are realized will also depend on how the public sector R&D is financed—whether by patents, federal or state government revenues, industry levies, sales of services or products, or gifts. The economic gains achieved by intervening to provide government-produced R&D also depend on the details of the institutional arrangements affecting the organization of research (between, say, SAESs and the ARS) and management of research resources (in terms of incentives and procedures for allocating resources). Hence, these administrative aspects, too, are the subject of policy.

The optimal intervention by the government, aiming to reduce the distortions arising from inadequate private sector incentives for agricultural R&D, would seek to

- minimize the distortions involved in raising the revenues to finance public sector R&D
- use economic criteria to allocate and use those resources efficiently
- allow decentralized decision making where effective incentive mechanisms are possible
- minimize the application of political criteria in decision making

---

9. One possible exception to this general position is that it may be economically efficient to use agricultural R&D rather than existing farm programs if the objective of the farm programs is to transfer income from taxpayers to farmers. While raising net income to society as a whole, agricultural research also raises farm incomes, an outcome that is clearly superior to making society as a whole worse off in order to transfer income to farmers.

- minimize transactions costs and administrative and bureaucratic overhead

Financing Strategies—Spillovers and Efficient Jurisdictions for R&D. Under the present policy, a mixture of federal and state government funding is used to support agricultural research conducted by the SAESs. In addition, federal and state governments conduct separately administered programs of research. The primary source of funding for these expenditures is the general tax revenues of the federal and state governments, an expensive source of revenues. Recent studies have shown that it costs society well over a dollar to provide a dollar of general taxpayer revenues to finance public expenditures. It is also an increasingly politically scarce source of revenues. Alternative sources of revenue may be less expensive, fairer, and politically more sustainable when used to finance certain types of research to achieve an expanded total public sector R&D budget.

Incentive problems in agricultural R&D arise from inappropriability of benefits and free riding due to the public good nature of research results. Sometimes this problem is manifested as spillovers of results from research conducted in one place, or by one group of producers, to producers or consumers in another place. Where spillovers are important, incentive problems will be serious unless some way can be found to ensure that beneficiaries share appropriately in R&D costs. Hence, a criterion for efficiency, as well as fairness, is to whom the benefits accrue. If benefits spill over beyond a particular state, from a national perspective the state is too small a jurisdiction since it will underinvest in R&D relative to a national optimum.

Different agricultural R&D programs and projects call for different funding arrangements. But research that is a public good, or a partial public good, need not benefit everybody in the nation. Consequently, the public good nature of agricultural R&D alone does not justify arrangements where everybody in the nation pays for the research. Funding research so that, as much as possible, the costs are

265

borne in proportion to the benefits promotes both fairness and efficiency. Funding arrangements that reflect the geographic focus and the commodity orientation of the research promote these goals. In particular, a greater use of commodity check-off funding and of multistate (but subnational) regional or commodity R&D programs is suggested. The federal role in both instances may be to develop the institutional arrangements, to provide incentives such as matching grants, or both.

Check-off Funding. Industry contributes little directly to U.S. public sector agricultural R&D; it is mostly funded by the general revenues of federal and state governments. This funding pattern should change for three reasons: (1) industry funding is a potential complement to other sources of funds, which, as a practical matter, are likely to continue to leave total funding inadequate from the viewpoint of both the nation and the industry; (2) commodity check-offs are likely to be a relatively efficient (and fair) tax base; and (3) industry funding arrangements can be organized to provide incentives for efficient use of both check-off funds and other research resources.

Check-off programs, as a major form of agricultural R&D funding, can be a practical reality. In 1985 the Australian federal government introduced legislation that provides for groups of commodity producers to establish R&D funds based on a check-off (or industry levy), which the government will match up to 0.5 percent of the gross value of production of the commodity. These arrangements (revised in 1989) have been very effective in increasing total resources available for agricultural R&D. Indeed, for several commodities the 0.5 percent constraint is binding, and the R&D body administering the combination of industry check-offs and matching government funds is spending 1 percent or more of the gross value of production.

Check-off funding is clearly applicable to research on a particular commodity. By definition, this is not basic research. Similarly, check-off schemes tend to be less applicable to research that affects multiple commodities or that applies to particular factors of production or that has an environmental focus. These issues notwithstanding, however, commodity check-offs could be used more extensively to support the significant proportion of research that can be identified with a well-defined commodity (or other) interest group. Some of these mechanisms are already in place in the United States but are relatively underused in the sense that only a small fraction of total R&D resources is generated in this fashion, and the check-off funds are directed mainly toward market promotion.

The federal government could encourage greater use of such funds for agricultural R&D by providing matching (or more than matching) support for programs funded through industry check-offs.[10] When funds from industry levies and general revenues are combined to finance publicly or privately executed R&D, there is a clear role for government involvement in the administration, management, and allocation of those funds to ensure that the public interest is adequately considered. It is important to understand that industry check-off funding is not to be regarded solely as a producer "self-help" arrangement, that is, producers collectively funding research on their own behalf and to serve only their own ends. Consumers and taxpayers are affected by, have an interest in, and should be involved in such enterprises as much as producers. Producer-dominated boards allocating such funds are likely to direct research resources toward work that benefits a narrower set of interests than may be socially optimal. In addition, incentive problems may still occur if, within the group of producers and consumers of a commodity, there are different distributions of benefits from different research programs (for example, producers from a particular region may prefer research specific to their own needs that may not benefit other producers).

---

10. The federal government may also encourage state government support of industry funds by matching the state's contribution as well. Federally matched state funding of agricultural research features in some of the formula funding schemes already in place.

What seems to be equally or more important, to secure industry support for this type of program, is an assurance that funds raised through check-offs will not crowd out other federal or state research funding. If commodity check-offs do not yield an increase in total research funding, some efficiency gains might be obtained in lower social costs of funding and greater efficiency in allocation of resources for research. But the total gains might be much less than if the check-off funds were additional, particularly since check-off funds are likely to be spent on applied work, where the social returns may be lower. If the check-off funds were not additional, some efficiency might be lost through the effective diversion of funds from more basic to more applied research.

Research Organization. The appropriate regional and institutional structure for organizing research programs ought to vary according to the nature of the research. Clearly national issues are appropriately addressed by federal programs. But the federal government can choose whether to address an issue by using federal funds in federal research institutes or in state organizations (or, for that matter, in private organizations) or by using incentives to encourage state organizations to take joint action.

Institutional structure. In the land-grant system, the SAESs are substantially and physically integrated with colleges of agriculture (and, in many cases, extension agencies). This institutional structure was initially justified on the grounds of "complementarity" between research and teaching and extension. While it is still a widely cited rationale for the continued support of the land-grant system, the precise nature and magnitude of these complementary effects remain largely speculative. In any event, it is questionable whether the current number and structure of land-grant colleges, which have changed little over the years, can be justified on grounds of economic efficiency. For one thing, students are much more mobile these days than they were when the land-grant colleges were first formed.

Whether economic efficiency criteria justify a land-grant college for every state (from a federal, if not a state, perspective) warrants serious study. It may be economic to consolidate some college programs and, perhaps, some research programs among states.

Similar questions can be raised about the organization of extension. Sources of supply for agricultural extension services are expanding rapidly. This factor, coupled with accelerating improvements in communication and information technologies, and better-educated farmers, raises similar questions about the cost effectiveness of public investments in agricultural extension services in the current organizational structures.

Regional issues. Research spillovers are important, and individual states may not be able to capture economies of size and scope in research programs that pertain to larger jurisdictions. As a consequence, state-level arrangements are often inadequate. The intramural work of the USDA scientific bureaus has often been directed at solving problems that touch several states but are beyond the research capabilities of individual states. At the same time, federal funding of *national* programs is not always the right policy for addressing underinvestment in research issues that involve multiple states. Congress and the USDA have also adopted a variety of approaches to encourage multistate cooperation in agricultural research. Support for regional research in the SAESs has been provided both on a formula basis, as earmarked funds, and more recently (as in the regional centers supervised by the Alternative Agricultural Research and Commercialization Board, created in the 1990 farm bill) on a competitive basis. The most concrete development was the institution of the nine regional research laboratories under the Bankhead-Jones Act in 1935 to study specific crops, livestock, and resources issues and the four introduced in 1938 to study new industrial uses for agricultural products. To many, those developments might appear to have been driven as much by political and perhaps scientific factors as economic ones.

On the whole, too little progress seems to have been made in developing institutions to deal efficiently with problems for which the jurisdiction is neither a state nor the nation as a whole. What should be done differently from what was done in the past, given that regional research has been a prominent priority for decades? One possibility may be to combine the development of industry research funds from check-offs with the development of corresponding research institutes. The federal role could be limited to facilitating such developments, or it might, and probably should, extend to providing significant core support—perhaps on a matching basis with either industry check-off funds, funds provided by the relevant states (perhaps also based on their shares of the industry in question), or both.

Research Management. A sizable share of the potential benefits from the agricultural research enterprise may have been wasted in inefficient resource allocation. The current set of institutional arrangements apportions research funds among alternative research-executing agencies in ways that have little economic foundation. Increasingly, buzzwords and fads seem to dominate the evolving research agenda. Processes that establish and enforce an economic efficiency criterion as the primary (preferably sole) basis for allocating research resources and for evaluating research performance must become institutionalized so that resources are allocated to achieve the most good.

A simple, singular, economic efficiency objective coincides with the rationale for public sector R&D. Resolving a simple objective also allows the development of simple and clear criteria for making decisions about how to allocate resources, about how to evaluate the outcome from research, and, perhaps, about how to reward effort. With a single objective, decision making is *relatively* easy.[11]

---

11. While R&D ought to be directed according to economic efficiency considerations at the strategic or programmatic level, different criteria may be more applicable for individual projects or individual scientists. Research within broad programs may be best directed according to well-structured and well-executed peer review. At that

Whether it is through the special grants approach or in the details of the authorization bills themselves, recent congressional direction of research funding has increasingly mixed technical science policy management with the inherently political processes of Congress. It is questionable whether politicians, even with the best of motives, could have the information required to make informed judgments about specific allocations of research resources at the level of detail implied by their earmarked funds.

The current system of formula funding is uneconomic and may be unfair. It may, however, be superior to earmarked special grants. Special grants have been rising relative to other components of the research pot. If these earmarked grants do not crowd out other uses of the funds, they may not be as bad as if they compete for funds with projects that are justified on merit. Indeed, if they are additional funds, special grants might even be a profitable use of society's resources—but that seems unlikely. On the negative side, much of what is done in the name of special grants is of questionable intrinsic merit, and it is visible "pork" that looks bad and taints an otherwise, at least potentially, clean portfolio. Although it is not clear what can be done to reduce the politicization of research, one possibility is to heighten demands for demonstrated benefits as a criterion for funding. Another is to expose systematically the costs (or their orders of magnitude) of the elements that cannot be justified on merit through regular formalized system reviews.

Competitive grants, perhaps under the National Research Initiative, have a great deal to recommend them as a way of allocating public sector research resources. Competing for grants, however, is hard work and expensive, and if competitive grants are to deliver the promised benefits of greater allocative efficiency, they have to be allocated according to efficiency criteria. The same arguments can be

---

level, the critical issues may be scientific merit and technical considerations such as the probabilities of research success and the likely lags involved in the research, more than the other economic variables.

271

applied to the intramural research efforts of the USDA. There is no reason why non-SAES organizations should not be allowed to compete for extramural funds, and this aspect was incorporated into the 1990 National Research Initiative. Likewise, why such a large share of the USDA agricultural R&D budget should be quarantined from competition is unclear. The ARS will be superior to SAESs in some research areas, and vice versa; in some other areas, they should collaborate, while a large number of gray areas require specific evaluation and decisions.

Such decisions should be based on economic considerations rather than precedence. In general, there should be more open competition, greater public scrutiny, and greater accountability for the public sector R&D effort, and this research should be conducted with an eye on its economic impacts. What implications this competition would have for the balance of funding between the intra- and extramural research programs is not obvious, but it would likely enhance the total net benefits through more efficient use of the funds.

Arrangements should be instituted to reduce reliance on politically based formula funds and special grants for the SAESs and to open up the USDA intramural funds for competition in the same way as other federal research agencies do, and thereby strengthen funding for competitive grants. But this process must be subject to some caveats. Proposals should undergo review based on the sole criterion of the expected economic benefits. A poorly administered and corrupted system of competitive grants could easily be worse than the antiquated, inefficient, and inflexible system of formula funding.

Conclusions and Recommendations

Problems Identified. What is wrong with rural research? In short, the total quantity is wrong (with too little research being produced), the mixture of financing methods is wrong (with not enough support from state government and industry), the balance of executing institutions is wrong (or at least wrong procedures are being used to make decisions about intra- versus extramural research), and the criteria for allocating research resources are wrong. By implication, the commodity, locational, and thematic focus of the research (that is, basic versus applied, environmental versus privately productive, and so on) may be less than optimal as well.

Agricultural research institutions and policies have evolved. The public sector U.S. agricultural R&D enterprise is now big business—worth over $2.6 billion per year. Correspondingly, private sector investment in agriculture-related research grew to total $3.3 billion per year by 1992. In spite of tremendous growth, the public system is small in that U.S. public sector agricultural research intensity ratios are smaller than corresponding public sector ratios in competing countries and the total (public plus private sector) U.S. intensity ratios for agricultural research are smaller than such ratios in many other knowledge-based U.S. industries.

Government intervention is warranted if the benefits will exceed the costs. The best intervention is the one with the greatest net national benefit. In the case of agricultural R&D, the unfettered workings of the free-market mechanism produce too little research and not enough agricultural scientists. What should the government do? Government production is only one of several options. Government R&D funded by general government revenues is not obviously the best policy in all cases, but it is by far the dominant element of U.S. government response to a private sector underinvestment in agricultural R&D. High rates of return to this investment justify the government intervention and at the same time testify to a substantial persistent underinvestment. In spite of the government's efforts, too little agricultural R&D is being produced. The current intervention is inadequate. A significant increase in federal funding, or federal government action to stimulate increased funding by either state government or industry, seems to be warranted.

As well as getting the total quantity wrong, we seem to

have gotten the mixture of agricultural R&D wrong (in terms of the types of R&D being undertaken), and the ways funds are obtained, disbursed, and managed are also questionable. Other public research institutions, such as the National Science Foundation and the National Institutes of Health, typically distribute the lion's share of their total research budget through competitive grants, based on peer review. The USDA spends about half its total research budget on intramural programs. Questions can reasonably be raised about the distribution of the total between the intra- and extramural alternatives and about the incentives within the USDA's administration of the two programs. Questions can also be raised about the processes and procedures that allocate research resources within the two broad programs. Of the extramural funding through CSRS, very little is allocated according to economic, or even scientific, criteria. Only one-quarter of the total extramural funding goes to competitive grants. Over half the extramural funds are distributed among states by formulas based on their values of agricultural production and rural and farm populations, essentially political criteria that are unlikely to yield the maximum social payoff to the investment. Other extramural funds are allocated according to other political criteria, through the special (earmarked) grants program.

Financing arrangements, as well as spending patterns, can be improved. The contributions by state governments have been declining as a share of the total. And, while private sector R&D and industry contributions to public sector R&D have been rising, the general taxpayer still bears the brunt of the burden.

Some would say that the system has worked very well (high reported rates of return testify to that) and, by implication, that we should not spoil a good thing. There is some truth in that. The public sector agricultural R&D system has achieved a great deal, and it would be undesirable to change it in ways that would diminish its capacity to contribute to the economy into the future. By the same token, the fact that it has done well does not mean that it could not have done better. Moreover, having done well in the past might not guarantee continued future success, especially considering recent trends in the evolving structure and management of the system that, if allowed to continue, may threaten its future effectiveness. These concerns include, in particular, the rising politicization of research, including the rise of earmarked funds and the contamination of the competitive grant system, and declining state government support. The rapidly changing economic environment in which the research system finds itself is also relevant in this regard. Things that worked in the past may not work in the future. The public sector may need to reconsider and revamp the way it goes about its business.

Allocating scarce research resources is an economic problem. In the system as it stands, too little use is made of economic analysis, economic incentives, and the economic way of thinking about problems. The current system emphasizes processes and politics (the inputs side) and pays scant attention to actual performance (the outputs side). Notably, no systematic attempt has been undertaken to perform economic evaluation studies on agricultural research investments as an integral part of the process of allocating resources. Resources are allocated according to ad hoc approaches that may simply serve to ratify prejudice.

Policy Proposals. Getting research right may involve several related elements:

- *Emphasize economic efficiency.* The rationale for intervention leads to a single criterion for designing public policy for agricultural R&D and for organizing and managing the institutions used to implement that policy—economic efficiency.
- *Alternative interventions.* Greater use could be made of alternatives to public sector R&D (that is, alternatives to government production) and of less costly ways of financing public sector agricultural R&D (that is, alternatives to government funding) such as commodity check-offs with, perhaps, matching grants from state or federal government.
- *Alternative institutions.* The current system emphasizes two types of institutions (that is, SAES versus intramural

USDA institutes) funded by a combination of state and federal government funding, and there is potential to develop new institutions serving subnational multistate regional or commodity interests, on the basis of efficient research jurisdictions, with a mixture of check-off and government funding.

• *Alternative administrative arrangements.* To achieve the greatest social payoff from public sector R&D, the current arrangements (formula funding and special grants for extramural R&D, and an earmarked pot for intramural R&D) should give way to a greater use of competitive grants allocated according to the economic efficiency criterion (without political constraints and without bureaucratic buzzwords).

• *Rural adjustment policy.* To take best advantage of the economic potential of agriculture, policies should be developed that assist the adjustment of human and other resources out of agriculture when conditions change (whether because of R&D or not) rather than policies that hamper adjustment or restrict the development or adoption of new technologies.

The main messages in this chapter are simple ones. There is scope for a more economic approach to financing, organizing, and managing U.S. public sector agricultural R&D. Financing can be made more efficient—with a more efficient total quantity of research resources, a lower cost of raising the revenues, and greater allocative efficiency—by using more check-off funds. The provision of matching grants from the state and federal governments may stimulate the development of this type of arrangement appropriately. The organization of research could be made more efficient by the development of alternative institutions to bridge the gap between state and federal jurisdictions and by the greater use of economic efficiency criteria to determine the balance between different types of R&D organizations. Finally, substituting economic incentives for central direction, clarifying the economic objective of research and ensuring that resources flow according to the achievement of that singular purpose, and using competition rather than committees to allocate resources would improve the management of research and development.

References

Alston, J. M., G. W. Norton, and P. G. Pardey. *Science Under Scarcity: Principles and Practice for Agricultural Research Evaluation and Priority Setting*. Ithaca: Cornell University Press, 1995.

Alston, J. M., and P. G. Pardey. *Making Science Pay: The Economics of Agricultural R&D Policy*. Washington, D.C.: AEI Press, forthcoming.

Executive Office of the President. *Budget of the United States Government: Historical Tables, Fiscal Year 1995*. Washington D.C.: Government Printing Office, 1994.

Fox, G. C. "Is the United States Really Underinvesting in Agricultural Research?" *American Journal of Agricultural Economics* 67 (November 1985): 806–12.

Fullerton, D. "Reconciling Recent Estimates of the Marginal Welfare Cost of Taxation." *American Economic Review* 81 (1991): 302–8.

Huffman, W. E., and R. E. Evenson. *Science for Agriculture: A Long-Term Perspective*. Ames: Iowa State University Press, 1993.

Kerr, N. A. *The Legacy: A Centennial History of the State Agricultural Experiment Stations, 1887–1987*. Columbia: Missouri Agricultural Experiment Station, 1987.

Kislev, Y., and W. Peterson. "Induced Innovations and Farm Mechanization." *American Journal of Agricultural Economics* 63 (August 1981): 562–65.

Moore, E. G. *The Agricultural Research Service*. New York: Praeger Publishers, 1967.

Pardey, P. G., B. J. Craig, and K. W. Deininger. "A New Look at State-Level Productivity Growth in U.S. Agriculture." In *Evaluating Agriculture in an Era of Resource Scarcity*. Department of Agricultural and Applied Economics staff paper P94-2. St. Paul: University of Minnesota, February 1994.

Pardey, P. G., W. Eveleens, and M. L. Hallaway. "A Statistical History of U.S. Agricultural Research." Department of

Agricultural and Applied Economics, St. Paul: University of Minnesota, mimeo, forthcoming.

Rasmussen, W. D., and G. L. Baker. *The Department of Agriculture.* New York: Praeger Publishers, 1972.

U.S. Department of Agriculture. "Budgetary Tables." Washington, D.C.: U.S. Department of Agriculture, mimeo, various fiscal years.

————. *Inventory of Agricultural Research.* Washington, D.C.: Government Printing Office, various fiscal years.

Index

Acreage reduction programs,
61–64, 69–71, 160, 163
  Conservation Reserve Program, 171–75
  export price subsidies and,
101–2
Adams Act of 1906, 243
Adverse selection
  in cost-of-production insurance programs, 146
  crop insurance and, 31,
125–26, 127, 147, 148,
149
  definition, 122
Agency for International Development, 109
Agricultural Adjustment Act of
1933, 84
Agricultural and Consumer
Protection Act, 134
Agricultural Research Service,
242, 249, 272
Agricultural Stabilization and
Conservation Service, 118–
19, 124, 222
Alternative Agricultural Research and Commercialization Board, 269
Antitrust considerations, 39
Area yield insurance, 128–29
Argentina, in trade policy, 103
Asset structure of U.S. farms,
117
Australia, 31, 86, 146, 266

Bankhead-Jones Act of 1935,
243, 244, 269

Baseline specification methodology, 47, 70, 75
Bush administration, 67

Campaign for Sustainable
Agriculture, 177
Canada, 31–32, 144
  wheat trade, 91–92
Clayton Bill, 228
Clinton administration, 55, 67
CoBank Bill, 228
Commodity Credit Corporation, 48–50, 57–59, 93
  grain loan rates, 57–58
  milk supply interventions,
65
Conservation Reserve Program,
$47n$, 55, 61–63, 73, 171–77,
$179n$
Consulting, service delivery
trends, 20–21
Consumer assistance programs, 36–37
Consumption
  consumer assistance programs, 36–37
  consumer knowledge in
functioning of food
safety market, 193–97,
201–4, 205
  response to income fluctuations, 26–29
  risk-management behavior, 25
Cooperative Extension Service,
20
  See also Extension services

279

supply management,
61–64
See also Corn; Wheat

Hatch Experiment Station Act,
243
Hazard Analysis Critical Control Points systems, 187, 189,
208
Health and safety
pesticide use as subject of
regulation, 154–55
rationale for government
intervention, 40
See also Food safety

Import of agricultural products
beef, 86
cotton, 88
dairy products, 87
environmental effects,
167–68
nontariff barriers, 84–88
peanuts, 88
perception of, 83–84
quotas, 84
sugar, 85–86, 167–68
tariffs, 88–89, 112
tobacco barriers, 89–90
wheat trade, 90–92
Income
agriculture risk modeling,
24–25
consumption smoothing
relative to, 26–27
export policy and, 96
farm parity, 11–12
farm size and, in policy objectives, 20
individual response to
fluctuations in, 26–30
making current farmers
wealthier as policy goal,
21–23
off-farm sources for farmers, 12, 26

redistribution through
agriculture policy, 15–
17, 21, 147, 178
risk protection objectives,
24
rural trends, 11–12
stabilization, farm value
and, 17
Income insurance
land value and, 14–16
versus price-yield insur-
ance, 31
Income supports
international context, 4
versus revenue insurance,
143–44
Information
in functioning of food
safety market, 191, 193–
98, 201–4
for policy evaluation,
39–40
International comparisons
agricultural deregulation,
19
agricultural research and
development, 249
farm credit programs, 229
farm ownership patterns,
19
International context
international food aid programs, 109–11
price and income support
policy in, 4
See also Trade policy
Iowa Farm Bill Study, 143

Livestock market, 52
meat import regulation, 86

Market failure
agricultural risks, 24–25
in agriculture research and
development, 239, 240
food safety market, 200

as justification for government intervention, 21, 32–33, 148
Market promotion, international, 107–9, 111
Market Promotion Program, 107–8
Marketing loan provisions, 163–64
McIntire-Stennis Forestry Research Act of 1962, 244
Means testing, 66–69
Mexico, 84
Monopolies, 38–39
Moral hazard
in cost-of-production insurance programs, 146
in crop insurance, 31, 138
crop insurance empirical research, 141
definition, 122

NAFTA. *See* North American Free Trade Agreement
National Research Initiative, 245
New Zealand, 19
in beef trade, 86
consumption response to deregulation, 27–28
in dairy trade, 103
export competitor, 103
farm structure, 20
fertilizer use, 35
policy reforms, 27
North American Free Trade Agreement (NAFTA), 2, 4, 55, 84
Nutrition labels, 190–91, 205, 207

Omnibus Budget Reconciliation Act of 1990, 47, 48–50, 103, 161
Organization for Economic Co-

operation and Development, 84
Ownership patterns, farm, 18–20

Patent rights, 21
Peanuts, 88, 166
Pesticides
cancer risk and, 186, 192
regulation of, 154–55, 190
Policy reform
alternatives to crop insurance, 142–47
crop insurance, 148–49
Crop Insurance Reform Act, 130–33
current environment for, 7–8, 45, 54–56
disaster relief, 148–49
environmental issues in, 179–81
farm policy as welfare versus industrial policy, 78–79
food safety choices, 185–88
food safety recommendations, 189–90, 206–9
foreign trade and, 81, 113–14
goal-oriented analysis in, 10–11
obstacles to, 41–42
opportunities for, 3–8, 41
performance of green support programs, 177–78
research and development recommendations, 239–40, 275–77
social and political environment for, 1–2
social values in, 78–79
versus new policy development, 40–42
Political context
of agricultural policy objectives, 14–15

285

Board of Trustees

Wilson H. Taylor, *Chairman*
Chairman and CEO
CIGNA Corporation

Tully M. Friedman, *Treasurer*
Hellman & Friedman

Edwin L. Artzt
Chairman and CEO
The Procter & Gamble
Company

Joseph A. Cannon
Chairman and CEO
Geneva Steel Company

Raymond E. Cartledge
Retired Chairman and CEO
Union Camp Corporation

Albert J. Costello
President and CEO
W.R. Grace & Co.

Christopher C. DeMuth
President
American Enterprise Institute

Malcolm S. Forbes, Jr.
President and CEO
Forbes Inc.

Christopher B. Galvin
President and COO
Motorola, Inc.

Robert F. Greenhill
Chairman and CEO
Smith Barney Inc.

M. Douglas Ivester
President and COO
The Coca-Cola Company

James W. Kinnear
Former President and CEO
Texaco Incorporated

Martin M. Koffel
Chairman and CEO
URS Corporation

Bruce Kovner
Chairman
Caxton Corporation

Kenneth L. Lay
Chairman and CEO
ENRON Corp.

Marilyn Ware Lewis
Chairman
American Water Works Company, Inc.

**The American Enterprise Institute
for Public Policy Research**

Founded in 1943, AEI is a nonpartisan, nonprofit, research and
educational organization based in Washington, D.C. The Institute
sponsors research, conducts seminars and conferences, and
publishes books and periodicals.

AEI's research is carried out under three major programs:
Economic Policy Studies; Foreign Policy and Defense Studies;
and Social and Political Studies. The resident scholars and
fellows listed in these pages are part of a network that also
includes ninety adjunct scholars at leading universities
throughout the United States and in several foreign countries.

The views expressed in AEI publications are those of the
authors and do not necessarily reflect the views of the staff,
advisory panels, officers, or trustees.

Alex J. Mandl
Executive Vice President
AT&T

Craig O. McCaw

Paul H. O'Neill
Chairman and CEO
Aluminum Company of America

Paul F. Oreffice
Former Chairman
Dow Chemical Co.

George R. Roberts
Kohlberg Kravis Roberts & Co.

John W. Rowe
President and CEO
New England Electric System

Edward B. Rust, Jr.
President and CEO
State Farm Insurance Companies

James P. Schadt
President & CEO
The Reader's Digest Association, Inc.

John W. Snow
Chairman, President, and CEO
CSX Corporation

Henry Wendt
Chairman
The Finisterre Fund

James Q. Wilson
James A. Collins Professor
of Management
University of California
at Los Angeles

Officers

Christopher C. DeMuth
President

David B. Gerson
Executive Vice President

**Council of Academic
Advisers**

James Q. Wilson, *Chairman*
James A. Collins Professor
of Management
University of California
at Los Angeles

Gertrude Himmelfarb
Distinguished Professor of History
Emeritus
City University of New York

Samuel P. Huntington
Eaton Professor of the
Science of Government
Harvard University

D. Gale Johnson
Eliakim Hastings Moore
Distinguished Service Professor
of Economics Emeritus
University of Chicago

William M. Landes
Clifton R. Musser Professor of
Economics
University of Chicago Law School

Glenn C. Loury
Professor of Economics
Boston University

Sam Peltzman
Sears Roebuck Professor of Economics
and Financial Services
University of Chicago
Graduate School of Business

Nelson W. Polsby
Professor of Political Science
University of California at Berkeley

George L. Priest
John M. Olin Professor of Law and
Economics
Yale Law School

Murray L. Weidenbaum
Mallinckrodt Distinguished
University Professor
Washington University

Research Staff

Leon Aron
Resident Scholar

Claude E. Barfield
Resident Scholar; Director, Science
and Technology Policy Studies

Cynthia A. Beltz
Research Fellow

Walter Berns
Resident Scholar

Douglas J. Besharov
Resident Scholar

Jagdish Bhagwati
Visiting Scholar

Robert H. Bork
John M. Olin Scholar in Legal Studies

Karlyn Bowman
Resident Fellow

John E. Calfee
Resident Scholar

Richard B. Cheney
Senior Fellow

Lynne V. Cheney
W.H. Brady, Jr., Distinguished Fellow

Dinesh D'Souza
John M. Olin Research Fellow

Nicholas N. Eberstadt
Visiting Scholar

Mark Falcoff
Resident Scholar

John D. Fonte
Visiting Scholar

Gerald R. Ford
Distinguished Fellow

Murray F. Foss
Visiting Scholar

Suzanne Garment
Resident Scholar

Jeffrey Gedmin
Research Fellow

Patrick Glynn
Resident Scholar

Robert A. Goldwin
Resident Scholar

Robert W. Hahn
Resident Scholar

Robert B. Helms
Resident Scholar; Director, Health
Policy Studies

James D. Johnston
Resident Fellow

Jeane J. Kirkpatrick
Senior Fellow; Director, Foreign and
Defense Policy Studies

Marvin H. Kosters
Resident Scholar; Director,
Economic Policy Studies

Irving Kristol
John M. Olin Distinguished Fellow

Dana Lane
Director of Publications

Michael A. Ledeen
Resident Scholar

James Lilley
Resident Fellow; Director, Asian
Studies Program

Chong-Pin Lin
Resident Scholar; Associate Director,
Asian Studies Program

John H. Makin
Resident Scholar; Director, Fiscal
Policy Studies

Allan H. Meltzer
Visiting Scholar

Joshua Muravchik
Resident Scholar

Charles Murray
Bradley Fellow

Michael Novak
George F. Jewett Scholar in Religion,
Philosophy, and Public Policy;
Director, Social and
Political Studies

Norman J. Ornstein
Resident Scholar

Richard N. Perle
Resident Fellow

William Schneider
Resident Scholar

William Shew
Visiting Scholar

J. Gregory Sidak
Resident Scholar

Herbert Stein
Senior Fellow

Irwin M. Stelzer
Resident Scholar; Director, Regulatory
Policy Studies

W. Allen Wallis
Resident Scholar

Ben J. Wattenberg
Senior Fellow

Carolyn L. Weaver
Resident Scholar; Director, Social
Security and Pension Studies

A Note on the Book

*This book was edited by the publications staff
of the American Enterprise Institute.
The figures were drawn by Hordur Karlsson.
The index was prepared by Robert Elwood.
The text was set in Palatino, a typeface
designed by the twentieth-century Swiss designer
Hermann Zapf. Coghill Composition Company of
Richmond, Virginia, set the type,
and Edwards Brothers Incorporated
of Lillington, North Carolina,
printed and bound the book,
using permanent acid-free paper.*

The AEI Press is the publisher for the American Enterprise Institute for Public Policy Research, 1150 Seventeenth Street, N.W., Washington, D.C. 20036; *Christopher
DeMuth,* publisher; *Dana Lane,* director; *Ann Petty,* editor;
Leigh Tripoli, editor; *Cheryl Weissman,* editor; *Lisa Roman,*
editorial assistant (rights and permissions).

www.ingramcontent.com/pod-product-compliance
Lightning Source LLC
Jackson TN
JSHW011932131224
75386JS00041B/1345

* 9 7 8 0 8 4 4 7 3 9 1 3 7 *